Coercive Control and Vulnerable Adults

Law and Practice in the Court of Protection and under the Inherent Jurisdiction of the High Court

Liebst du um Schätze,	If you love me for wealth,
O nicht mich liebe!	Do not love me!
Liebe die Meerfrau,	Love the mermaid,
Sie hat viel Perlen klar!	She has many clear pearls.

From the song, *Liebst du um Schönheit* (If you love for beauty).

Words by Friedrich Rückert, music by Gustav Mahler.

Coercive Control and Vulnerable Adults

Law and Practice in the Court of Protection and under the Inherent Jurisdiction of the High Court

Oliver Lewis

Barrister, Doughty Street Chambers

Bloomsbury Professional

LONDON • DUBLIN • EDINBURGH • NEW YORK • NEW DELHI • SYDNEY

BLOOMSBURY PROFESSIONAL

Bloomsbury Publishing Plc
50 Bedford Square, London, WC1B 3DP, UK
1359 Broadway, New York, NY 10018, USA

Bloomsbury Publishing Ireland Ltd
29 Earlsfort Terrace, Dublin 2, D02 AY28, Ireland

2

British Library Cataloguing-in-Publication Data

A catalogue record for this book is available from the British Library.

ISBN: PB 978 1 52653 591 7
ePDF 978 1 52653 593 1
ePub 978 1 52653 592 4

Typeset by Evolution Design & Digital Ltd (Kent)
Printed and bound in Great Britain by TJ Books, Padstow, Cornwall

FSC www.fsc.org MIX Paper | Supporting responsible forestry FSC® C013056

For product safety related questions contact productsafety@bloomsbury.com

To find out more about our authors and books, visit www.bloomsburyprofessional.com. Here you will find extracts, author information, details of forthcoming events and the option to sign up for our newsletters.

Foreword

Controlling and coercive behaviour first became a crime in England and Wales on 29 December 2015 under s 76 of the Serious Crime Act 2015. The scope of this 'new' crime was subsequently extended in 2023 by s 68 of the Domestic Abuse Act 2021 to remove the requirement that the abuse must have taken place when the parties were living together.

These bald facts do nothing to give one any understanding of the corrosive, psychologically destructive and traumatic impact of such behaviour on an individual. Nor do they expose the challenges faced in identifying coercive control where a vulnerable adult or a person lacking capacity is the victim and the control is masked, as it so often is, by assertions that the perpetrator is only 'caring for' and 'loving' a person incapable otherwise of caring for themselves.

In *A County Court v LW & Anon* [2020] EWCOP 50, Hayden J, then Vice President of the Court of Protection, highlighted the need for vigilance in the Court of Protection when seeking to understand and identify coercive and controlling behaviour in the context of, in particular, vulnerable adults. Fortunately, since then, there has been an increasing understanding in the courts, amongst professionals and by the public of this insidious form of abuse, albeit there is still some way to go.

Through the Judicial College, the judges, magistrates and coroners of England and Wales all have specialist training on domestic abuse with an emphasis on coercive control and they are taught to take a trauma-informed approach to court proceedings. But what this most welcome book does, is to improve awareness and understanding of coercive and controlling behaviour in a way to make it accessible not only to the lawyers, but also to safeguarding professionals and to those lay people who are concerned that someone they know is, or may be, a victim of coercive control. Having developed the reader's understanding in Chapter 2: 'Coercive control', the author then moves on to explain the relevant law and procedure. Crucially, throughout the book he separates out the law as it applies to persons who lack capacity and whose best interests are determined under the umbrella of the Court of Protection, from those vulnerable adults who fall within the inherent jurisdiction of the High Court. Too often the two are confused and confusing for non-lawyers, particularly as it is sometimes unclear whether a vulnerable person also lacks capacity.

Also invaluable are the practical guides in Chapters 11–13. In these chapters the role of the legal representatives of the various parties to this type of litigation is discussed, that is to say: the victim/survivor, the local authority and the controlling person. These chapters are far more than 'tips for trials', but rather they provide fascinating and invaluable information and guidance, for example, on how best to take a trauma-informed approach to representing and advising a victim/survivor or, how to look out for, and avoid, the attempts of a controlling person to manipulate their legal team and the court.

The publication of this book is most welcome. Dr Oliver Lewis' expertise in medical ethics and human rights law adds a depth and breadth to its content which takes it beyond that of practitioner's guide to being an authoritative work covering all aspects of this important topic.

The Rt Hon Lady Justice King

13 February 2026

Biography

Oliver Lewis is a barrister at Doughty Street Chambers, London, practising in the areas of healthcare law, disability and human rights. He is frequently instructed in medical treatment cases and complex welfare cases in the Court of Protection and in the inherent jurisdiction of the High Court by NHS bodies, local authorities, the Official Solicitor and family members. He also acts in public law challenges, civil claims, and inquests touching on health or social care.

He is a Governing Bencher of Inner Temple where he regularly trains advocacy to Bar students. He is co-chair of Respond, a charity providing psychotherapy to autistic people and people with learning disabilities who have experienced trauma. He serves as trustee of Bild, the British Institute of Learning Disabilities.

Before returning to the Bar in 2017, Oliver lived in Budapest for several years, serving as Legal Director and then Executive Director of Validity (formerly the Mental Disability Advocacy Centre), an international disability rights NGO. During this time, he oversaw the world's largest docket of international disability litigation, and took several cases to the European Court of Human Rights, including the leading cases of *Shtukaturov v Russia* (2008) and *Stanev v Bulgaria* (2012).

He participated in the drafting of the UN Convention on the Rights of Persons with Disabilities (2006) and maintains an international practice, providing advice and capacity-building to governments and civil society on its implementation. With Peter Bartlett and Oliver Thorold, he co-authored *Mental Disability and the European Convention on Human Rights* (Brill, 2007).

Oliver studied law at LSE and then medical ethics and law at King's College, London. In 2015, he was awarded a PhD from Leiden University on the development of legal capacity in international human rights law.

Acknowledgements

Lady Justice King is the most senior member of the judiciary to have sat as a judge in the Court of Protection. I am very grateful to her for taking time to read the manuscript in draft, and for writing such a generous Foreword.

Alex Ruck-Keene KC (Hon) encouraged me to write this book, reviewed the legal chapters and introduced me to Bloomsbury Publishing. There, I would like to thank my publisher Kiran Goss and my editor Susan Ghaiwal.

I am fortunate to work alongside such smart and collegial people at Doughty Street Chambers, barristers and staff alike. I thank them for their encouragement and support of this writing project. My former pupil, Jordan Briggs, undertook invaluable legal research at the outset of the project, collating, categorising, and summarising the relevant case law.

The staff at Inner Temple Library patiently guided me to shelves I could not locate myself. Lizzie Moss at Heron Books in Bristol introduced me to representations of coercive control in fiction, a theme I look forward to continuing to explore.

The following people made helpful suggestions on draft chapters along the way: Michael Barrett, HHJ Simon Burrows, Victoria Butler-Cole KC, Elizabeth Cleaver, Professor Rod Dubrow-Marshall, Dr Foziha Hamid, Louise Haverson, Camille Ivinson, Amelia Nice and Dr Keio Yoshida. Malcolm Chisholm and Timothy Hutchinson reviewed family law remedies.

On the otherwise lonely journey writing this book, my Doughty Street colleague Zoe Harper became my critical friend extraordinaire. She generously shared her deep knowledge of combatting domestic abuse and working with victims/survivors. And she carefully reviewed, and thereby improved, many draft chapters. Any remaining errors are mine.

Two people control my life. My clerk, Emily Norman, juggled the competing demands of my diary and somehow managed to protect precious writing time. My husband, István, cooked brain-nourishing meals, walked the dogs when I was mid-chapter, and has patiently supported me through the emotional rollercoaster of my cases.

My former and current clients include social workers, clinicians, solicitors, lay advocates, family members, and, most importantly, those who have experienced coercive control. I thank them for sharing their insights into human relationships, for offering thoughtful perspectives on how the justice system might be improved, and for showing me the possibility of healing.

This book is dedicated to my mother, Dr Sylvia Carpenter. A Viennese-trained psychiatrist, she devoted her career in the UK to supporting people with learning disabilities to heal from institutional trauma and build fuller lives in the community. She has not only provided the perfect Freudian explanation for my interest in learning disability and the law, but, through her love and unwavering support, has guided my career and shaped my life. Vielen Dank!

Contents

Foreword *v*
Biography *vii*
Acknowledgements *ix*
Table of Statutes *xvii*
Table of Statutory Instruments *xix*
Table of International Legislation *xxi*
Table of Cases *xxiii*

Chapter 1 Introduction
Purpose and roadmap 1
Objectives of the book 1
Terminology 2
The legal frontline 3
Reported and unreported cases 4
Overview of the cases 6
The two jurisdictions 8
Conclusions 11

Chapter 2 Coercive control
Introduction 13
Elements of coercive control 13
The behaviours 13
Tactics of control 14
Entrapment 16
Post-separation abuse 19
Homicide and suicide 20
Coercive control in international human rights law 21
United Nations 22
Council of Europe 23
Coercive control in the criminal law of England and Wales 25
Definition of domestic abuse 25
The criminal offence of controlling or coercive behaviour in an intimate or family relationship 25
The criminal offence of putting people in fear of violence 27
Coercive control statutory guidance 28
Historical context 31
Coercive control and disabled people 33
Conclusions 34

Chapter 3 Determining capacity
Introduction 37
Capacity and coercive control 38
Presumption of capacity 39
All practicable steps 40
Unwise decisions 41

Determining lack of capacity 42
The first question: Is P unable to make the decision? 44
The second question: Is P unable to make the decision 'because of' an impairment or disturbance? 47
Interim and final declarations of capacity 49
Obtaining capacity evidence 50
A party 50
A non-party local authority or NHS body 51
A Court of Protection Visitor 53
An independent expert 53
Summary 54

Chapter 4 Decision-making domains
Introduction 57
Preliminary points 57
Articulating the matter 58
Tailoring the relevant information 58
Putting the relevant information to P 59
Reasonably foreseeable consequences 59
Avoiding silos 60
Decision-making areas 61
Conducting proceedings 61
Deciding about residence 64
Deciding about care 65
Deciding about contact with others 67
Deciding about disclosure of information to others 69
Managing property and financial affairs 69
Deciding on internet and social media use 70
Executing and revoking a lasting power of attorney 72
Engaging in sexual relations 73
Deciding to marry 74
Testamentary capacity 74
Conclusions 75

Chapter 5 Coercive control cases in the Court of Protection
Introduction 77
Learning disabilities 77
Miss KP lived with her sex-offender stepfather 78
Ms KF wanted to see her violent partner one more time 78
Mrs A was being pressured to become pregnant 79
Elder abuse 81
Ms BU 81
Ms LC 85
Mental illness 87
Ms LW 87
Brain injury 88
Mrs PB 88
Conclusions 89

Chapter 6 Law and procedure under the inherent jurisdiction
Introduction 93
Principles of the inherent jurisdiction 95

The foundational cases	95
The vulnerable adult	96
Permitted versus undue influence	101
Avoiding the protective imperative	101
Human rights considerations	101
Article 3 ECHR	102
Article 8 ECHR	102
Article 5 ECHR	104
Deprivation of liberty in practice	107
Procedure	108
Civil Procedure Rules	108
Form of application	108
Level of judiciary	109
Funding	109
Transfer from/to the Court of Protection	109
Determining capacity or undue influence	109
Litigation friend	110
Without notice applications	110
Interim orders	111
Conclusions	111

Chapter 7 Coercive control cases under the inherent jurisdiction

Introduction	113
Control of a partner	113
Control by a parent	115
Mr TT and his mother	115
Ms KP and her cousin/step-father	116
Ms P and her father	118
Control of a parent	120
Forced relationships	123
Ms AG	123
Ms EF	124
Amina	125
Conclusions	125

Chapter 8 Finding facts

Introduction	127
Fact-finding in the Court of Protection	127
Why establish facts?	127
Facts before capacity	128
Determining whether to hold a fact-finding hearing	128
Interim findings	130
Fact-finding in the inherent jurisdiction	130
Schedules of allegations	131
Fact-finding hearings	132
Timetabling a fact-finding hearing	132
Witnesses	133
The hearing itself	134
The judgment	137
Conclusions	137

Chapter 9 Remedies
Introduction 139
Best interests decisions in the Court of Protection 140
Conducting proceedings 141
Residence 141
Care 142
Contact with others 142
Information sharing 143
Property and financial affairs 143
Internet and social media 144
Lasting power of attorney 144
Engaging in sexual relations 145
Marrying 145
Making a will 145
Orders under the inherent jurisdiction 145
Objectives of remedies 145
LPAs 146
Removal from home 147
Undertakings and injunctions 147
Agreements 147
Undertakings 148
Injunctions 148
Injunctions against a person other than the victim/survivor 148
Just and convenient 148
Wording of injunctions 149
Interim remedies 150
Court of Protection 150
Capacity evidence at the start of proceedings 151
Substantive test 152
Inherent jurisdiction 152
Deprivation of liberty 155
Remedies available elsewhere 155
Non-molestation order 155
Occupation order 155
Forced marriage protection order 156
Injunction to protect a person from harassment 156
Domestic abuse protection order 157
Domestic abuse protection notice 157
Conclusion 157

Chapter 10 The traumatic effects of coercive control
Introduction 159
Coercive control and trauma 159
Trauma responses 160
Traumatic memory recall 162
Shutting trauma away 162
Collage, not chronology 162
Substance abuse 163
Mental health: diagnoses 163
Mental health: therapy and healing 165
Physical health 169
Learning disabilities and autism 171

Conclusions 172

Chapter 11 Representing the victim/survivor
Introduction 175
Preparing for the meeting with the client 176
Reviewing records 176
Obtaining mental health and other advice 176
Determining methods of communication 176
Avoiding a power dynamic 177
Arranging the appointment 177
Preparing questions 178
Ensuring consistency 178
Being prepared to meet the client 179
At the meeting 179
Small choices increase agency 179
Online meetings 180
Grounding 181
Introductions and explaining the process 182
Explaining the litigation friend role 182
Starting before the abuse 183
Active listening 183
Suggestibility 184
Discussing abuse 184
Physical contact 185
The effects of trauma during the meeting 186
Emotional shut down 187
Dissociation 187
Flashbacks 188
Shame 189
Guilt 190
Intrusive thoughts 190
Grief 191
Rage 191
Confusion 192
Minimising 192
Other presentations 193
Ending the meeting 193
Summing up with positivity 193
Forthcoming court hearings 194
Story stewardship 194
What happens next 194
The litigation friend 195
Funding 196
Attendance notes of the client's wishes and feelings 197
Participation in proceedings 198
Supporting the client at court 199
Lawyer self-care 201
Conclusions 202

Chapter 12 Representing the local authority
Introduction 203
Legal strategy 203

Access to the victim/survivor 206
Speed and creativity 207
Gathering evidence 209
The role of healthcare professionals 210
Issues that arise during proceedings 211
Conclusions 211

Chapter 13 Representing the controlling person
Introduction 213
The controlling client Trauma responses 213
Typologies of those who harm 213
Controlling the proceedings 214
Perpetrator views of the victim/survivor 216
Conspiracies 217
Fighting all the way 217
Complaints and being dismissed 218
Compliance with orders 218
Actions the lawyer can take 219
Risk assessments 219
Funding 220
Evidence 220
Signposting to services 221
Capacity concerns 221
Fact-finding 221
Conclusions 222

Chapter 14 Conclusions 225

Index 235

Table of Statutes

Care Act 2014 .... 1.36; 4.38; 7.51; 9.13, 9.33
s 9 .... 4.40; 9.55
11 .... 7.31; 9.55
(2) 4.41
42 .... 9.55
Crime and Security Act 2010
s 27, 28 .... 9.70
Domestic Abuse Act 2021 .... 2.42; 9.69, 9.71
s 1 .... 2.42
22 .... 9.72
27–49 .... 9.70
64 .... 11.119
68 .... 2.43
Equality Act 2010 .... 10.50
Family Law Act 1996 .... 9.62
s 33 .... 9.64
42 .... 9.61
63B 9.65
Forced Marriage (Civil Protection) Act 2007 .... 7.56
Human Rights Act 1998 .... 6.31
Legal Aid, Sentencing and Punishment of Offenders Act 2012
Sch 1
para 9 .... 6.62
Mental Capacity Act 2005 .. 1.06, 1.39, 1.45, 1.46; 3.01, 3.02, 3.06, 3.09, 3.21, 3.22, 3.47, 3.50; 4.14, 4.29, 4.52, 4.68, 4.74; 5.69; 6.01, 6.02, 6.13, 6.18, 6.43, 6.59, 6.64, 6.66, 6.70; 7.35, 7.51; 8.08; 9.06; 11.100; 12.22, 12.25; 14.07, 14.08, 14.12, 14.13
s 1 .... 3.08, 3.15, 3.17
(2), (3) 3.22
(4) 3.17
(6) 9.07; 12.22
2 .... 3.21, 3.23, 3.43, 3.44, 3.53; 7.19
(1) 3.22, 3.23, 3.41, 3.45; 7.35; 14.12
(2), (4) 3.22
3 .... 3.21, 3.23
(1) 3.22, 3.25, 3.26, 3.27, 3.40, 3.41; 4.01; 7.38
(a) 3.26
(b) 3.26, 3.32
(c) 3.04, 3.26
(d) 3.26
(2) 3.28
(3) 3.32
(4) 4.14, 4.16, 4.34
(a) 3.22
4 .... 9.07
(1)(a), (b) 9.07
(2) 6.01, 6.02; 8.37; 9.05, 9.07; 13.35
(3) 9.07
(4) 9.07; 11.113
(6) 1.42; 6.02; 11.108; 14.11
(a)–(c) 9.07
(7) 9.07
(11) 9.07
15 .... 3.50, 3.51, 3.55; 9.47, 9.49
16 .... 12.35
18(1)(i) 9.27
20(2)(a) 4.49
21A 6.43; 11.103; 12.35
21ZA 6.43
22 .... 9.24
(2)(a) 9.22
(3)(a), (b) 9.22
(4) 9.22
27(1)(a) 9.26
(b) 9.25
44 .... 2.68
48 .... 3.52, 3.55; 9.46, 9.49, 9.52
49 .... 3.61, 3.62, 3.64, 3.71, 3.72
(2) 3.59
(3) 3.69
(5), (7), (8), (9) 3.62
58(1)(d) 3.70
61 .... 3.70
Sch AA1 .... 6.43
Sch A1 .... 6.43
para 15 .... 4.19
Sch 1
para 2(e)(ii) 9.22
Mental Health Act 1983 .... 6.43, 6.50
National Assistance Act 1948
s 47 .... 9.33
Online Safety Act 2023 .... 2.54
Protection from Harassment Act 1997 .... 2.75
s 3 .... 10.31
3A 9.68
4 .... 2.51, 2.53

Senior Courts Act 1981
s 9 .... 6.61
37(1) 9.39
Serious Crime Act 2015 .... 2.75; 6.22
s 76 .... 2.43, 2.47, 2.49, 2.51, 2.52, 2.53; 5.33
77 .... 2.56
Serious Organised Crime and Police Act 2005
s 125(5) 9.68
Social Services and Well-being (Wales) Act 2014 .... 1.36; 4.38; 9.33
s 19, 20, 126 .... 9.55

Table of Statutory Instruments

Care and Support (Eligibility Criteria) Regulations 2015, SI 2015/313 .... 4.38
reg 2(2) 4.38
Care and Support (Eligibility) (Wales) Regulations 2015, SI 2015/1578 .... 4.38
Civil Legal Aid (Merits Criteria) Regulations 2013, SI 2013/104
reg 52 .... 13.27
69 .... 11.104
Civil Procedure Rules 1998, SI 1998/3132 .... 6.58, 6.59, 6.66; 8.09, 8.29
PD 1A 11.99
Pt 21 (rr 21.1–21.13) 11.100
r 25.1(1) 9.51
(a), (b), (k) 9.51
(3) 9.51
Pt 32 (rr 32.1–32.20) 8.29
r 32.5 .... 8.29
(1) 8.29
Pt 33 (rr 33.1–33.9) 8.29
Court of Protection Rules 2017, SI 2017/1035 .... 6.58; 8.07, 8.25, 8.27, 8.29, 8.31
r 1.1 .... 8.07
(3) 8.07
1.2 .... 3.72; 11.113
1.3(3)(f) 8.07
1.4(2)(e) 13.24
(3) 13.24
3.1(2)(h) 8.07
10.10 .... 9.46
(b) 3.52
Pt 14 (rr 14.1–14.25) 8.29
r 14.2 .... 8.25
(e) 8.25
14.3(4) 8.27
14.5 .... 8.28
14.26 .... 3.63
PD 14E 3.64, 3.66, 3.67, 3.68, 3.71
Pt 15 (rr 15.1–15.13) 3.72
15.3 .... 3.72
15.4(1), (2) 3.75
Pt 17 (rr 17.1–17.14) 11.113
r 17.1–17.3 .... 9.10
17.4 .... 4.32; 9.10
17.5–17.8 .... 9.10
Domestic Abuse Protection Orders (County Court: Relevant Proceedings) Regulations 2024, SI 2024/253 .... 9.71
Family Procedure Rules 2010, SI 2010/2955 .... 6.58
PD 12J 2.12; 8.08

Table of International Legislation

Convention on the Elimination of All Forms of Discrimination Against Women (CEDAW) (New York, 18 December 1979) 2.30
Art 1 .... 2.30, 2.32
2 .... 2.32
16 .... 2.30
CEDAW General Recommendation No 19 on Violence against Women (Adopted at 11th Session A/47/38) 2.32
CEDAW General Recommendation No 28 on the core obligations of States parties under Article 2 (CEDAW/C/GC/28) (16 December 2010) 2.32
European Convention on Human Rights (Rome, 4 November 1950) 6.31; 9.17; 11.104
Art 2 .... 6.23
3 .... 2.35, 2.37; 6.23, 6.31, 6.32, 6.33, 6.34, 6.41; 7.33
5 .... 6.31, 6.42, 6.45, 6.51, 6.54; 9.34
(1) 6.54
(e) 6.42, 6.71; 7.60
(4) 6.43
6 .... 12.25
8 .... 6.31, 6.35, 6.36, 6.37, 6.41; 7.33, 7.37, 7.49, 7.55; 8.04; 9.17, 9.31
(2) 6.37
14 .... 2.35, 2.36
Council of Europe Convention on Preventing and Combatting Violence Against Women and Domestic Violence (Istanbul Convention) (Istanbul, 11 May 2011) 2.39, 2.49
Art 3 .... 2.39
United Nations Convention on the Rights of Persons with Disabilities (New York, 30 March 2007) 14.06
Art 3(a) 14.06
12 .... 2.66; 14.06
19 .... 14.06

Table of Cases

All references are to paragraph numbers

A

A v X [2012] EWHC 2400 (COP), [2012] 7 WLUK 953, [2013] WTLR 187 .... 4.53
A (a child: fact-finding hearing: speculation), Re [2011] EWCA Civ 12, [2011] 1 WLUK 260, [2011] 1 FLR 1817 .... 8.30
A (capacity: refusal of contraception), Re [2010] EWHC 1549 (Fam), [2011] Fam 61, [2011] 2 WLR 878 .... 1.31; 2.57; 5.10
A (capacity: social media & internet use: best interests), Re [2019] EWCOP 2, [2019] Fam 586, [2019] 3 WLR 59 .... 4.57
AE v Bulgaria (Application 53891/20) [2023] 5 WLU 609, (2023) 77 EHRR 19........ 6.33
A-G v De Keyser's Royal Hotel *see* De Keyser's Royal Hotel Ltd, Re
A-G v Edwards [2010] EWHC 2160 (Admin), [2010] 7 WLUK 9.......... 7.01
AMDC v AG [2020] EWCOP 58, [2020] 4 WLR 166, [2020] 11 WLUK 201..........3.10; 4.13
Al-Jeffery v Al-Jeffery [2016] EWHC 2151 (Fam), [2018] 4 WLR 136, [2016] 8 WLUK 58 .... 2.57; 7.56
Avon & Wiltshire Mental Health Partnership v WA [2020] EWCOP 37, [2020] 7 WLUK 271 .... 3.35

B

B v A Local Authority [2019] EWCA Civ 913, [2020] Fam 105, [2019] 3 WLR 685 ......3.21; 4.00, 4.08, 4.09, 4.11, 4.35
B (a child) (habitual residence: inherent jurisdiction), Re [2016] UKSC 4, [2016] AC 606, [2016] 2 WLR 557 .... 7.58
B (children) (sexual abuse: standard of proof), Re [2008] UKHL 35, [2009] 1 AC 11, [2008] 3 WLR 1 .... 8.30
B, Re *see* B v A Local Authority
BU, Re *see* WU v BU
Banks v Goodfellow (1869-70) LR 5 QB 549, [1870] 7 WLUK 15 .... 4.72

C

C (mental patient: contact), Re [1993] 1 WLUK 41, [1993] 1 FLR 940, [1993] Fam Law 404 .... 6.22
CA (Fact Finding – Capacity – Inherent Jurisdiction – Injunctive Relief), Re *see* Norfolk County Council v CA
CC v KK [2012] EWHC 2136 (COP), [2012] 7 WLUK 861 ....3.22, 3.35; 6.30
CT v London Borough of Lambeth [2025] EWCOP 6 (T3), [2025] 4 WLR 46, [2025] 4 All ER 173 .... 3.00, 3.18, 3.19, 3.44; 4.17
Cheshire & Wirral Partnership NHS Foundation Trust v JMC [2023] EWCOP 14, [2023] 4 WLUK 358 .... 3.68
County Council v K, D & L *see* Local Authority, a v K
County Council, a v LW [2020] EWCOP 50, [2020] 4 WLR 164, [2020] 7 WLU 673 .....2.56; 5.00, 5.52; 12.26
Croydon LBC v KR [2019] EWHC 2498 (Fam), [2019] 9 WLUK 291, [2020] COPLR 285 .... 9.51; 12.30
Cumbria County Council v A [2020] EWCOP 38, [2020] 1 WLR 4008, [2020] 7 WLUK 321 .... 14.12
Cumbria, Northumberland Tyne & Wear NHS Foundation Trust v EG [2021] EWHC 2990 (Fam), [2021] 11 WLUK 83, [2022] COPLR 83 .... 6.54

D

D v R (The Deputy of S) *see* S, Re
DL, Re *see* L (vulnerable adults with capacity: court's jurisdiction), Re
DP (revocation of Lasting Power of Attorney), Re [2014] 2 WLUK 301, [2014] COPLR 188, [2014] WTLR 979 .... 9.23
DP (by his accredited legal representative) v London Borough of Hillingdon [2020] EWCOP 45, [2020] COPLR 769, (2021) 180 BMLR 179 .... 9.49
De Keyser's Royal Hotel Ltd, Re [1920] AC 508, [1920] 5 WLUK 46 .... 1.46
Dudgeon v United Kingdom (A/59) [1983] 2 WLUK 243, (1983) 5 EHRR 573 .... 6.39
Dunhill (a protected party by her litigation friend Tasker) v Burgin [2014] UKSC 18, [2014] 1 WLR 933, [2014] 2 All ER 364, [2014] COPLR 199 .... 4.26

E

E, Re *see* Sheffield City Council v (1) E (2) S
EG, Re *see* Cumbria, Northumberland Tyne & Wear NHS Foundation Trust v EG
EO, Re [2024] EWCA Civ 1579, [2024] 12 WLUK 315, [2025] 2 COPLR 179 .... 13.33
EOA, Re *see* Greenwich RLBC
Edwards (decs'd), Re [2007] EWHC 1119 (Ch), [2007] 5 WLUK 72, [2007] WTLR 1387 .... 4.73

F

F v M [2021] EWFC 4, [2021] 1 WLUK 112 .... 2.13; 8.00, 8.08, 8.16, 8.18; 12.07; 13.08; 14.01, 14.21
F v West Berkshire Health Authority [1990] 2 AC 1, [1989] 2 WLR 1025, [1989] 2 All ER 545 .... 6.09
F (mental patient: sterilisation), Re *see* F v West Berkshire Health Authority
FH, Re *see* Wakefield Metropolitan District Council v FH

G

G, Re *see* ICB v G (by her litigation friend the Official Solicitor)
G (Court of Protection: injunction), Re [2022] EWCA Civ 1312, [2023] Fam 107, [2022] 3 WLR 1339 .... 8.31; 9.40
GP, Re *see* Local Authority, a v GP (capacity: care, support & education)
Giorgi v Italy (Application 23735/19) (judgment 16 June 2022) 2.38
Greenwich RLBC [2021] EWCOP 20, [2021] 1 WLUK 514, [2021] COPLR 564 .... 4.48, 4.59

H

HBCC v LC (by her litigation friend, the Official Solicitor) ; IIBCC v LG [2010] EWHC 1527 (Fam), [2010] 6 WLUK 582 .... 2.57; 5.41
H-C (Children), Re [2016] EWCA Civ 136, [2016] 4 WLR 85, [2016] 3 WLUK 309 .... 8.33
H-N (Children) (domestic abuse: finding of fact hearings), Re [2021] EWCA Civ 448, [2022] 1 WLR 2681, [2022] 1 All ER 475 .... 2.11; 8.03, 8.08, 8.09, 8.17, 8.19, 8.23; 14.00, 14.01
Hall v Hall (1865-69) LR 1 P & D 481, [1868] 3 WLUK 24 .... 6.28
Harbin v Masterman (No 2) [1896] 1 Ch 351, [1895] 12 WLUK 55 .... 6.64; 12.34
Heart of England NHS Foundation Trust v JB [2014] EWHC 342 (COP), [2014] 2 WLUK 529, (2014) 137 BMLR 232 .... 3.18, 3.22, 3.30; 4.37, 4.67
Hertfordshire County Council v AB [2018] EWHC 3103 (Fam), [2019] Fam 291, [2019] 2 WLR 1084, [2019] COPLR 192 .... 6.50
Hokkanen v Finland (A/299-A); K v Finland (Application 19823/92) [1994] 9 WLUK 123, [1996] 1 FLR 289, [1995] 2 FCR 320 .... 6.35
Hillingdon London Borough Council v Neary [2011] EWHC 1377 (COP), [2011] 4 All ER 584, [2011] 6 WLUK 166 .... 12.31

Hull City Council v KF [2022] EWCOP 33, [2022] 7 WLUK 382, [2022] COPLR 540 ... 2.57; 5.06
Humphreys v Humphreys [2004] EWHC 2201 (Ch), [2004] 10 WLUK 307, [2005] 1 FCR 712 ... 9.19
Hwang v Kim [2021] EWHC 3327 (QB), [2021] 12 WLUK 99 ... 2.43

I

ICB v G (by her litigation friend the Official Solicitor) [2024] EWCOP 13, [2024] 2 WLUK 532 ... 8.01, 8.19, 8.30; 12.02
IH (observence of Muslim practice), Re [207] EWCOP 9, [2017] 6 WLUK 176, [2017] COPLR 281 ... 9.13
IM v LM *see* M (an adult) (capacity: consent to sexual relations), Re
Ilnseher v Germany (Application 10211/12) [2018] 12 WLUK 770, [2019] MHLR 278 ... 6.54

J

JB, Re *see* Heart of England NHS Foundation Trust v JB and *see* Local Authority, a v JB

K

K v K [2022] EWCA Civ 468 ... 8.08
K (forced marriage: Passport Order), Re [2020] EWCA Civ 190, [2020] Fam 283, [2020] 2 WLR 1279 ... 2.57; 6.33, 6.41; 7.01; 14.22
KH v Nottinghamshire NHS Foundation Trust [2025] UKUT 128 (AAC), [2025] 1 WLR 4263, [2025] 4 WLUK 637 ... 3.54
KK v STC *see* CC v KK
KP, Re *see* Local Authority, a v KP (acting by the Official Solicitor as her litigation friend)

L

L v J [2010] EWHC 2665 (Fam), [2010] 9 WLUK 378, [2011] 1 FLR 1279 ... 3.30; 6.11; 9.30
L (vulnerable adults with capacity: court's jurisdiction), Re [2010] EWHC 2675 (Fam), [2011] Fam 189, [2011] 3 WLR 445 ... 6.64
L (vulnerable adults with capacity: court's jurisdiction), Re [2012] EWCA Civ 253, [2013] Fam 1, [2012] 3 WLR 1439 ... 1.43; 6.12, 6.16, 6.21, 6.26, 6.38, 6.50, 6.64; 9.31; 14.14, 14.17, 14.21
L (vulnerable adults with capacity: court's jurisdiction), Re [2011] EWHC 1022 (Fam), [2011] 4 WLUK 566, [2012] 1 FLR 1119 ... 9.31, 9.45, 9.58
LBL v RYJ & VJ *see* L v J
LBX, Re [2011] EWHC 2419 (Fam) ... 2.73
LBX v K *see* X v K
LBX v TT [2014] EWCOP 24, [2014] WLUK 1009, [2014] COPLR 561 ... 8.11
LDV, Re [2013] EWHC 272 (Fam), [2013] 2 WLUK 453 ... 4.19
LW, Re *see* County Council, a v LW [2020] EWCOP 50
Lancashire & South Cumbria NHS Foundation Trust v Q [2022] EWCOP 6, [2022] 2 WLUK 369, [2022] COPLR 315 ... 4.26
Local Authority, a v A (by the Official Solicitor) *see* A (capacity: refusal of contraception), Re
Local Authority v B [2024] EWCA Civ 572, [2024] 5 WLUK 335, [2024] 1 COPLR 243 ... 13.35
Local Authority, a v BF [2018] EWCA Civ 2962, [2018] 12 WLUK 584, [2019] COPLR 150 ... 6.10, 6.16, 6.46, 6.51, 6.53

Local Authority, a v DL [2012] EWCA Civ 253 *see* L (vulnerable adults with capacity: court's jurisdiction), Re [2012] EWCA Civ 253
Local Authority, a v DL [2011] EWHC 1022 (Fam) *see* L (vulnerable adults with capacity: court's jurisdiction), Re [2011] EWHC 1022 (Fam),
Local Authority, a v GP (capacity: care, support & education) [2020] EWCOP 56, [2020] 9 WLUK 449, [2021] COPLR 1 ....4.37, 4.43, 4.46
Local Authority, a v JB [2021] UKSC 52, [2022] AC 1322, [2021] 3 WLR 1381 ...3.22, 3.23, 3.30, 3.41; 4.04, 4.07, 4.15, 4.16; 14.08, 14.10, 14.11
Local Authority, a v K [2005] EWHC 144 (Fam), [2005] 1 FLR 851, [2005] Fam Law 450.... 8.30
Local Authority, a v KP (acting by the Official Solicitor as her litigation friend) [2023] EWHC 3102 (Fam), [2023] 12 WLUK 438....1.32, 1.33, 1.34; 2.57; 5.03; 7.15
Local Authority, a v LD [2023] EWHC 1258 (Fam), [2024] 1 WLR 1052, [2023] 5 WLUK 363....6.54; 9.49
Local Authority, a v M [2014] EWCOP 33, [2015] COPLR 6.... 8.30
Local Authority, a v Mrs A (by the Official Solicitor) [2010] EWHC 1549 (Fam), [2011] Fam 61, [2011] 2 WLR 878 .... 9.42
Local Authority, a v NP (by her litigation friend the Official Solicitor) *see* Southwark LBC v NP [2019] EWCOP 48
Local Authority, a v P (by her litigation friend, the Official Solicitor) *see* P (vulnerable adult: withdrawal of application), Re
Local Authority, a v RS (capacity) [2020] EWCOP 29, [2020] 6 WLUK 375, [2020] COPLR 705.... 4.18
Local Authority A v ZZ (by his litigation friend the Official Solicitor) [2024] EWCOP 21, [2024] 4 WLUK 160, [2024] 1 COPLR 397 ....4.21, 4.70
Local Authority A, a v ZZ [2023] EWCOP 61, [2023] 7 WLUK 736.... 4.54
Local Authority, a (Inquiry: restraint on publication), Re [2003] EWHC 2746 (Fam), [2004] Fam 96, [2004] 2 WLR 926 .... 6.27
Local Authority X v M [2007] EWHC 2003 (Fam), [2007] 8 WLUK 178, [2009] 1 FLR 443 ....14.15, 14.25
London Borough of Brent v NB [2017] EWCOP 34, [2017] 10 WLUK 602 .... 3.15
London Borough of Croydon v KR [2019] EWHC 2498 (Fam), [2019] 9 WLUK 291, [2020] COPLR 285....6.36, 6.38, 6.41; 9.51
London Borough of Enfield v SA [2010] EWHC 196 (Admin), [2010] 2 WLUK 230, [2010] 1 FLR 1836.... 8.31
London Borough of Islington v EF [2022] EWHC 803 (Fam), [2022] 3 WLUK 548 ....6.49; 7.54; 9.51
London Borough of Southwark v NP [2019] EWCOP 48, [2019] 4 WLR 141, [2019] 10 WLUK 379....3.74, 3.76
London Borough of Tower Hamlets v A [2020] EWCOP 21, [2020] 4 WLUK 262, [2020] COPLR 609 .... 4.20
London Borough of Tower Hamlets v PB [2019] EWCOP 27, [2019] 7 WLUK 255, [2019] COPLR 398 ....14.09, 14.10, 14.12
London Borough of Tower Hamlets v PB [2020] EWCOP 34, [2020] 4 WLR 94, [2020] 7 WLUK 27 ....3.09, 3.19
London Borough of Wandsworth v M [2017] EWHC 2435 (Fam), [2017] 10 WLUK 34, [2018] 1 FLR 919.... 9.39
Luton Borough Council v G [2024] EWCOP 18, [2024] 3 WLUK 564 ....2.57; 7.51; 12.30

M

M v N [2015] EWCOP 76, [2015] 11 WLUK 514, [2016] COPLR 88 .... 14.16
M (An Adult) (capacity: consent to sexual relations), Re [2014] EWCA Civ 37, [2015] Fam 61, [2014] 3 WLR 409 .... 3.26

M (Children) (contact refusal: appeal), Re [2013] EWCA Civ 1147, [2013] 9 WLUK 473, [2014] 2 FLR 685 .... 8.31
MB v PB [2022] EWCOP 14 *see* Newcastle upon Tyne Hospitals NHS Foundation Trust v H (a child) [2022] EWCOP 14
MM (an adult), Re *see* Local Authority X v M [2007] EWHC 2003 (Fam)
MacPherson v Sunderland City Council (Rev 1) *see* EO, Re [2024] EWCA Civ 1579
MacPherson (by her litigation friend the Official Solicitor) v Sunderland City Council [2025] EWCOP 18 (T3) [2025] 5 WLUK 392 .... 3.09
Masterman-Lister v Brutton & Co *see* Masterman-Lister v Jewell
Masterman-Lister v Jewell; Masterman-Lister v Brutton & Co [2002] EWCA Civ 1889, [2003] 1 WLR 1511, [2003] 3 All ER 162 .... 4.26, 4.52
Mazhar, Re *see* Mazhar v Birmingham Community Healthcare Foundation NHS Trust
Mazhar v Birmingham Community Healthcare Foundation NHS Trust [2020] EWCA Civ 1377, [2021] 1 WLR 1207, [2021] 2 All ER 693, [2021] COPLR 115 .... 6.52, 6.68; 12.30
Meyers, Re *see* Southend-on-Sea Borough Council v Meyers

N

N v ACCG; N (an adult) (Court of Protection: jurisdiction) [2017] UKSC 22, [2017] AC 549, [2017] 2 WLR 1011 .... 9.08
N, Re [2015] EWCOP 76 *see* M v N [2015] EWCOP 76, [2015] 11 WLUK 514, [2016] COPLR 88
N (a child), Re [2019] EWCA Civ 1997, [2019] 4 WLR 154, [2019] 11 WLUK 230.. 13.33
NB v MI (capacity to contract marriage) [2021] EWHC 224 (Fam), [2021] 2 WLUK 109, [2021] 2 FLR 786 .... 4.69, 4.70
NHS Trust, an v A [2013] EWHC 2442 (COP), [2014] Fam 161, [2014] 2 WLR 607. 6.53
NHS Trust, an v P [2021] EWCOP 27, [2021] 4 WLR 69, [2021] 4 WLUK 379 .... 4.26, 4.28
NHS Trust v WA *see* Avon & Wiltshire Mental Health Partnership v WA
NK v RK [2023] EWCOP 37, [2023] 8 WLUK 132, (2023) 26 CCL Rep 565 .... 6.28; 9.53
NS v MI [2006] EWHC 1646 (Fam), [2006] 7 WLUK 102, [2007] 1 FLR 444 .... 14.15
Newcastle upon Tyne Hospitals NHS Foundation Trust v H (a child) [2022] EWCOP 14, [2022] 3 WLUK 81, (2023) 194 BMLR 126 .... 1.34; 2.57; 5.57; 8.03, 8.08; 9.16, 9.41
Newcastle Upon Tyne City Council v TP (best interests) [2016] EWCOP 61, [2016] 12 WLUK 623 .... 1.31, 1.32
Newcastle-Upon-Tyne City Council v TP (best interests of TP No 1) [2016] EWCOP B3 .... 1.31; 2.57
Newcastle-Upon-Tyne City Council v TP (best interests of TP No 2) [2016] EWCOP B4 .... 12.27
Norfolk County Council v CA [2024] EWCOP 64 (T3), [2024] 10 WLUK 696 .... 1.32, 1.35; 2.57; 3.15; 5.66; 6.66; 7.00, 7.35; 8.31, 8.32; 9.24; 10.13; 12.21, 12.33; 13.14
Norfolk County Council v CA [2025] EWCOP 16 (T3), [2025] 4 WLUK 647 .... 7.50
Norfolk County Council v Grady [2025] EWCOP 15 (T3), [2025] 1 WLUK 698 .... 7.50
Norfolk CC v PB & TB [2014] EWCOP 14, [2014] 3 WLU 641, [2015] COPLR 118 .... 2.57; 3.06
North Bristol NHS Trust v R [2023] EWCOP 5, [2023] 2 WLUK 451 .... 3.22, 3.23, 3.43
Nottinghamshire County Council v SV [2025] EWCOP 37 (T3), [2025] 10 WLUK 610 .... 8.01, 8.02, 8.08

O

Opuz v Turkey (Application 33401/02) [2009] 6 WLUK 179, (2010) 50 EHRR 28, 27 BHRC 159 .... 2.35

P

P, Re *see* NHS Trust, an v P
P (abortion), Re [2013] EWHC 50 (COP), [2013] COPLR 405 .... 1.42
P (vulnerable adult: withdrawal of application), Re [2024] EWHC 1882 (Fam), [2024] 7 WLUK 480, [2025] 1 FLR 588 .... 1.31, 1.34; 6.00, 6.33, 6.59, 6.64; 7.24, 7.34
PB, Re *see* Norfolk County Council v PB
PC v City of York Council *see* York City Council v C [2013] EWCA Civ 478, [2014] Fam 10, [2014] 2 WLR 1
PC (by her litigation friend the Official Solicitor) v City of York Council *see* York City Council v C
PCT v P [2009] 12 WLUK 670, [2011] 1 FLR 287, (2010) 13 CCL Rep 636............. 3.34
PH v A Local Authority [2011] EWHC 1704 (Fam), [2011] 6 WLUK 749................. 3.76
PS (incapacitated or vulnerable adult), Re *see* Sunderland City Council v P
Primary Care Trust, a v LDV *see* LDV, Re
Public Guardian v RI [2022] EWCOP 22, [2022] 6 WLUK 23, [2022] COPLR 420... 4.65

Q

Q, Re *see* Lancashire & South Cumbria NHS Foundation Trust v Q
QJ v Local Authority [2020] EWCOP 7, [2020] 1 WLUK 374 .... 3.09; 9.47

R

R v C [2009] UKHL 42, [2009] 1 WLR 1786, [2009] 4 All ER 1033 .... 3.22
R v Cooper *see* R v C
R v Lucas (Lyabode Ruth) [1981] QB 720, [1981] 3 WLR 120, [1981] 2 All ER 1008 ....8.30, 8.32, 8.33
R v Middleton [2000] TLR 293 .... 8.32
R (on the application of Aguilar Quila) v Secretary of State for the Home Department [2011] UKSC 45, [2012] 1 AC 621, [2011] 3 WLR 836...................................... 6.36
R (on the application of Ali) v Secretary of State for the Home Department; R (on the application of Bibi) v Secretary of State for the Home Department [2015] UKSC 68, [2015] 1 WLR 5055, [2016] 2 All ER 193 .... 6.40
RK (capacity: contact: inherent jurisdiction), Re *see* NK v RK
RT & LT v A Local Authority *see* T v T
Redcar & Cleveland Borough Council v PR [2019] EWHC 2305 (Fam), [2019] 9 WLUK 37, [2019] COPLR 446..6.50; 9.54

S

S, Re [2009] EWHC 2115 (Fam)... 8.30
S, Re [2010] EWHC 2405 (Fam), [2010] 10 WLUK 13, [2011] WTLR 449 .... 4.27
SA (vulnerable adult with capacity: marriage), Re [2005] EWHC 2942 (Fam), [2005] 12 WLUK 514, [2006] 1 FLR 867..6.16, 6.17, 6.22, 6.24, 6.27, 6.56; 7.13; 8.13, 8.14; 9.29, 9.31, 9.34, 9.52; 14.15, 14.16, 14.18
SAD v SED [2017] EWCOP 3, [2016] 11 WLUK 139, [2017] WTLR 1439.............. 4.64
SB (a patient) (capacity to consent to termination), Re [2013] EWHC 1417 (COP), [2013] 5 WLUK 518, [2013] 3 FCR 384.. 3.22
Scott v Scott [1913] AC 417, [1913] 5 WLUK 10... 8.15
Sheffield City Council v E; E (alleged patient), Re [2004] EWHC 2808 (Fam), [2005] Fam 326, [2005] 2 WLR 953 .... 4.24
Shtukaturov v Russia (Application 44009/05) [2008] 3 WLUK 555, (2012) 54 EHRR 27, (2008) 11 CCL Rep 440... 6.37
Southend-on-Sea Borough Council v Meyers [2019] EWHC 399 (Fam), [2019] 2 WLUK 406, [2019] COPLR 202 ....6.20, 6.46, 6.55; 9.35
Southwark LBC v NP [2019] EWCOP 48, [2019] 4 WLR 141, [2019] 10 WLUK 379.. 12.25

Spencer v Spencer; Anderson v Spencer [2018] EWCA Civ 100, [2019] Fam 66, [2018] 3 WLR 972 .... 6.26
Stockport Metropolitan Borough Council v EKK (Rev 1) [2025] EWCOP 42, [2025] 11 WLUK 523 .... 4.68, 4.69
Sunderland City Council v P [2007] EWHC 623 (Fam), [2007] 3 WLUK 256, [2007] 2 FLR 1083 .... 6.53

T

T v T [2010] EWHC 1910 (Fam), [2010] 7 WLUK 733, [2011] 1 FLR 594 .... 3.22
T, Re [1993] Fam 95 *see* T (adult: refusal of treatment), Re
T, Re [2004] EWCA Civ 458, [2005] 2 FLR 838 .... 8.30
T (adult: refusal of treatment), Re [1993] Fam 95, [1992] 3 WLR 782, [1992] 4 All ER 649 .... 6.22, 6.28; 14.16
TB v KB & LH (capacity to conduct proceedings) [2019] EWCOP 14, [2019] 4 WLUK 486, [2020] COPLR 149 .... 4.27
TP, Re *see* Newcastle-upon-Tyne City Council v TO (Capacity of TP No 2)
TT (injunctive relief) (by his litigation friend the Official Solicitor), Re [2022] EWHC 2185 (Fam), [2022] 8 WLUK 72 .... 2.57; 6.66; 7.11, 7.13; 9.43
Tunikova v Russia (Application 55974/16) [2021] 12 WLUK 649, (2022) 75 EHRR 1 .... 2.37; 6.32

V

Vertigo v Philippines (CEDAW/46/D/18/2008, 29 November 2007) 2.33
Volodina v Russia (Application 41261/17) (judgment 9 July 2019) 2.36

W

W (a child) (non-accidental injury), Re [2002] EWCA Civ 710, [2002] 4 WLUK 631, [2003] 2 FCR 346 .... 8.30
WU v BU [2021] EWCOP 54, [2021] 9 WLUK 334, [2022] COPLR 46 .... 1.32, 1.33, 1.34; 2.57; 4.46; 5.19; 9.05, 9.48, 9.58, 9.66; 10.34; 14.28
Wakefield Metropolitan District Council v FH [2024] EWHC 830 (Fam), [2024] 3 WLUK 622 .... 1.32; 2.57; 7.03; 12.28
Wakefield Metropolitan District Council v DN [2019] EWHC 2306 (Fam), [2019] 9 WLUK 38, [2019] COPLR 525 .... 6.50; 9.56
Wakefield Metropolitan District Council v R [2019] EWHC 3581 (Fam), [2019] 12 WLUK 412 .... 8.33
Warrington Borough Council v Y [2023] EWCOP 27, [2023] 6 WLUK 373 .... 4.09; 14.10
Wiltshire County Council v RB (by her litigation friend the Official Solicitor) [2023] EWCOP 26, [2023] 6 WLUK 326 .... 4.05
Wingrove v Wingrove (1885) 11 PD 81, [1885] 11 WLUK 67 .... 6.22
Winterwerp v The Netherlands (A/33) (Application 6301/73) [1979] 10 WLUK 201, [1979] ECHR 4, (1979-80) 2 EHRR 387 .... 6.44, 6.50, 6.52
Wookey v Wookey; S (a child) (injunction), Re [1991] Fam 121, [1991] 3 WLR 135, [1991] 3 All ER 365 .... 9.54

X

X v K [2013] EWHC 3230 (Fam), [2013] 6 WLUK 532 .... 4.33, 4.35, 4.38, 4.47
X, Re *see* A v X

Y

York City Council v C [2013] EWCA Civ 478, [2014] Fam 10, [2014] 2 WLR 1 .... 3.22, 3.45; 4.45, 4.68; 14.09

Z

Z v Kent County Council [2018] 10 WLUK 517, [2019] 1 FCR 830, [2019] COPLR 79 .... 4.29
Z NHS Foundation Trust v Patricia [2023] EWCOP 41, [2023] 5 WLUK 612 .... 14.11
Z (Local Authority: Duty), Re [2004] EWHC 2817 (Fam), [2005] 1 WLR 959, [2005] 3 All ER 280 .... 6.22
ZZ, Re *see* Local Authority A v ZZ (by his litigation friend the Official Solicitor)

CHAPTER 1

Introduction

'The love of power and the love of liberty are in eternal antagonism'[1]

PURPOSE AND ROADMAP

1.01 The intended readers of this book include lawyers (barristers, solicitors and legal executives) practising in the Court of Protection and in the Family Division of the High Court, as well as judges and their clerks. Lawyers practising in healthcare, community care, and adult safeguarding may also find the book informative. In addition, the book may sadly be useful to lawyers representing bereaved families in inquests where the deceased was killed by an abuser or died by suicide in the context of coercive control.

1.02 The book has been written in a manner that aims to be accessible to non-lawyers too. These include social workers, members of safeguarding adult boards, safeguarding professionals in NHS trusts, police officers involved in multi-agency responses to safeguarding, those involved in the regulation of adult health and social care, those working in the Office of the Public Guardian, lay advocates such as Independent Mental Capacity Advocates, persons who act as litigation friend, and those concerned that a loved one is the victim of coercive control.

Objectives of the book

1.03 The book has three objectives:

(1) **To improve awareness of coercive and controlling behaviour and how people with mental disabilities may become victims and may heal.**[2] Chapter 2 provides an introduction to the phenomenon of coercive control, makes connections with the criminal law, and discusses how an understanding of contemporary abuse requires appreciation of the historical degradation of women and the devaluation of disability. Research evidence from the trauma literature that is relevant to coercive control is considered in Chapter 10, which explains how those who are victims/survivors of coercive control may access trauma therapies to enable them to heal.

1 John Stewart Mill, *The Subjection of Women* (London, Longmans, Green, Reader & Dyer, 1869).
2 By mental disabilities, I include people with learning disabilities, those who are neurodiverse, those with mental health problems, those with brain injury or a cognitive disability such as dementia.

(2) **To make the law in relation to coercive control in the Court of Protection and under the inherent jurisdiction of the High Court more accessible.** Chapters 3 and 4 explain what it means to 'lack capacity' to make certain decisions in the context of coercive control, while Chapter 5 provides illustrative examples of coercive control jurisprudence in the Court of Protection. Chapters 6 and 7 cover the law, procedure and cases under the inherent jurisdiction. Chapter 8 deals with fact-finding processes, and Chapter 9 covers remedies, including interim relief to prevent imminent harm, and injunctions.

(3) **To strengthen the skillset of legal professionals** who represent one of the three main parties in coercive control cases:

(a) The victim/survivor of coercive control

The victim/survivor may have endured years of lies, manipulation, and devaluation, leading to a distorted sense of reality and fragmented memory. Chapter 11 suggests that lawyers representing a victim/survivor of coercive control operate by adopting biopsychosocial and trauma-informed approaches to their legal practice.

(b) The public body, usually a local authority

Chapter 12 provides tips to those representing public bodies, including how to avoid common pitfalls such as delay and imprecision.

(c) The controlling person

Representing the person who has been accused of coercive and controlling behaviour is extremely challenging, and Chapter 13 makes suggestions for lawyers to progress their client's case without falling into the trap of becoming controlled by the client.

Terminology

1.04 The book uses the term 'coercive control' as an umbrella term to include coercive and controlling behaviour and undue influence: see Chapter 2.

1.05 In a 2025 report, the Domestic Abuse Commissioner noted that domestic abuse is a gendered crime and that survivors of all genders face significant barriers to accessing a justice response. There is no term that is preferred by those with lived experience of domestic abuse, and the Commissioner has chosen to use the terms 'victim', 'survivor', and 'victim and survivor' in a gender-neutral way while recognising that domestic abuse is a gendered crime that disproportionately affects women.[3] Similarly, this book uses the term 'victim/survivor' inclusively to respect people's own language preferences. The word 'victim' is used in a legal context, as the behaviour is a crime and responsibility lies with the perpetrator. In

3 Dame Nicole Jacobs, Domestic Abuse Commissioner for England and Wales, *Shifting the scales: Transforming the criminal justice response to domestic abuse*, January 2025.

the domestic abuse context, the term 'survivor' may be preferred, as it recognises agency, resilience and recovery. I apologise if I have used one term when the other might have been more appropriate. While recognising the gendered nature of domestic abuse, the book uses gender-neutral pronouns which is the house-style of Bloomsbury Law.

1.06 The Mental Capacity Act 2005 uses the letter 'P' to donate the person who lacks capacity, as does this book where appropriate. In the context of the inherent jurisdiction, the word 'adult' is preferred.

1.07 The terms 'controlling person', 'abuser' and 'perpetrator' are used interchangeably, depending on context. The book does not use the term 'alleged abuser' or 'alleged victim' because while allegations must be tested and, where required, determined through a fact-finding process, the rider of 'alleged' risks discounting the victim's account and is stylistically cumbersome. Where status is genuinely in issue, the text will make that clear by reference to the procedural stage or the court's findings.

1.08 The word 'lawyer' is a shorthand for a barrister, solicitor or legal executive practising in England and Wales.

1.09 The law in this book relates to England and Wales, and is correct at 1 March 2026.

The legal frontline

1.10 My practice in the Court of Protection has exposed me to the extraordinary dynamics that can unfold in private settings, often revealed only when the court authorises intervention. Among the most complex matters are those involving a person said to lack capacity who is simultaneously the victim/survivor of coercive or controlling behaviour by another (see Chapter 2 on coercive control). Unlike other Court of Protection work where an experienced practitioner may navigate a case by drawing on previous experience or by seeking collegial advice, cases involving coercive control rarely feel intuitive. There is a notable scarcity of practical guidance for lawyers practising in this field.

1.11 At times, I am instructed by a local authority to advise whether proceedings should be commenced. Key questions include: Is there sufficient evidence of abuse, or is an application premature? Is there evidence that the person lacks capacity in the relevant domains so that the Court of Protection can make orders, or would relief be better sought under the High Court's inherent jurisdiction? What exactly is the local authority proposing to do, and why? If the person wishes to remain at home, how – if at all – can their removal or separation be lawfully and ethically achieved? Is the objective to facilitate separation and adjustment away from the perpetrator, or to support the person to resume the relationship with appropriate guardrails to mitigate risk? What arrangements can be made to ensure timely access to psychotherapy and other therapeutic support to help the victim/survivor heal from their trauma?

1.12 In other cases, I act for the perpetrator. This raises practical, regulatory and human challenges. How should I advise the client on a schedule of allegations of coercive control? How can a productive conference be conducted when the client is hostile, shouts at me, or believes I am part of a conspiracy? How can my solicitor and I manage a client whose focus is on discrediting professionals rather than engaging with the court's welfare inquiry? How should I approach repeated attempts to amend my position statement (a document that a barrister writes for their client before each court hearing) with points that are, in my professional judgment, unarguable?

1.13 I am also instructed to represent the victim/survivor, commonly via a litigation friend such as the Official Solicitor. I will typically review substantial case materials and, where possible, meet the person I represent (I realise that barristers meeting clients in advance is quite rare, but where possible, I try to meet clients in their home).). Should I discuss the abuse directly with the client, or leave that to psychologists? Does direct enquiry risk harm or retraumatisation? On might avoidance inadvertently silence the client or suggest that I am not interested? If the client becomes emotionally dysregulated, what should I do to ensure their safety and preserve trust? If the client starts crying, should I avoid meeting the client again?

Reported and unreported cases

1.14 Chapters 5 and 7 discuss cases reported in the National Archive, typically authored by High Court judges who are 'tier 3 judges' of the Court of Protection: Family Division judges exercising the inherent jurisdiction of the High Court. However, most Court of Protection cases are heard by district judges (tier 1) or circuit judges (tier 2), whose judgments are less frequently published.

Mary

1.15 Two unreported cases illustrate key issues, and I have changed the names and identifying features in both. The first concerned Mary, aged 83. She had been married to Richard for over 55 years. She developed mild dementia and was hospitalised with pneumonia. During her admission, a social worker assessed her care needs and Mary revealed that Richard had recently demeaned her by calling her a dog and forcing her to eat from a bowl on the floor.

1.16 Mary's son had observed bruises on her body. He told the social worker that Mary had suffered physical, emotional, and psychological abuse from Richard for decades. Richard controlled every aspect of her life, including her clothing, social interactions, diet, and finances, resorting to violence if she disobeyed.

1.17 The local authority applied to the Court of Protection. I was Mary's barrister, and took my instructions from the litigation friend who had been appointed by the court. During proceedings, Mary described Richard as 'good in lots of ways, but not when he's hitting me though'. When asked about her response to his violence, she said, 'I just take it'. An independent psychologist was appointed, to whom Mary expressed admiration for Richard, feeling inadequate compared to his independence and cooking skills.

1.18 The judge determined that Mary lacked capacity to decide on her residence, care, and contact with others, leading to her temporary relocation to a care home for safety. The local authority presented a schedule of allegations (see Chapter 8 on fact-finding) detailing a pattern of abuse. Richard denied most of the allegations but admitted to a past assault that caused Mary to lose an eye. He dismissed the dog bowl incident as a joke.

1.19 As Richard refused carers entry to their home and as he could no longer meet Mary's needs, a return home was ruled out. Richard denied many violent incidents recorded in medical records, blaming others, including his sons, from whom he had isolated Mary.

1.20 Mary's dementia progressed in the care home, where she formed close bonds with staff. She occasionally exhibited sexually disinhibited behaviours, necessitating a brief admission to a mental health unit before returning to the care home. Both Mary and Richard desired unsupervised contact at home. Supervised contact occurred weekly, until Richard's death two years later.

1.21 Mary was fortunate to survive, given the data on homicide and suicide, as discussed in Chapter 2. Hospital clinicians and social workers were pivotal in raising the alarm, sharing safeguarding information, and ensuring her safety.

1.22 Her case underscores another recurring issue in coercive control cases. While it was beneficial for Mary not to return to her abusive husband, Richard's behaviour resulted in Mary losing the right to live in her home. Despite her wish to return, the Court of Protection could not remove Richard to facilitate her return without him. This appears unjust: the victim/survivor lost her home, while the abuser remained. This perpetuates a gender imbalance, as most domestic abuse victims/survivors are women.

Jessica

1.23 In the second case, I represented Jessica, a 30-year-old woman with mild learning disabilities. She had moved from her mother's home to live with her older sister, following a family dispute. The local authority sought a decision from the Court of Protection. Social workers said that it was in Jessica's best interests to remain with her sister rather than return to her controlling mother. Although Jessica did not wish to live with her mother, her mother claimed that Jessica was being manipulated by her sister. The mother said only she, the mother, knew Jessica's true wishes.

1.24 The fact-finding hearing was challenging but essential. The older sister bravely gave evidence, and the court ensured her physical and psychological safety by allowing a separate entrance and exit, and using a screen to shield her from her mother. The sister's testimony was both detailed and moving. It enabled the judge to find that the mother had engaged in controlling and coercive behaviour towards Jessica over several years, and that this had adversely affected Jessica's life, independence, and happiness, leading to her social isolation.

1.25 The mother had made unfounded allegations against educational services, care providers, and activity centres, withdrawing Jessica from these services and further isolating her. She disregarded Jessica's views and needs, took her to unnecessary medical appointments, and made false allegations against the older sister in an effort to influence Jessica's living arrangements.

1.26 The court determined that the mother upset and manipulated Jessica, fed her lines to say, lacked insight into her actions, and undermined Jessica's activities and placements to keep her dependent. The judge granted the local authority's application for Jessica to continue living with her sister and issued an injunction against the mother, prohibiting any contact with Jessica by any means: this aligned with Jessica's wishes and feelings, and representations I made to the court on Jessica's behalf.

1.27 This case exemplified human rights in action, delivered by a district judge in a rural court. The justice system protected Jessica from her mother's toxic influence, allowing her to thrive in her sister's care. As the hearing concluded, there was a poignant moment when the judge and advocates stood and bowed to each other, silently acknowledging for a moment the profundity of the decision and the court having paved the way for Jessica to get on with her life. As the judge departed, the mother shouted at the judge: 'I love Jessica: It's not me but her sister who's abusing her. You've misunderstood everything!'

OVERVIEW OF THE CASES

1.28 In writing this book, I have reviewed all reported cases on coercive control in the Court of Protection, the Family Division (in relation to the inherent jurisdiction for adults) and the family courts (in relation to children). Many of the cases are cited in the book. Expected themes emerged: power and domination, arrogant abusers, enmeshed relationships, trauma bonds, and the challenge of achieving a satisfactory resolution for the victim/survivor. What I had not realised until categorising the cases is the frequency and veracity with which perpetrators dress up power and domination as 'love' like Jessica's mother did. Abusers justify acts of violence and campaigns of control by asserting their love for the person they have harmed.

1.29 When a strong trauma bond exists between two people, it can be challenging for a non-psychology trained person (such as a lawyer) to discern an *intention* to abuse, even if the effects on the victim/survivor are evident. Especially so where the relationship contains a care dynamic, common in Court of Protection cases. Forensic psychologist Ahona Guha helps us understand:

> The reality for people who offend is not often born of fantastic psychological twists and dark desires, but instead of the mundane: crushing need; anger; secret fears; repressing instead of confronting; trying to control a world that seems dangerous and out of control; avoidance; hostility; difficulties with communicating (and thus showing instead of telling). Harms and abuse are often born of a mixture of these few ingredients.[4]

1.30 People abuse for all these reasons and more. I will suggest in Chapter 13 that while a lawyer can have empathy for an abuser who professes their love for the victim/survivor, an appreciative enquiry into the mind of an abuser is no substitute for harm reduction, victim/survivor safety and healing, and the pursuit of justice.

1.31 The cases in this book involve relationships with a 'completely unequal dynamic',[5] where one person is the controlling 'dominant leader',[6] and the other has 'no space to have a thinking mind of her own'.[7] For instance, a father controlled his daughter so strictly that she was forced to wear covert recording equipment outside the home for him to monitor her interactions. He rationed food to £1.50 per day for his family of four.[8]

1.32 The book describes a sex offender who was so 'serious, determined, persistent, manipulative and obsessive' that he prohibited his stepdaughter from speaking to social workers.[9] Another case involved an abuser whose behaviour towards their disabled relative showed an 'unacceptable and, in some measure, shocking level of intolerance, abuse and lack of empathy'.[10] The book details cases where the abuser was 'bullish and brutish',[11] 'misleading' and 'unkind',[12]

4 Ahona Guha, *Reclaim: Understanding Complex Trauma and Those who Abuse* (Scribe, 2023), p 132.
5 *A Local Authority v Mrs A (by the Official Solicitor)* [2010] EWHC 1549, para 73.
6 *Newcastle-Upon-Tyne City Council v TP (Best Interests of TP No. 1)* [2016] EWCOP B3, para 55.
7 *Newcastle-Upon-Tyne City Council v TP (Best Interests)* [2016] EWCOP 61, para 34.
8 *A Local Authority v P (by her litigation friend, the Official Solicitor) and others* [2024] EWHC 1882, para 8.
9 *A Local Authority v KP (Acting by the Official Solicitor as her litigation friend) and another* [2023] EWHC 3102 (Fam).
10 *Wakefield Metropolitan District Council v FH & Ors* [2024] EWHC 830, para 17.
11 *In the Matter of CA (Fact Finding – Capacity – Inherent Jurisdiction – Injunctive Relief)* [2024] EWCOP 64 (T3), para 66.
12 *Re BU* [2021] EWCOP 54, para 93.

and who took actions 'the opposite of what one would expect a supportive family member or a concerned person to do'.[13]

1.33 There are also cases where a disabled person is targeted as easy prey: in one case the female victim/survivor was beaten – physically and mentally – into submission until she 'craved' the perpetrator.[14] In another, the abuser's manipulation was so successful that the victim/survivor had 'closed her mind to the possibility of his motives being anything other than benign'.[15]

1.34 There is then is the case of a 'determined, persistent, manipulative and obsessive'[16] person who controlled every aspect of his partner's life, including her movements and diet, rather than inviting her for a romantic meal.[17] A case of a lover so jealous that he monitored his partner whenever she left the home,[18] and another where the abuser socially isolated the victim/survivor, creating 'cult-like' dynamics.[19]

1.35 These are all cases about power, domination and the quest for control: behaviours that leave behind the mental scars of enduring trauma. In one of the cases, the victim/survivor said that the abuse by her daughter was, 'so traumatic that I can't even remember what happened'.[20] One of the central lenses of this book is trauma, whose effects are explained more fully in Chapter 10. Practical suggestions for trauma-informed approaches to legal representation are provided in Chapter 11 for those representing the victim/survivor, Chapter 12 for those working for or on behalf of a local authority, and Chapter 13 for legal representatives of the perpetrator.

THE TWO JURISDICTIONS

1.36 A local authority has limited statutory powers to protect a vulnerable adult from harm. Neither the Care Act 2014 (in England) nor the Social Services and Well-being (Wales) Act 2014 confer a power upon social workers to enter a person's property without consent, nor can they compel third parties, such as family carers, to change their behaviour towards a vulnerable adult. For instance, if a disabled adult is living in unsanitary conditions and their personal care needs are unmet, social workers cannot simply go into the property and remove the adult to a place of safety.

1.37 While a local authority may apply for a domestic abuse protection notice from the police, or a non-molestation order, a local authority may find

13 *Newcastle-Upon-Tyne City Council v TP (Best Interests)* (n 7), para 35.
14 *Re KP* (n 9), para 89.
15 *Re BU* (n 12), para 91.
16 See *Re KP* (n 9) (see Chapter 5).
17 *Re BU* (n 12), para 93.
18 *MB v PB* [2022] EWCOP 14, para 27.
19 *A Local Authority v P (by her litigation friend, the Official Solicitor) and others* (n 8).
20 *Norfolk CC v CA & Ors* [2024] EWCOP 64, para 118.

the remit of those orders insufficient. It may determine that longer-term orders are merited, and therefore deem an application to the Court of Protection (or under the inherent jurisdiction of the High Court) appropriate, seeking an order that protects the victim/survivor of coercive control, potentially with adjunctive injunctions against the controlling person: These, and other remedies, are dealt with in Chapter 9.

1.38 Local authorities typically apply to the court when social workers are concerned that they cannot adequately assess a person's care needs, or when it appears that someone is obstructing the assessment or provision of care for the person (P).

1.39 Applications should be made to the Court of Protection if: (a) it is established that the person lacks capacity in accordance with the Mental Capacity Act 2005 (MCA 2005) regarding the subject matter, (b) it is not possible to assess capacity but there is reason to believe the person lacks capacity, or (c) there is evidence that the person lacks capacity, but capacity is disputed. Assessing and determining capacity are considered in Chapter 3.

1.40 Applications may concern one or multiple decision-making areas such as decisions about residence, care, medical treatment, contact with others, lasting power of attorney, internet and social media use, sexual relations, contraception, marriage, or management of property and finances. These are explained in Chapter 4. Applications can seek remedies in relation to decisions that the person lacks capacity to make. These decisions are made in the person's best interests, and can include interim decisions, and injunctions against the controlling person: remedies are considered in Chapter 9.

1.41 Coercive control cases often involve family relationships, such as an overbearing partner, a domineering parent, or a controlling adult child. Victims/survivors may have lifelong disabilities, like learning disabilities, affecting their capacity to manage money, decide on living arrangements, care, or social contact. Others may lose capacity gradually due to conditions like dementia or suddenly due to brain injury. As they become more vulnerable, they attract the attention of adult social services, losing resilience skills that previously helped them cope with coercive control. This vulnerability allows the controlling person to further isolate the victim under the guise of love, care, and 'I know best'. Sometimes the perpetrator will seek out a potential victim because of some perceived vulnerability they can exploit, such as forced marriage of people with learning disabilities, or fraud against older people with dementia.

1.42 The court's approach is 'not to dress an incapacitous person in forensic cotton wool but to allow them as far as possible to make the same mistakes that all other human beings are at liberty to make and not infrequently do'.[21] Even if a person lacks capacity, the court may make a best interests decision that aligns

21 *Re P (Abortion)* [2013] EWHC 50 (COP), para 10.

with the person's 'wishes and feelings', and any beliefs and values that would be likely to influence the decision if the person had capacity.[22]

1.43 When a person *has* capacity to make the relevant decision, and is under influence, duress, control, or coercion, an application can be made to the Family Division of the High Court requesting the court to make orders under its inherent jurisdiction. Chapters 6 and 7 will explain how this area of law is intended to be 'facilitative, rather than dictatorial',[23] and its orders aim to restore the person's autonomy, free from coercive control. Due to the victim/survivor's trauma, this may be difficult to achieve without specialist psychotherapeutic interventions.

1.44 Deciding whether to apply to the Court of Protection or under the inherent jurisdiction can be challenging when a person appears to be a victim of coercive control and has a disability, but their capacity is unclear due to the controlling person's interference, or where the controlling person has blocked professionals' access to the person. In such cases, if there is sufficient evidence, the local authority can apply under the inherent jurisdiction for an order directing the controlling person to allow professionals access to the property. This enables an initial needs assessment, evaluation of any safeguarding concerns, and assessment of the person's capacity regarding residence, care, and contact, with further assessments arranged as needed.

1.45 Decision-making under the inherent jurisdiction has its critics, notably Lady Hale, former President of the UK Supreme Court. In her foreword to Rob George KC's book on the inherent jurisdiction,[24] Lady Hale noted that the MCA 2005 'laid down principles, criteria and safeguards. It did not abolish any inherent jurisdiction because none was thought to exist. Yet the High Court decided that it had the very jurisdiction that the House of Lords had decided that it did not have.'

1.46 A key principle of the MCA 2005 is that a person is not to be treated as unable to make a decision simply because they make an unwise one. Lady Hale suggests that the High Court's creation of the inherent jurisdiction is unconstitutional, as it breaches the principle that where Parliament has legislated – in this case by declining to enact a limited protective scheme for those with capacity – it is not for the courts to use the Royal Prerogative to circumvent the limits that Parliament has laid down, 'and it is worse still when there was no Royal Prerogative in the first place'.[25]

22 MCA 2005, s 4(6).
23 *A Local Authority v DL* [2012] EWCA Civ 253, para 67.
24 Lady Hale, 'Foreword', in Rob George KC, *Wards of Court and the Inherent Jurisdiction* (Hart Publishing, 2024), vi.
25 *Attorney-General v De Keyser's Royal Hotel* [1920] AC 508.

1.47 Despite criticisms of its 'nebulous and ill-defined nature',[26] its constitutional overreach, its imprecision, and its overly-broad approach to 'vulnerability', the inherent jurisdiction remains available in appropriate cases until Parliament decides otherwise.

CONCLUSIONS

1.48 We make decisions every day, decisions that are influenced by family, friends, advertising, media, social networks, religious organisations, teachers, and various sources of information, misinformation, opinion, and gossip. We weigh these influences before making the decision. Advertising, for instance, aims to persuade us to spend money, often unwisely. Our family may hold strong views about certain topics.

1.49 At what point does a judge decide that an everyday influence has become undue, warranting intervention? What does the label of 'vulnerability' of the person making the decision truly add? How far will the law go to protect a person from another's control when they do not seek such protection? If a person like Mary chooses to live with or maintain contact with someone who harms them, should the law intervene? How do civil courts handle coercive and controlling behaviour, given its status as a criminal offence? What remedies exist for victims/survivors whose decision-making is dominated by a controlling person?

1.50 What happens when caregivers, initially well-intentioned, become increasingly controlling as care needs grow, crossing into abuse? When does compromise in a relationship turn into control? When does monitoring a disabled person via video become an unjustified invasion of privacy? When does assisting someone confused about finances turn into exploitation? When does ensuring proper nutrition become force-feeding? When do numerous minor incidents, seemingly harmless alone, form a pattern of coercive control? How severe must the control be for a local authority to seek court intervention, and which court should handle such applications?

1.51 This book does not pretend that the answers to those questions are straightforward. Rather, it aims to offer practical approaches for social workers, healthcare professionals, family members, victims/survivors of coercive control, and, of course, lawyers and judges, to find solutions to these dilemmas.

1.52 Harriet Taylor Mill and her husband John Stuart observed that those who crave power and control over others inevitably clash with the ideal of liberty: the right to self-govern without undue interference. We return to them in the next chapter, which examines the phenomenon of coercive control.

26 Margaret Hall, 'The vulnerability jurisdiction: Equity, *parens patriae*, and the inherent jurisdiction of the High Court' (2016) 2(1) CJCCL 185–225, at 187.

CHAPTER 2

Coercive control

> 'In this abusive environment, minor assaults and humiliations can occur so regularly that they become as unremarkable as breathing.'[1]

INTRODUCTION

2.01 This chapter provides an overview of behaviours considered coercive or controlling in England and Wales and their effects on victims/survivors. The section headed 'Elements of coercive control' (at para 2.03) offers a holistic description of coercive control and explains the tactics that abusers use to manipulate and dominate victims/survivors. Of particular importance to readers of this book will be efforts to limit the victim's access to justice: be that access to social workers, police, or the Court of Protection.

2.02 The section headed 'Coercive control in international human rights law' (at para 2.29) looks at the treatment of coercive control in international human rights law, while the commentary under the heading 'Coercive control in the criminal law of England and Wales' (at para 2.40) explains the development of coercive control offences in the criminal law in England and Wales, including the 2023 statutory guidance which provides a non-exhaustive list of coercive and controlling behaviours. The section headed 'Historical context' (at para 2.59) explains how disabled people are especially vulnerable to coercive control, and discusses how contemporary forms of coercive control could be viewed through the lens of two historical trends of the degradation of women and the invalidity of disability, and take an intersectional approach.

ELEMENTS OF COERCIVE CONTROL

The behaviours

2.03 Coercive control is a form of abuse characterised by a pattern of restrictive regulation in a relationship, by instilling fear and maintaining dominance through micro-management of everyday life, threats, psychological manipulation, economic abuse, technology-facilitated control, stalking, and physical and/or sexual violence. Coercive control may persist after separation, including through institutional, legal, and economic mechanisms.

1 Jess Hill, *See What You Made Me Do: Power, Control and Domestic Abuse* (Hurst, 2020), p 7.

2.04 A recent meta-analysis of the literature on coercive control has found at least 22 definitions or schemas of coercive control,[2] reflecting ongoing debates in psychology and sociology about, for example, landing on a definition that recognises the gendered nature of coercive control while retaining flexibility for application beyond heterosexuality.

2.05 Coercive control can happen in any sort of relationship: a genuinely romantic relationship or a so-called romance scam. It can exist outside intimate partner relationships too. It can involve parents controlling their adult children, an adult controlling their parent(s), or a person controlling their sibling. In the context of disabled adults, it could be that a paid carer's behaviour tips over into being coercive and controlling, or a person who develop a relationship with a vulnerable person with criminal intent to financially exploit or otherwise abuse that person.

2.06 Coercive control robs the victim's autonomy and sense of self, entrapping them in a state of constraint even when physical violence or confinement are absent. A person who has been the victim of power, control and psychological manipulation over time may develop trauma, a phenomenon that will be examined in detail in Chapter 10.

Tactics of control

2.07 Coercive control may coexist with other types of abuse, such as physical, sexual, emotional, or financial abuse. It is linked to the denial or restriction of the victim's freedoms, including speech, movement, property ownership, autonomous decision-making, and social connectedness, as well as access to justice.

2.08 Domination and control within relationships were inadequately captured in domestic violence frameworks in which abuse centred on physical violence. Susan Schechter was among one of the first feminist scholars to discuss coercive and controlling behaviour, noting its manifestation in men who dominate their female partners through multiple methods of abuse.[3] Evan Stark further developed the term 'coercive control' in 2007, describing it as a pattern of intimidation tactics designed to create fear and humiliation, impacting the victim's security, dignity, autonomy, and liberty.[4]

2.09 Stark categorised the 'technology' used by abusers into three main areas: isolation, intimidation and exhaustion, and monopolisation of perception. Isolation involves cutting the victim off from support systems, while intimidation

2 L Kevin Hamberger, Sadie E Larsen and Amy Lehrner, 'Coercive control in intimate partner violence' (2017) 37 *Aggression and Violent Behavior* 1–11.

3 Susan Schlechter, *Women and Male Violence: The Visions and Struggles of the Battered Women's Movement* (South End Press, 1982).

4 Evan Stark, *Coercive Control: How Men Entrap Women in Personal Life* (2nd edn, OUP, 2023).

and exhaustion tactics wear down the victim physically and emotionally. Monopolisation of perception includes psychological manipulation, such as gaslighting, to distort the victim's sense of reality.

2.10 The coercive control statutory guidance, considered below at para 2.56, lists an array of behaviours that are considered coercive and controlling, and many of these tactics are drawn out in the legal case studies in Chapters 5 and 7. The tactics include a range of control measures over daily life (what to eat, what TV programmes to watch, who to meet etc), psychological methods of control (menace, fear, isolation, intimidation, mockery, gaslighting, dependence), financial control, physical abuse or sexual abuse. Coercive control can involve the use of people close to the victim/survivor (eg, their children) as weapons of control. In this way, the abuse may affect people other than the person considered to be the primary victim/survivor.

2.11 The psychology and sociology literature are at one with the law in that violence may be a feature of coercive control, but is not a defining feature. Stark described coercive control as a 'liberty crime', where coercive control is a pattern of domination in which the abuser may use violence (or the threat of violence) strategically to instil fear and enforce control, although he stressed that violence is not always present.[5] The Court of Appeal has held that, 'it is possible to be a victim of controlling or coercive behaviour or threatening behaviour without ever sustaining a physical injury'.[6] Similarly, as this chapter will explain further below (at para [2.48]), violence need not be present to secure a conviction of the criminal offence of controlling or coercive behaviour in an intimate or family relationship.

2.12 In family law, the Family Procedure Rules 2010 Practice Direction 12J (PD12J) provides guidance and mandatory requirements for the family court in cases where domestic abuse is alleged, admitted, or there is other reason to believe that a child or party has experienced, or is at risk of experiencing, domestic abuse perpetrated by another party. PD12J defines behaviour as abusive if it, among other behaviours, consists of controlling or coercive behaviour. These are terms it defines as follows:

(a) Coercive behaviour is 'an act or a pattern of acts of assault, threats, humiliation and intimidation or other abuse that is used to harm, punish, or frighten the victim'.

(b) Controlling behaviour is 'an act or pattern of acts designed to make a person subordinate and/or dependent by isolating them from sources of support, exploiting their resources and capacities for personal gain, depriving them of the means needed for independence, resistance and escape and regulating their everyday behaviour'[7].

5 Stark, ibid.
6 *H-N And Others (Children) (Domestic Abuse: Finding of Fact Hearings)* [2021] EWCA Civ 448.
7 Ibid, para 3.

2.13 Sitting as a judge in the Family Division, Hayden J has held that coercive and controlling behaviour is unambiguous and needs no embellishment:

> Understanding the scope and ambit of the behaviour however, requires a recognition that 'coercion' will usually involve a pattern of acts encompassing, for example, assault, intimidation, humiliation and threats. 'Controlling behaviour' really involves a range of acts designed to render an individual subordinate and to corrode their sense of personal autonomy. Key to both behaviours is an appreciation of a 'pattern' or 'a series of acts', the impact of which must be assessed cumulatively and rarely in isolation.[8]

2.14 These comments can be read across into the Court of Protection and into the inherent jurisdiction concerning adults. There, social workers, lawyers and other professionals should be alert to the full range of behaviours that may be coercive or controlling. They should take any allegation of abuse seriously, and act in accordance with their ethical and regulatory duties, including helping the victim to report potential criminal offences to the police (and ensuring that social workers have done so where the victim/survivor lacks capacity to do so). A theme running throughout the book is the victim's access to justice and to healing services, and for professionals to be aware of the abuser's efforts to thwart it.

Entrapment

2.15 Deep-rooted structural problems can cause victims/survivors of coercive control and other types of domestic abuse to be trapped in abusive relationships and unable to leave.[9] Such structural barriers include the following.

(a) Lack of financial resources may entrap victims/survivors by limiting the means available to them to live independently, for example, through the impact of economic abuse, poverty, reduced earning power or labour market skills, unemployment, poor housing, lack of childcare or transport. Isolation from family, friends and support systems make it harder to leave or imagine life beyond abuse.

(b) Inadequate, discriminatory, or inaccessible services, including institutional racism, ableism, pathologising attitudes, and risk of institutionalisation or criminalisation further deter victims/survivors from approaching services.

(c) Lack of funded specialist domestic abuse services, and few resources for improving public awareness of them, may result in people who need such

8 *F v M* [2021] EWFC 4, para 4.

9 This section draws on the domestic abuse research, in particular RK Thiara and C Harrison, *Reframing the Links: Black and Minoritised Women, Domestic Violence and Abuse, and Mental Health – A Review of the Literature* (Bristol: Women's Aid, 2021); and *Women's Aid, Mental health and Domestic Abuse: A Review of the Literature* (Bristol: Women's Aid, 2021).

services not knowing about them or being denied access to appropriate provision.

(d) Lack of accessibility, specialist awareness and long waiting lists for statutory services such as social services or general practitioners, hinder the availability of support.

(e) Disabled victims/survivors may find it harder to remove themselves from the abusive situation. They may 'choose' to stay at home with a difficult controlling partner who provides some care, fearing that without the abuser-carer they will be left without care, or enter institutional care with its own level of control and loss of autonomy. Their home may have special adaptations for them which they may lose if they move out. For certain victims/survivors, 'the coercive and controlling behaviour of a partner may be seen as more tolerable than the coercive and controlling responses of the state and its authorities'.[10]

(f) Disabled victims/survivors may face inaccessible domestic abuse services, and ableist responses. Victims/survivors with learning disabilities may not understand that they are experiencing domestic abuse and may be unable to access help. In response they may display 'behaviours that challenge' which are not understood properly as an indication of an unmet need or as help-seeking communication.

(g) Support services are not geared up to meet the needs of disabled people. For example, only 18% of accommodation-based services could provide support to victims/survivors with learning disabilities, autism or both.[11]

(h) Some victims/survivors have insecure immigration status or no recourse to public funds, which limits their access to statutory services, welfare benefits, and safe housing: in those situations, perpetrators may exploit these vulnerabilities and fears of immigration consequences.

(i) Parent-victims/survivors may fear that disclosing abuse or mental ill-health will lead to their children being taken into care.

2.16 Black and minoritised women in particular face cultural and social barriers that limit access to safety and recovery from abusive relationships. Among these are:

(a) institutional racism and discrimination embedded in services, which act as a strong disincentive to approach services;

(b) services that culturally stereotype women, for example, that certain communities are self-reliant, strong not in need of help. Alternatively, services may pathologise certain women, for example, the 'Strong Black Woman' stereotype and its association with unconditional caregiving may mean services view women as strong and resilient even when they are in

10 Charlotte Barlow and Sandra Walklake, *Coercive Control* (Routledge, 2022), p 76.
11 Domestic Abuse Commissioner, *A Patchwork of Provision*, 2022, p 23.

danger. There is evidence of internalising this expectation, leading to under-reporting and delayed disclosure of abuse;[12]

(c) lack of identification of culturally and linguistically specific ways of interpreting mental distress, for example, through describing physical symptoms or dealing with mental distress solely through the lens of mental illness;

(d) lack of funded 'by and for' specialist and inclusive domestic abuse organisations;[13]

(e) confidentiality issues, lack of interpreting access with respect to communication support and reliance on abuser/others, concern that professionals, interpreters may leak information; and

(f) shame, stigma, notions of honour and other community pressures in which a victim may fear bringing shame upon the family. Disclosure may be seen as a betrayal, and women may fear ostracisation, gossip, or exclusion from their communities or may fear contributing towards essentialist, racist attitudes towards their communities through disclosure.

2.17 Intersecting with structural and cultural issues are psychological explanations as to why a victim may stay in an abusive relationship. The effects of trauma (see Chapter 10) can significantly impact a victim/survivor, as follows.

(a) The impact of mental health caused by the abuse, such as depression, anxiety, suicidality or (as this chapter seeks to explain more fully) trauma responses, may make help-seeking difficult. The person may have a sense of powerlessness (sometimes described as 'coerced choice') leading them to stay, as they feel there is no viable alternative.

(b) A 'trauma bond' between victim and abuser may develop, wherein the push and pull of good and bad elements of the relationship) traps the victim and creates a power imbalance and a system of intermittent reward and punishment.[14]

(c) The development of 'totalistic identity', whereby the core aspects of the victim's self-identity are stymied in their development, becoming obscured and beyond reach, may result in the victim's identity becoming overwhelmed by the abuser's.[15] In cases of trauma-coerced attachment, the victim is left

12 Claudia Bernard, *Intersectionality for Social Workers* (Routledge, 2021).

13 'By and for' provision is defined by Imkaan and End Violence Against Women Coalition, *Joint Briefing: Adjournment Debate: Black Women and Domestic Abuse*, 30 June 2020, as specialist dedicated services that are delivered in consultation with or which directly involve Black and minoritised survivors. They are trusted by women because they recognise and understand the multiple forms of disadvantage and discrimination experienced by Black and minoritised women.

14 This was developed by Donald G Dutton and Susan Painter in 'Emotional attachments in abusive relationships: a test of traumatic bonding theory' (1993) *Violence and Victims/Survivors* 8(2) 105–120.

15 Rod Dubrow-Marshall, 'The influence continuum – the good, the dubious and the harmful – evidence and implications for policy and practice in the 21st Century' (2010) 1(1) *International Journal of Cultic Studies* 1–13.

feeling grateful and loyal to the abuser, believing they have no alternative but to be with them.[16]

(d) Young people may find it especially difficult to leave, as their psychological subjugation and domination is likely to be even deeper and quicker in its aetiology and prevents other aspects of identity development, thus locking in the domination by the abuser.[17]

(e) Prolonged abuse can lead to diminished self-worth, confusion, internalised guilt, and belief that the abuse is the victim's fault, reducing agency and the ability to take action to leave, and the fear of not being believed by those who may be able to help.

2.18 Locating entrapment solely at the psychological level risks establishing a threshold of trauma (however defined) that a victim is required to experience to be recognised as proper victims/survivors. The problem with this approach is that it locates the site of difficulty within the victim, rather than focus on the perpetrator and the wider structural reasons that maintain the abuse. A further critique is that it focuses on the reason why a victim does not leave rather than asking why abusers continue to abuse.

2.19 None of these factors operate in isolation. The cumulative effect has been described as 'compound oppressions', operating at the intersection of disadvantage on the grounds of, for example, disability and gender. [18] Structural inequalities (such as economic disadvantage, ableism, sexism and racism), cultural pressures, and individual psychological consequences reinforce each other, create a web of coercive control and a 'continuum of oppression' that powerfully constrain victims/survivors' freedom to leave.[19]

2.20 On top of this, perpetrators – often expertly – manipulate and exploit these factors to maintain control and prevent escape. They may use mental health history against victims/survivors, instil fear in the victim of authorities or the community, foster isolation, or weaponise stigma.

Post-separation abuse

2.21 Coercive control happens while the abuser and the victim are in a relationship (not necessarily a romantic relationship), and it can continue after the victim has left. Staying in a relationship with the abuser may have been a rational safety strategy deployed by a victim, given the evidence that they are at greater

16 Kendra Doychak and Chitra Raghavan, '"No voice or vote": trauma-coerced attachment in victims/survivors of sex trafficking' (2018) 6(3) *Journal of Human Trafficking* 339–357.

17 See Janja Lalich and Karla McLaren, *Escaping Utopia: Growing Up in a Cult, Getting Out, and Starting Over* (Routledge, 2017).

18 J Radford, L Harne and J Trotter, 'Disabled women and domestic violence as violent crime' (2006) 18(4) *Practice: Social Work in Action* 233–246.

19 A Kanyeredzi, *Race, Culture, and Gender: Black Female Experiences of Violence and Abuse* (Palgrave Macmillan, 2018).

risk when they try to leave. Domestic abuse researchers have observed that, 'the abusive partner often has an extensive repertoire of means, both significant and seemingly miniscule, by which to continue interfering in the women's and their children's lives post-separation'.[20]

2.22 If the abuser cannot have control of the victim/survivor, they may track them physically or digitally and seek to continue to control them. They may harass them, go to the ostensibly safe place where they now live, make complaints about them to the authorities, defame them online, or make counter-claims against them whereby the abuser accuses them of abuse. This common manipulation strategy used by perpetrators is known as 'DARVO': Deny, Attack, Reverse Victim and Offender.

2.23 Attempted or actual separation is a prominent risk for intimate partner homicide. The Femicide Census of 2022 looked at women killed by male perpetrators and reported that of the 112 women killed by men in the UK in 2022, 40% of those killed by a current/former partner had left or were taking steps to leave him, of which 44% were killed within one month after taking steps to separate.[21]

Homicide and suicide

2.24 Coercive control is a strong risk factor in homicide and suicide:

> Of the 124 domestic homicide reviews[22] that took place in the year to October 2020, coercive control was identified in 65% of the cases.[23] In the year to March 2024 there were 262 recorded domestic abuse related deaths in England and Wales. The number of 'suspected victim suicide following domestic abuse' (SVSDA) exceeded intimate partner homicides for the second year running.[24] Of the homicides, all but six were by men. In the four years to 2024, the most commonly recorded risk factors in relation to the suspects were mental ill health (43%), a history of coercive and controlling behaviour (39%), alcohol use (33%) and drug misuse (30%).

20 LM Tutty, Lorraine H Radtke and KL Nixon, '"He tells people that I am going to kill my children": Post-separation coercive control in men who perpetrate IPV' (2023) 30(11) *Violence Against Women* 2853–2876.

21 Femicide Census, *Femicide Census 2022: Annual report*, 2023, p 19.

22 Domestic homicide reviews (DHRs) are multi-agency reviews, commissioned by community safety partnerships, into the deaths of adults which may have resulted from violence, abuse, or neglect; by a person to whom they were related or with whom they had an intimate relationship, or where they were a member of the same household.

23 Home Office, *Key findings from analysis of domestic homicide reviews: October 2019 to September 2020*, 2021 (at https://www.gov.uk/government/publications/key-findings-from-analysis-of-domestic-homicide-reviews/key-findings-from-analysis-of-domestic-homicide-reviews?utm_source=chatgpt.com#introduction).

24 Home Office, Vulnerability Knowledge and Practice Programme, 'Domestic Homicides and Suspected Victim Suicides 2020-2024 Year 4 Report', Home Office, March 2025 (at https://www.vkpp.org.uk/assets/Year-4-Report_publication-with-footnote.pdf).

2.25 Campaigners have called for suicides of victims/survivors of domestic abuse, including coercive control, to be investigated as homicides. Families of deceased victims highlight systemic failures by the police to investigate their loved ones' domestic abuse-related suicides as potential homicides, following failures to adequately protect and support them whilst alive.[25]

2.26 Criminologist Jane Monckton Smith has described controlling relationships as 'practices in possession', wherein the controlling person seeks to secure a commitment from the victim/survivor to them, often very rapidly in a relationship.[26] She has examined over 400 cases of intimate partner homicide from which has emerged 'The Homicide Timeline' which contains eight stages of escalating risk, from a pre-relationship history of stalking or abuse, to a relationship being dominated by control, to an escalation, to a change of thinking by the perpetrator that may lead to planning and homicide.

2.27 This research has implications for judges of the Court of Protection and exercising powers under the inherent jurisdiction when, for example, the court authorises the removal of the victim/survivor from their home, regulates contact with the abuser, or makes decisions about who can make decisions about the victim/survivor's property and financial affairs.

2.28 In chapter 1, I explained how the Court of Protection had authorised Mary[27] to be taken from her home, which her husband controlled, to a care home. The litigation friend (my client) feared what her husband might do to Mary during contact, and on her behalf I argued that it was in Mary's best interests for contact to be supervised, contrary to Mary's wishes and feelings. In that case, the risks were well-assessed. Appropriate risk assessments need to be in place to identify *all* risks, not only the risk of homicide and suicide. Judges and lawyers should be aware of these broader assessments, and cannot be complacent. If the victim/survivor has disclosed abuse, and the court has made best interests decisions putting in place supervised contact, the abuser may feel they have nothing to lose if they have been prevented from having unsupervised contact with the person they feel entitled to control: this may place the victim/survivor at risk of abduction, serious injury and homicide. All cases should be thoroughly risk-assessed.

COERCIVE CONTROL IN INTERNATIONAL HUMAN RIGHTS LAW

2.29 Having considered the development and elements of coercive control in the legal, sociology and psychology literature, we turn to the treatment of coercive control in international human rights law.

25 The Guardian, 'Suicides linked to domestic abuse should be investigated as potential homicides, say UK families', 25 October 2025.

26 Jane Monckton Smith, *Control: Dangerous Relationships and How They End in Murder* (Bloomsbury Publishing, 2022), p 69.

27 In reference to the case of Mary discussed in Chapter 1 (an unreported case, names changed).

United Nations

2.30 The UN adopted the Convention on the Elimination of All Forms of Discrimination Against Women (CEDAW) in 1979. [28] Under CEDAW, States must take all appropriate measures to eliminate discrimination against women, including in all matters relating to marriage and family relations and to ensure equality between men and women.[29] States have a duty to take all appropriate measures to eliminate discrimination against women, including in family relations.[30]

2.31 In 1989, the UN Commission on the Status of Women posited a theory of domestic violence based on 'the pervasiveness and acceptability of violence against women in the home and roots its cause in the structure of society itself' which is 'a reflection of the broad structures of sexual and economic inequality in society.[31] In this analysis:

> women are regarded as inferior to men, suffering discrimination in employment and education and being grossly underrepresented in all areas of social and political life. This inferiority is confirmed particularly within intimate relationships wherein men are assumed to be dominant and women are legally and financially dependent. The analysis further suggests that the subordination of women within relationships and therefore, domestic violence, is condoned by cultural values that emphasize the privacy and autonomy of the family, rendering outside agencies loath to interfere, or if they do so, to stress reconciliation.

2.32 In 1992, CEDAW's specialist committee recognised gender-based-violence as a form of discrimination against women, addressed in Article 1 of the Convention, that States have duties to eliminate.[32] It recognised that gender-based violence impairs or nullifies the enjoyment by women of their human rights and fundamental freedoms. In doing so, it considered the impact of family violence and the role of coercion:

> Family violence is one of the most insidious forms of violence against women. Within family relationships women of all ages are subjected to violence of all kinds, including battering, rape, other forms of sexual assault, mental and other forms of violence, which are perpetuated by traditional

28 Convention on the Elimination of All Forms of Discrimination against Women (New York, 18 December 1979). The Convention came into force on 3 September 1981 and the UK ratified it on 22 July 1981.

29 CEDAW, Article 1.

30 CEDAW, Article 16.

31 UN Office at Vienna, Centre for Social Development and Humanitarian Affairs, 'Violence against women in the family', 1989.

32 General Recommendation No. 19 on Violence against Women, adopted at its eleventh session, A/47/38. See also paragraph 19 of General Recommendation No. 28 on the core obligations of States parties under Article 2 of the Convention on the Elimination of All Forms of Discrimination against Women, CEDAW/C/GC/28, 16 December 2010.

attitudes. Lack of economic independence forces many women to stay in violent relationships. The abrogation of their family responsibilities by men can be a form of violence, and coercion. These forms of violence put women's health at risk and impair their ability to participate in family life and public life on a basis of equality.[33]

2.33 In 2017, the CEDAW Committee updated its 1992 recommendation, reiterating the position that violence against women is a form of discrimination which may take many forms, including physical, sexual, psychological or economic harm or suffering to women, threats of such acts, harassment, coercion and arbitrary deprivation of liberty.[34] Among the legislative measures identified to address the elimination of gender-based violence against women, the Committee recommended that States ensure that the definition of sexual crimes take into account coercive circumstances.[35] The CEDAW Committee drew on the case of *Vertigo v Philippines*[36] where it had recommended an amendment to the criminal law of the Philippines that where a definition of sexual offences based on 'coercive circumstances' is adopted, it should ensure that any circumstances listed are expansive, and do not revert to an emphasis on use of force or violence.[37]

2.34 The CEDAW Committee has therefore recognised coercion within its understanding of gender-based violence, as a form of discrimination against women, and has acknowledged that coercive control need not involve violence. These are developments that have subsequently taken place in England and Wales: see 'Coercive control in the criminal law of England and Wales' (para 2.40, below).

Council of Europe

2.35 The European Court of Human Rights (in this section, 'the court') has recognised that domestic abuse may amount to torture, inhuman and degrading treatment or publishment, contrary to Article 3 of the European Convention on Human Rights (ECHR). In *Opuz v Turkey*, the court discussed domestic violence under Article 3 as well as article (right to life) and Article 14 (discrimination, here, gender-based), and noted the ineffectiveness of available remedies to keep the applicant safe from her violent husband.[38]

2.36 In the 2019 judgment of *Volodina v Russia*, the applicant had received death threats from her ex-partner, and had experienced stalking, beating

33 Ibid, para 6.
34 UN Committee on the Elimination of Discrimination Against Women, General Recommendation No. 35 on gender-based violence against women, updating General Recommendation No. 19, CEDAW/C/GC/35, 26 July 2017, para 14.
35 Ibid, para 29(e).
36 CEDAW Committee, CEDAW/C/46/D/18/2008, 29 November 2007.
37 'Handbook for legislation on violence against women', UN Department of Economic and Social Affairs, Division for the Advancement of Women, 2010.
38 (2010) 50 EHRR 28.

(including while pregnant, resulting in the termination of her pregnancy) and abduction.[39] The abuser published the applicant's private photographs, placed a GPS tracker in her purse, and damaged or took away her property and identity papers. She was injured many times, and alerted the police, but the authorities never prosecuted her abuser.

2.37 The Court emphasised the psychological aspects of the abuse which the applicant had endured at the hands of her former partner, finding a violation of Article 3 because of '[t]he feelings of fear, anxiety and powerlessness that the applicant must have experienced in connection with his controlling and coercive behaviour were sufficiently serious'. This was a milestone in which the court found the psychological impact of domestic violence could constitute ill-treatment on its own,[40] a finding reiterated in the December 2021 judgment of *Tunikova v Russia*.[41]

2.38 In 2022, the court decided the post-separation abuse case of *Giorgi v Italy*.[42] There, the woman was subjected to controlling and coercive behaviour specifically, including surveillance of movement, harassment and death threats. The court found that prosecutors failed to demonstrate an awareness of the specific nature and dynamics of domestic violence and failed in their duty to conduct an immediate and proactive assessment of the risk of recurrence of the violence and implement protective measures.[43] The court also found a failure in the duty to conduct an effective investigation into all acts of domestic violence as the prosecutors showed no real willingness to hold the perpetrator to account, and stating that leaving the woman to fend for herself in a situation of proven domestic violence is tantamount to a State abandoning its obligation to investigate all cases of ill-treatment.[44]

2.39 In July 2022, the UK ratified the 2011 Istanbul Convention on combatting violence against women and domestic violence.[45] This Convention places duties on States to address violence against women and domestic violence fully in all their forms and to take measures to prevent such violence, protect its victims/survivors and prosecute the perpetrators. It recognises the role of coercion within the definition of violence.

39 *Volodina v Russia*, Application No. 41261/17, judgment 9 July 2019, para 75. The Court also found a violation of Article 14 (prohibition of discrimination) in conjunction with Article 3 on gender grounds.

40 Niels Hedlund, 'The ECHR and the positive obligation to criminalise domestic psychological violence' (2024) 24(3) *Human Rights Law Review*. See https://academic.oup.com/hrlr/article/24/3/ngae019/7723322/.

41 (2022) 75 EHRR 1.

42 Application No. 23735/19, 16 June 2022.

43 Ibid, paras 77–78.

44 Ibid, para 85.

45 The Council of Europe Convention on preventing and combating violence against women and domestic violence (Istanbul Convention), Article 3.

COERCIVE CONTROL IN THE CRIMINAL LAW OF ENGLAND AND WALES

2.40 The focus of this book is coercive control in the Court of Protection and the inherent jurisdiction of the High Court in England and Wales. This section outlines other legal areas that are relevant to coercive control. It explains the development of coercive and controlling behaviour as a criminal offence and introduces the reader to statutory guidance with a list of the types of abuse that can constitute coercive control, and how the statutory guidance is relevant to cases of coercive control in the Court of Protection and in the inherent jurisdiction of the High Court. It also introduces the reader to civil remedies, that are more fully explained in Chapter 9.

Definition of domestic abuse

2.41 In 2013, England became the first jurisdiction in the world to adopt a cross-government definition of victims/survivors of domestic violence that included coercive control.[46] Since then, definitions of domestic abuse have been put on a legislative footing.

2.42 The Domestic Abuse Act 2021 provides that the behaviour of a person (A) towards another person (B) is domestic abuse if A and B are both aged 16 or over and are personally connected to each other, and the behaviour is abusive. Behaviour is abusive if it consists of any of the following: (a) physical or sexual abuse; (b) violent or threatening behaviour; (c) controlling or coercive behaviour; (d) economic abuse (which means any behaviour that has a substantial adverse effect on B's ability to acquire, use or maintain money or other property, or to obtain goods or services); or (e) psychological, emotional or other abuse. It does not matter whether the behaviour consists of a single incident or a course of conduct. Additionally, A's behaviour may be considered abusive behaviour towards B even if it is directed at another person, such as B's child.[47]

The criminal offence of controlling or coercive behaviour in an intimate or family relationship

2.43 The Serious Crime Act 2015 (SCA 2015), s 76 (as amended by the Domestic Abuse Act 2021, s 68) created an offence of controlling or coercive behaviour in an intimate or family relationship. A High Court judge has described the criminalisation of this behaviour as 'something of a societal shift. It put a label, and a criminal law deterrent, to something – a species of "toxic

46 Home Office Circular 003/2013, 'New government domestic violence and abuse definition', 14 February 2013.
47 Domestic Abuse Act 2021, s 1.

relationship" – which had been ruining lives but lacked a name by which it could be recognised as such, including by its own victims'.[48]

The offence has four elements:

(1) Person A (who must be 16 or over) must have engaged in repeated or continuous behaviour towards Person B (who must also be 16 or over) that is controlling or coercive; and

(2) A and B must be personally connected (which includes being or having been married to each other, being or having been civil partners of each other, being engaged, cohabiting, being or having been in an intimate personal relationship with each other, or having or having had parental relationship in relation to the same child, or being relatives),[49] and

(3) A's behaviour has a 'serious effect' on B, which means either:

  (a) it causes B to fear on at least two occasions that violence will be used against B; or

  (b) it causes B serious alarm or distress which has a substantial adverse effect on B's usual day-to-day activities;[50] and

(4) A knows or ought to know that the behaviour will have a serious effect on B.

2.44 Person A has a defence if they can show that in engaging in the behaviour, they believed that they were acting in Person B's best interests (subjective element), and the behaviour was in all the circumstances reasonable (objective element). This defence is not available in relation to behaviour that causes Person B to fear violence will be used against them.

2.45 Prosecution guidance issued by the Crown Prosecution Service (CPS) states that 'a suspect will often tailor the conduct to the victim, and this conduct can vary to a high degree from one person to the next'.[51] The wide variety of controlling techniques is borne out also in the case law in the Court of Protection and the inherent jurisdiction, as will be explained in Chapters 5 and 7. As Chapter 12 on representation of the local authority will point out, it is incumbent

48 *Mr Sueng Ha Hwang v Ms Mi Soon Kim* [2021] EWHC 3327 (QB), para 45.

49 Previously, A and B had to live together. The scope was broadened by the Domestic Abuse Act 2021, s 68. The offence therefore applies to partners, ex-partners, or family members, regardless of cohabitation, so is available also for cases of post-separation abuse. In July 2022, the Home Office published, 'Domestic Abuse: Statutory guidance' which at paras 47–54 comments on coercive control in similar terms as the 2023 statutory guidance on controlling or coercive behaviour, considered below.

50 Crown Prosecution Service, 'Prosecution guidance: Controlling or Coercive Behaviour in an Intimate or Family Relationship', 24 April 2023, updated 7 February 2025. This document states that examples of 'substantial adverse effect on the victim' include 'physical or mental health deterioration; no longer socialising or withdrawing from activities such as physical exercise; needing to put in place measures at home to safeguard themselves or their children, including CCTV; self-harming; no longer eating properly; putting in place measures in their home to safeguard themselves or their children; changing working patterns, employment status or routes to work'.

51 Crown Prosecution Service, 'Prosecution guidance: Controlling or Coercive Behaviour in an Intimate or Family Relationship', 24 April 2023, updated 7 February 2025.

on social workers to ensure that the police investigate crimes properly, irrespective of whether the victim has a learning disability or other cognitive impairment.

2.46 A person guilty of the offence is liable to a term of imprisonment not exceeding five years on indictment (not exceeding 12 months on summary conviction), or a fine, or both.

2.47 While coercive control is thought of by psychologists to occur over a non-trivial period, a minimum duration of coercive and controlling behaviour is not required to secure a conviction under SCA 2015, s 76. What is required is repeated or continuous behaviour.

2.48 Actual violence is not an element of this offence. Rather it is the effect on the victim that is important: they must have feared violence on at least two occasions or experienced serious alarm or distress which has had a substantial adverse effect on their usual day-to-day activities.

2.49 In a case where there is no violence, a victim/survivor of coercive control may not be entitled to compensation (where compensation is not available elsewhere) through the government-funded Criminal Injuries Compensation Scheme 2012 which provides compensation for impairment of mental health caused by a 'crime of violence' in which where there is no physical attack, a threat 'causing fear of immediate violence' is required.[52] Immediacy is not a requirement of the SCA 2015, s 76 offence.

2.50 The scheme is unavailable to the domestic abuse offences of harassment and stalking, online sexual offending, disclosing private sexual photographs and films with intent to cause distress and malicious communications offences. The Council of Europe body that monitors compliance with the Istanbul Convention has noted this lacuna and expressed its 'concern that obtaining compensation from the perpetrator in civil procedures is made very difficult in practice for victims/survivors'.[53]

The criminal offence of putting people in fear of violence

2.51 Section 4 of the Protection from Harassment Act 1997 (PHA 1997) criminalises a course of conduct that causes another to fear, on at least two occasions, that violence will be used against them. No family or intimate relationship is required. The maximum penalty is 10 years' imprisonment. The CPS guidance states that, the offence of harassment may overlap with the SCA 2015, s 76 offence of coercive and controlling behaviour in an intimate of

52 The Criminal Injuries Compensation Scheme 2012, para 4, and Annex B.

53 Group of Experts on Action against Violence against Women and Domestic Violence (GREVIO), 'Baseline evaluation report: United Kingdom' (Council of Europe, June 2025), para 272.

family relationship where there are threats to hurt or harm the victim or their family members and threats of sexual assault.

2.52 Prosecution under the SCA 2015, s 76 is likely where the conduct was controlling or coercive, causing serious alarm or distress which affects the usual day-to-day activities of the victim but did not amount to stalking and where no violence was used. For example, the offender controlling when the victim can leave the house, who they can and cannot socialise with, control of their finances.

2.53 The CPS favours consideration of prosecution under PHA 1997, s 4 given that an offender may be sentenced to 10 years' imprisonment rather than five years' imprisonment for the commission of an offence under the SCA 2015, s 76.

2.54 Alternative offences may be relevant, including communications offences under the Online Safety Act 2023, four distinct offences for 'revenge porn', offences against the person, stalking or harassment, and other sexual offences and offences involving violence.[54]

2.55 Other remedies such as domestic abuse prevention orders, non-molestation orders, forced marriage protection orders are considered in Chapter 9 on remedies.

Coercive control statutory guidance

2.56 In April 2023, the Home Office published the 'Statutory guidance: Controlling or coercive behaviour: statutory guidance framework' pursuant to SCA 2015 s 77. It was published primarily for the police and criminal justice agencies in England and Wales involved in the investigation of criminal behaviour. The Court of Protection has made reference to the statutory guidance,[55] and it is essential reading for those involved in coercive control cases in the Court of Protection and cases under the inherent jurisdiction.

2.57 The statutory guidance elucidates a non-exhaustive list of behaviours that are coercive and controlling. These are reproduced in full:

Physical and sexual violence/abuse and violent behaviour

- Physical violence, and threats of physical violence;[56]
- Physical intimidation e.g. blocking doors, clenching or shaking fists, slamming doors, hitting walls, pretending to hit or swing, throwing objects at or around the

54 See the section on 'Offences available to prosecutors' in CPS, Domestic Abuse Prosecution Guidance, 2022.

55 See, for example, *A County Council v LW & Anor* [2020] EWCOP 50 in Chapter 5.

56 An example is *A Local Authority v Mrs A (by the Official Solicitor)* [2010] EWHC 1549 (Fam) in Chapter 5.

victim, displaying weapons or harmful objects, driving dangerously or erratically with the victim in the car; and

- Sexual assault, coercion or abuse, and threats of sexual assault.[57]

Emotional and psychological abuse[58]

- Abuse relating to faith or beliefs;[59]
- Verbal abuse;
- Constant criticism of the victim's role as a partner, spouse or parent;
- Criticising the victim's choice of friends and associates;
- Intentionally undermining and/or manipulating the victim;[60] and
- Posting unwanted messages on the victim's social media.

Controlling behaviours

- Controlling or monitoring the victim's daily activities and behaviour, for example making them account for their time, dictating what they can wear, what and when they can eat, when and where they may sleep, who they meet or talk to, where they may work, restricting access to training/development etc.;[61]
- Using digital systems, such as smart devices or social media, to coerce, control, upset and monitor the victim (e.g. restricting and checking phone use, needing to know passwords for accounts, using location tracking on devices, posting of a possibly triggering image);[62]
- Controlling and monitoring the victim's access to their post;
- Acts of coercion or force to persuade the victim to do something that they are unwilling to do;
- Economic abuse (e.g. coerced debt, controlling spending/bank accounts/investments/mortgages/benefit payments);[63]
- Using a victim's workplace to control them, e.g. denying access to work, dictating where they work, turning up at work;
- Making and enforcing rules and regulations that the victim is expected to follow and using punishments to make them comply e.g. making accusations or humiliating a person in public or private for deviating from the rules;
- Coercing the victim into carrying out criminal behaviour such as selling drugs or carrying weapons;

57 See for example *A Local Authority v KP (Acting by the Official Solicitor as her litigation friend) and another* [2023] EWHC 3102 (Fam), and *Hull City Council v KF* [2022] EWCOP 33, both in Chapter 5.

58 Missing from this list are threats of suicide and self-harm.

59 See for example *Re LW* (n 55) in Chapter 5.

60 See for example *WU v BU* [2021] EWCOP 54 in Chapter 5.

61 See for example *Newcastle-Upon-Tyne City Council v TP (Best interests of TP No. 1)* [2016] EWCOP B3, *Re LW* (n 55) in Chapter 5, and *Re TT (Injunctive Relief)* [2022] EWHC 2185 (Fam) in Chapter 7.

62 See for example *In the Matter of CA (Fact Finding – Capacity – Inherent Jurisdiction – Injunctive Relief)* [2024] EWCOP 64 (T3) in Chapter 7.

63 See for example *WU v BU* (n 60) in Chapter 5, and *Re P (Vulnerable Adult: Withdrawal of Application)* [2024] EWHC 1882 (Fam) in Chapter 7.

- Following the victim and/or appearing unexpectedly, e.g. at their place of work or at places where they are meeting friends;
- Reproductive coercion, including restricting a victim's access to birth control;[64] refusing to use a birth control method; forced pregnancy; forcing a victim to get an abortion, to undergo in vitro fertilisation (IVF) or other procedure; or denying access to such a procedure;
- Using substances such as alcohol or drugs to control a victim through dependency, or controlling their access to substances;
- Using child arrangements and child maintenance to control the victim.

Restrictive behaviours

- Withholding and/or destroying the victim's immigration documents, e.g. passports and visas;[65]
- Preventing normal leisure activities such as volunteering, joining local clubs and groups, sports teams, civil/charitable activity, etc.;
- Preventing the victim from learning a language, improving their existing language skills, such as English if this is not their first language, or making friends outside of their ethnic/ or cultural background;
- Refusing to interpret (including British Sign Language, BSL, for deaf victims/ survivors) on behalf of the victim;
- Hindering access to communication, e.g. refusing to make information accessible, denying access to communication support tools, augmentative and alternative communication (AAC), and/or professionals who support communication;
- Restricting access to health and social care appointments, or preventing the victim from accessing health or social care, including refusing to allow the victim to attend appointments alone (especially relevant for victims/survivors with disabilities or long-term health conditions);[66]
- Preventing the victim from taking medication[67], or accessing medical equipment, or over-medicating them; and
- Isolating the victim from family, friends, colleagues and professionals who may be trying to support them,[68] intercepting messages or phone calls.

Threatening behaviours

- Threats of being placed in an institution against the victim's will, e.g. care home, supported living facility, mental health facility, etc. (particularly for disabled or elderly victims/survivors);[69]

64 See for example *A Local Authority v Mrs A (by the Official Solicitor)* [2010] EWHC 1549 (Fam) in Chapter 5.

65 See for example *Amina Al-Jeffery v Mohammed Al-Jeffery* [2016] EWHC 2151 (Fam); *Re K (Forced Marriage: Passport Order)* [2020] EWCA Civ 190 in and the case of *Luton Borough Council v G and others* [2024] EWCOP 18, all in Chapter 7.

66 See for example *HBCC v LC (by her litigation friend, the Official Solicitor), JG and SG* [2010] EWHC 1527 (Fam), and *MB v PB* [2022] EWCOP 14, both in Chapter 5.

67 See for example *Wakefield Metropolitan District Council v FH and others* [2024] EWHC 830 (Fam) in Chapter 7.

68 See for example *Re TP* (n 61) and *WU v BU* (n 55) in Chapter 5.

69 See for example *Re CA* (n 62) in Chapter 7.

- Threats to expose/exposure of sensitive information (e.g. sexual activity, private sexual photos or films, sexual orientation and/or transgender identity), or making false allegations to family members, friends, work colleagues, community or others, including via photos or the internet;
- Making false allegations to statutory agencies (e.g. Police, Children's Services, Jobcentre, Child Maintenance Services);
- Using children to control the victim, e.g. threatening to take the children away, threatening to harm the children;
- Using pets to control or coerce a victim, e.g. harming, or threatening to harm or give away pets;
- Intimidation and threats of disclosure of health status or an impairment to family, friends, work colleagues and the wider community, particularly where this may carry a stigma in the community;
- Threats to the victim, including to their family, friends and pets, that make them feel afraid;
- Threats to report a victim to immigration enforcement and/or the police, or threaten to remove the victim to their country of origin; and
- Intimidation or threats to go to the police to report alleged offending.

2.58 The CPS guidance for prosecutors acknowledges the possibility of 'confusion about where the "appropriate" dynamic of a relationship ends and where unlawful behaviour begins', and refers to College of Policing guidance which sets out that in regular relationships, partners have to compromise, but '[t]he difference in an abusive relationship is that decisions by a dominant partner can become rules that, when broken, lead to consequences for the victim'.[70]

HISTORICAL CONTEXT

2.59 I use the term disabled person to include those with learning disabilities, mental health issues, cognitive impairments such as dementia, and people who are neurodiverse.

2.60 In the year to March 2023, it was estimated that around one in 10 disabled people experienced domestic abuse on at least one occasion, compared with one in 30 non-disabled people. Disabled women were three times more likely to say they experienced domestic abuse than non-disabled women (12.4% compared with 4%) and for disabled men the numbers were 7% compared with 2.6%.[71]

2.61 When considering the ways in which disabled persons may experience coercive control it may be helpful to consider two trends to provide context and to consider contemporary abuse from an intersectional perspective.

70 The College of Policing, 'Authorised Professional Practice on Domestic Abuse', 16 September 2015.
71 House of Commons Library, *UK Disability Statistics: Prevalence and Life Experiences* (London, 2024), p 26.

2.62 The first is the degradation of women. Much has been written about this. For example, writing in the 1790s, Mary Wollstonecraft observed that education for girls was 'directed to one point – to render them pleasing'.[72] She observed how, '[t]aught from infancy that beauty is woman's sceptre, the mind shapes itself to the body, and, roaming round its gilt cage, only seeks to adorn its prison'. A woman's role was to please men, including by feeding them, caring for them, and having children for them.

2.63 In 1869, Harriet Taylor Mill and her husband John Stewart Mill sought to contribute to a 'moral regeneration of mankind' by righting the 'system of inequality of rights' between women and men.[73] It was inevitable that women sought to be attractive to men given that, 'the wife's entire dependence on the husband, every privilege or pleasure she has being either his gift, or depending entirely on his will'. Men held women in subjection 'by representing to them meekness, submissiveness, and resignation of all individual will into the hands of a man, as an essential part of sexual attractiveness'. A man wanted a willing wife who was submissive and yielded to her husband's control. The social subordination of women favoured men, who put in place arrangements to enslave women's minds.

2.64 The Mills' call to action was for the equal treatment of women, so that they could enjoy 'a life of rational freedom'. Their vision was for a woman to make her own decisions rather than being controlled by her husband. Equality of the sexes would bring about 'the freedom of action of the individual – the liberty of each to govern his conduct by his own feelings of duty, and by such laws and social constraints as his own conscience can subscribe to.' As we will see from the contemporary case law on coercive control in Chapters 5 and 7, the courts try to protect an individual's freedom of action when it has been disrupted, or repatriate it when it has been removed.

2.65 The second historical trend relevant to the topic of this book is the 'othering' of disability whereby society treats 'them' (disabled people) as fundamentally different, inferior, abnormal, or defective. Throughout history, disabled people have been subjected to humiliation, incarceration, brutality and murder. From the desire for physical perfection that led to the abandonment or killing of disabled children in ancient times, to the belief that a disabled person represented God's way of punishing a family who then kept the disabled person hidden or in chains. From the Victorian freak show fascination with disabled bodies, to the life-long institutionalisation and abuse of those deemed undeserving and a drain on the economy. From the eugenics movement that sterilised and segregated disabled people, to the Holocaust in which thousands of disabled children and adults were the first victims of the Nazi killing machine.

72 Mary Wollstonecraft, *A Vindication of the Rights of Woman* (J Johnson, 1792), Ch 2.
73 John Stewart Mill, *The Subjection of Women* (Longmans, Green, Reader & Dyer, 1869).

2.66 Disabled people were – and often still are – rendered *objects* of other people's management, treatment, pity, charity and – especially in relation to mental health issues – fear. The law has enabled and authorised restrictions of disabled people's autonomy and freedoms. Roman law equated disabled adults to children, and designed guardianship laws to keep wealth in the family by bypassing a male family member who was deemed incompetent. This is the foundation of modern guardianship laws across the world that strip a disabled adult from enjoying what the UN calls 'legal capacity',[74] handing many or all decisions about the person's life to a guardian who makes unimpeachable decisions, even those that go against a person's wishes and feelings or where less restrictive alternatives are available. A prominent contemporary example is the guardianship (in the US this is called conservatorship) of Britney Spears.[75]

COERCIVE CONTROL AND DISABLED PEOPLE

2.67 Many disabled people are dependent on others to provide care that meets their needs. This may include tasks, such as cooking meals, eating and drinking, washing and dressing, continence care, cleaning up, going out (called 'accessing the community' in social care), meeting friends ('contact with peers'), making and going to appointments, doing the shopping and managing money.

2.68 There are regulatory and inspection regimes for hospitals and care homes, and while there have been some prosecutions for wilful neglect by professional carers,[76] at-home and informal care arrangements by family or acquaintances are subject to less scrutiny. Many of the cases in Chapters 5 and 7 show how coercive control can take place in the victim/survivor's home, behind closed doors.

2.69 The care sector relies on many altruistic family members to look after loved ones, as well as under-paid and under-appreciated professional carers. The word 'burden' is sometimes associated with caregiving, reflecting oppressive notions of blame,[77] feelings that can be internalised by a disabled person who may have become resigned to substandard and precarious care. They may feel that enduring poor quality care is preferable to not having any care at all, or being placed in an institutional setting.

2.70 When a stranger enters a person's life with persistent offers of care, friendship, or romance, it can be hard to resist. If the abuser is already known to the disabled person, family dynamics might shift due to ageing, cognitive decline, or sudden events like a stroke. In such situations, the disabled person

74 See Article 12 of the UN Convention on the Rights of Persons with Disabilities.

75 Helena Moradi and Bojan Perovic, 'Britney Spears and systemic reform: Embracing vulnerability in conservatorship laws' (2024–2025) 76 *South Carolina Law Review* 355.

76 Mental Capacity Act 2005, s 44 creates an offence if a person (the defendant, D) has the care of a person (P) who lacks, or D reasonably considers to lack, capacity, and D ill-treats or wilfully neglects P.

77 See Tom Shakespeare, *Disability rights and wrongs* (Routledge, 2006).

may struggle to stand up to a dominant partner or relative. Without the ability to resist as before, the impact of control can be more severe.

2.71 A controlling relative may react negatively when their disabled loved one experiences illness, injury, or cognitive decline, reducing their control. Concerns about domestic abuse may be raised first by health and social care professionals, as seen with Mary in Chapter 1: she endured a violent relationship for decades before she became ill and made disclosures to health professionals.

2.72 A disabled person may be considered a 'vulnerable adult' not due to inherent weakness, but because their autonomy relies on others' cooperation. A carer-abuser may use coercive control, threatening to withhold care, medication, or restrict access to community and justice. They might claim to know what is best for the disabled person, intertwining care with control.

2.73 Disability can affect relationship navigation. Research shows that people with learning disabilities are more susceptible to acquiescence, suggestibility, compliance and confabulation.[78] Suggestibility may also be linked to social disablement where compliance is learned through paternalistic care systems and institutional dependence.[79] An example from the caselaw is *Re LBX*, where a young man with mild learning disabilities was eager to please his overbearing father, making his preferences unreliable. His capacity was affected not by his innate cognitive impairment, but, the expert said, by 'the overwhelming emotional issues of others which he is poorly equipped to resist'.[80]

CONCLUSIONS

2.74 The multifaceted phenomenon of coercive control intersects with sociology, psychology and law. A form of domestic abuse, coercive control encompasses a range of behaviours designed to dominate and isolate victims/survivors. Physical violence sometimes features in coercive control, but it is not an essential element.

2.75 While an in-depth examination of the criminal law lies outside the scope of this book,[81] this chapter has outlined how the SCA 2015 criminalised coercive and controlling behaviour in specific circumstances and provides a mechanism for victims/survivors to seek justice if the elements of harassment under the PHA 1997, which attracts greater sentencing powers, are not made out.

78 Isabel CH Clare and Gisli H Gudjonsson, 'The vulnerability of suspects with intellectual disabilities during police interviews: A review and experimental study of decision-making' (1995) 8(2) *Mental Handicap Research* 110–128.
79 Dan Goodley, *Disability Studies: An Interdisciplinary Introduction* (2nd edn, Sage, 2016).
80 *Re LBX* [2011] EWHC 2419 (Fam), para 93.
81 See Wiener Cassandra, *Coercive Control and the Criminal Law* (Routledge, 2023).

2.76 The chapter has discussed two phenomena that may be useful in thinking about coercive control cases in the Court of Protection and under the inherent jurisdiction. The first is the subjugation of women and gender inequality. The second is the degradation and segregation of disabled individuals and their legal 'othering'. The law can render a disabled person invisible, and their dependence on others for care provides an opportunity for abuse. While a pattern of coercive or controlling behaviour can take many forms, its traumatic impact may be profound, and developing an understanding is crucial for effective representation in court: this is considered in depth in Chapter 10. Before we get there, the next chapters examine how capacity is assessed and determined, and how coercive control cases have been decided both by the Court of Protection and under the inherent jurisdiction of the High Court.

CHAPTER 3

Determining capacity

> 'Those assessing capacity must vigilantly ensure that the assessment is evidence-based, person-centred, criteria-focussed and non-judgmental ...'[1]

INTRODUCTION

3.01 This first part of this chapter explains how coercive control was historically proposed as a way in which a person (P) could lack capacity, but the proposal did not feature in what became the Mental Capacity Act 2005 (MCA 2005). Instead, that Act requires capacity to be assessed by answering two questions: (1) whether P is able to make the relevant decision; and if the answer is no, (2) whether the inability is because of an impairment-related reason. The section headed 'Capacity and coercive control' (at para 3.04) explains how an assessor must take all practicable steps to help P to make the relevant decision. It explains the centrality of the presumption of capacity, which the Court of Protection requires robust evidence to rebut.

3.02 The chapter examines three principles of the MCA 2005 in relation to coercive control cases. The section headed 'Presumption of capacity' (at para 3.08) explains how the Court of Protection determines whether P has or lacks capacity to make a decision. The section headed 'All practicable steps' (at para 3.13) explains the information relevant to making decisions that may appear in coercive control cases. The section headed 'Unwise decisions' (at para 3.17) describes the law and procedure on interim capacity declarations and best interests decisions: that is, when the court has some evidence that P lacks capacity to make a certain decision, and must make urgent decisions to protect P's interests.

3.03 The section headed 'Determining lack of capacity' (at para 3.21) sets out the two questions that a capacity assessor (and where relevant, the Court of Protection) must answer in order to determine that P lacks capacity to make the revenant decision. The section on 'Interim and final declarations of capacity' (at para 3.50) explains how a declaration that P lacks capacity to make a decision permits the court to make best interests decisions (and as we shall see in Chapter 6, where P has capacity to make a relevant decision, the High Court can still intervene if certain criteria are met under the inherent jurisdiction). The section headed 'Obtaining capacity evidence' (at para 3.53) explains four

1 Mrs Justice Theis in *CT v London Borough of Lambeth & Anor* [2025] EWCOP 6 (T3), para 60(4).

ways how and from whom the Court of Protection can obtain further and better capacity evidence.

CAPACITY AND COERCIVE CONTROL

3.04 In its 1995 report 'Mental incapacity',[2] the Law Commission criticised the concept of 'using or weighing' information as part of the process of making a decision. Nevertheless, this concept was given statutory footing as s 3(1)(c) of the MCA 2005. The Commission's view was that P may be able to understand information, but may be unable to use it in cases involving: (a) compulsive conditions, like anorexia nervosa; (b) mental disability that disables P from exerting their will against *force majeure circumstances*, including a stronger person who wishes to influence P's decisions; or (c) mental disability that prevents P from being able to believe relevant information.

3.05 The Commission's view was that,

> [c]ommon to all these cases is the fact that the person's eventual decision is divorced from his or her ability to understand the relevant information. Emphasising that the person must be able to use the information which he or she has successfully understood in the decision-making process deflects the complications of asking whether a person needs to 'appreciate' information as well as understand it. A decision based on a compulsion, the overpowering will of a third party or any other inability to act on relevant information as a result of mental disability is not a decision made by a person with decision-making capacity.[3]

3.06 The MCA 2005 differs from the Commission's suggested framework: the Act does not say that P lacks capacity if P is unable to exert their will against some stronger person who wishes to influence their decisions. While it has been held that P's 'inability to exert the will against influence because of the impairment or disturbance is relevant' to the court's decision about whether P has or lacks capacity to make the relevant decision,[4] incapacity under the MCA 2005 requires an inability to make a decision because of an impairment-related reason. P's inability to fend off the stronger will of another person is insufficient.

3.07 This chapter explains how the Court of Protection determines whether P has or lacks capacity to make relevant decisions when P's decision-making is impacted by another person's influence.

2 Mental Incapacity, Item 9 of the Fourth Programme of Law Reform: Mentally Incapacitated Adults (Law Com No 231, 1995): https://www.bailii.org/ew/other/EWLC/1995/231.html (accessed 29 October 2025).

3 Law Commission, Report No. 231 of 1995, para 3.17.

4 *Re PB* [2014] EWCOP 14, para 101.

PRESUMPTION OF CAPACITY

3.08 Section 1 of the MCA 2005 establishes five principles of the Act. This chapter will consider the first three.[5] The first principle is: 'A person must not be assumed to have capacity unless it is established that he lacks capacity'. The burden of proof is on the assessor to provide evidence that P lacks capacity to make the relevant decision and the standard of proof is the balance of probabilities (ie, is it more likely than not that P lacks capacity?).

3.09 Despite the statutory verb 'assume', the Court of Protection prefers to 'presume'. As Vice-President of the court, Hayden J held that, 'the presumption of capacity is a fundamental safeguard of human autonomy. It requires cogent, clear and carefully analysed information before it can be rebutted'.[6] He described the presumption of capacity as 'the paramount principle'.[7] Theis J, the current Vice-President, has endorsed this approach.[8]

3.10 The court has previously noted that the assessor's interview with P 'need not be fully transcribed in the body of the report (although it might be provided in an appendix), but if the expert relies on a particular exchange or something said by P during interview, then at least an account of what was said should be included'.[9] In the author's experience it is always useful to have a full transcript, which is straightforward to produce using standard software at no extra cost.

3.11 In 2014, Parliament found that the presumption of capacity:

> is widely misunderstood by those involved in care. It is sometimes used to support non-intervention or poor care, leaving vulnerable adults exposed to risk of harm. In some cases this is because professionals struggle to understand how to apply the principle in practice. In other cases, the evidence suggests the principle has been deliberately misappropriated to avoid taking responsibility for a vulnerable adult.[10]

3.12 Capacity assessors must not allow themselves to be convinced (by the controlling person) that they need not assess capacity of the adult who may be a victim of coercive control. Chapter 6 explains how, if required, an application can be made under the inherent jurisdiction for orders to direct the controlling

5 The fourth is that decisions for a person who lacks capacity must be made in the person's best interests, and the fifth principle is to have regard to less restrictive ways to achieve the purpose for which the best interests decision is made. These are both considered in the coercive control case studies in Chapter 5.

6 *QJ v A local authority and another* [2020] EWCOP 7, para 23.

7 *London Borough of Tower Hamlets v PB* [2020] EWCOP 34, para 51.

8 *MacPherson (by her litigation friend the Official Solicitor) v Sunderland City Council* [2025] EWCOP 18, para 56(1).

9 *AMDC v AG & Anor* [2020] EWCOP 58, para 28.

10 House of Lords Select Committee on the Mental Capacity Act 2005, 'Mental Capacity Act 2005: post-legislative scrutiny', HL Paper 139, 2014, para 105.

person to step aside and allow social workers access to the adult where there is credible evidence that the adult is a vulnerable person in need of protection.

ALL PRACTICABLE STEPS

3.13 Where there are allegations of coercive control, the continued influence of the controlling person may pose challenges in assessing P's capacity. The controlling person may want to choose the assessor, coach P on what to say during the assessment or be present during the assessment.

3.14 On receipt of the assessment report, the controlling person may contest what P is reported to have said to the assessor or may dismiss what P said on the grounds that they have psychosis, memory problems or that their answers were influenced by social workers: this is a tactic of wrestling back control over P and control over the proceedings.

3.15 The second principle in MCA 2005, s 1 is that 'a person is not to be treated as unable to make a decision unless all practicable steps to help him to do so have been taken without success'. This is sometimes referred to as 'supported decision-making' and is intended to enable P as much as necessary to be able to make a decision. The following are five suggestions as to practicable steps an assessor could take when assessing capacity in a coercive control case:

(1) The assessor could collect and consider background material, ideally from a variety of sources. The assessor could obtain P's GP records, and – if they exist – P's hospital records and adult social services records. If there are allegations of financial exploitation or abuse, the assessor may want to see P's financial records. The assessor should have access to the court bundle which may contain statements from social workers that may contain collateral information from P's relatives, friends or neighbours. Drawing from a wide canvas of material will provide the assessor with a deeper understanding of P's situation and predicaments. This may illuminate curtailments of P's autonomy that may remain hidden during a capacity assessment.

(2) The assessor should resist any attempt by the perpetrator to chaperone P during the assessment. If the perpetrator is present, when the assessor puts to P the allegations concerning the alleged perpetrator, P would be in an impossible situation: either P would be reluctant to answer truthfully for fear of later consequences, or P may answer the questions in a manner to please the perpetrator. In *Re CA*, for example, the judge observed that 'P says what she thinks her family would like her to say'.[11] If P needs a chaperone, the assessor could instead involve a neutral third party, ideally someone P already knows and trusts, and who has signed an agreement to keep the conversation confidential.

11 *Re CA (Fact Finding – Capacity – Inherent Jurisdiction – Injunctive Relief)* [2024] EWCOP 64 (T3), para 70.

(3) Where there are concerns that the perpetrator is coaching P before the capacity assessment, the assessor could request no contact between P and the perpetrator(s) for a period of time before the assessment, to give P an influence-free period. If the perpetrator does not agree, either the public body or P's litigation friend could ask the court for an injunction against the alleged perpetrator not to have contact with P by any means during a specified period of time before the assessment.

(4) The assessor may consider that family therapy is merited before the assessment. This happened in *Re NB*.[12] There, the independent psychologist expert identified, 'occasions when [P] feels he should not express his opinion if it differs from the opinion of those he cares about, in particular his mother',[13] and considered that family therapy 'may help to reduce the enmeshment and anxiety within the relationship which may in turn enable [P] to regain his capacity in this area of decision-making'.[14] In some coercive control cases, the suggestion of family therapy will go nowhere, as the court cannot direct a person to engage in therapy. Indeed, where the controlling person denies allegations of control and undue influence, it is unlikely that they will agree to therapy, especially before any findings of fact have been made.

(5) The assessor may find that despite their best efforts, P is unwilling to engage in an assessment. In these circumstances, the assessor should try to establish what P does not like about the assessor or assessment process, and provide a workaround. For example, by arranging for another person to carry out the assessment.[15]

3.16 These suggestions are additional to any steps that might be used to support P with any disability-related needs by the provision of reasonable adjustments, for example, a social story for a person with learning disabilities, or written information for an autistic person.

UNWISE DECISIONS

3.17 The third principle in MCA 2005, s 1 is: 'A person is not to be treated as unable to make a decision merely because he makes an unwise decision'.[16] This principle is commonly misunderstood. An unwise decision is *not* an indicator of a capacitous decision, because P could both lack capacity and make an unwise decision.

12 *London Borough of Brent v NB* [2017] EWCOP 34.
13 Ibid, para 68(b).
14 Ibid, para 71(b).
15 This will avoid the stress and delay of the assessment taking place, only having to be repeated as the results of the first assessment cannot be relied on.
16 MCA 2005, s 1(4).

3.18 Capacity assessors should be careful not to fall into a different error, which is to conduct a capacity assessment through the lens of best interests.[17] In 2014, Peter Jackson J (as he then was) said,

> the temptation to base a judgement of a person's capacity upon whether they seem to have made a good or bad decision, and in particular upon whether they have accepted or rejected medical advice, is absolutely to be avoided. That would be to put the cart before the horse or, expressed another way, to allow the tail of welfare to wag the dog of capacity.[18]

3.19 Similarly, Hayden J has said that, 'the professional instinct to achieve that which is objectively in P's best interests should never influence the formulation of the criteria on which capacity is assessed'.[19] Theis J made the same point by warning against, 'the protection imperative and the risk of pathologising disagreements'.[20] Theis J has put it in the following way: '[t]hose assessing capacity must vigilantly ensure that the assessment is evidence-based, person-centred, criteria-focussed and non-judgmental, and not made to depend, implicitly or explicitly, upon the identification of a so-called unwise outcome'.[21]

3.20 Despite these judicial warnings, capacity assessments are commonly coloured by assessors' views of best interests, ie, P is assessed as lacking capacity because the alternative would lead to an outcome that the assessor dislikes. In these circumstances, the Court of Protection may require further and better capacity assessments, as described in the section headed 'Obtaining capacity evidence', at para 3.53 below.

DETERMINING LACK OF CAPACITY

3.21 The MCA 2005 places several demands on a capacity assessor (and if the matter is in the Court of Protection, the judge) before it can be established that P lacks capacity to make a particular decision. These are found in MCA 2005, ss 2 and 3, which are not reproduced here. The Court of Appeal has reminded judges to 'always be careful not to discriminate against persons suffering from a mental disability by imposing too high a test of capacity'.[22]

3.22 In *Re R* in 2023,[23] Macdonald J produced a succinct list of relevant considerations for assessing capacity. These are reproduced in full:

17 It is unfortunate that social workers qualified to assess capacity for the purposes of the Deprivation of Liberty Safeguards are called 'best interests assessors'.

18 *Heart of England NHS Foundation Trust v JB (by her litigation friend the Official Solicitor)* [2014] EWHC 342 (COP), para 7.

19 *London Borough of Tower Hamlets v PB* [2020] EWCOP 34, para 51.

20 *Re CT* (n 1), para 60(2).

21 *CT v London Borough of Lambeth & Anor* [2025] EWCOP 6 (T3), para 60(4).

22 *B v A Local Authority* [2019] EWCA Civ 913, para 37. The notion of 'suffering from a disability' is not language used by disabled people.

23 *North Bristol NHS Trust v R* [2023] EWCOP 5, para 41.

i) A person must be assumed to have capacity unless it is established that they lack capacity (Mental Capacity Act 2005 s. 1(2)). The burden of proof lies on the person or body asserting a lack of capacity, in this case the Trust, and the standard of proof is the balance of probabilities (Mental Capacity Act 2005 s. 2(4) and see *KK v STC and Others* [2012] EWHC 2136 (COP) at [18]);

ii) Determination of capacity under Part I of the Mental Capacity Act 2005 is always 'decision specific' having regard to the clear structure provided by ss 1 to 3 of the Act (see *PC v City of York Council* [2014] 2 WLR 1 at [35]). Thus, capacity is required to be assessed in relation to the specific decision at the time the decision needs to be made and not to a person's capacity to make decisions generally;

iii) A person is not to be treated as unable to make a decision unless all practicable steps to help him to do so have been taken without success (Mental Capacity Act 2005 s. 1(3));

iv) A person is not to be treated as unable to make a decision merely because he or she makes a decision that is unwise (see *Heart of England NHS Foundation Trust v JB* [2014] EWHC 342 (COP) at [7]). The outcome of the decision made is not relevant to the question of whether the person taking the decision has capacity for the purposes of the Mental Capacity Act 2005 (see *R v Cooper* [2009] 1 WLR 1786 at [13] and *York City Council v C* [2014] 2 WLR 1 at [53] and [54]);

iv) Pursuant to s. 2(1) of the 2005 Act a person lacks capacity in relation to a matter if at the material time he is unable to make a decision for himself in relation to the matter because of an impairment of, or a disturbance in the functioning of, the mind or brain. It does not matter whether the impairment or disturbance in the functioning of the mind or brain is permanent or temporary (Mental Capacity Act 2005 s. 2(2)). It is important to note that the question for the court is not whether the person's ability to take the decision is impaired by the impairment of, or disturbance in the functioning of, the mind or brain but rather whether the person is rendered unable to make the decision by reason thereof (see *Re SB (A Patient: Capacity to Consent to Termination)* [2013] EWHC 1417 (COP) at [38]);

vi) Pursuant to s. 3(1) of the 2005 Act a person is '*unable to make a decision for himself*' for the purposes of s.2(1) of the Act if he is unable (a) to understand the information relevant to decision, (b) to retain that information, (c) to use or weigh that information as part of the process of making the decision, or (d) to communicate his decision whether by talking, using sign language or any other means;

vii) An inability to undertake any one of these four aspects of the decision making process set out in s 3(1) of the 2005 Act will be sufficient for a finding of incapacity *provided* the inability is because of an impairment of, or a disturbance in the functioning of, the mind or brain (see *RT and LT v A Local Authority* [2010] EWHC 1910 (Fam) at [40]). For a person to be found to lack capacity there must be a causal connection between being unable to make a decision by reason of one or more of the functional elements set out in s. 3(1) of the Act and the diagnostic element of 'impairment of, or a disturbance in the functioning of, the mind or brain' required by s. 2(1) of the Act, i.e. for a person to lack capacity the former must result from the latter (*York City Council v C* [2014] 2 WLR 1 at [58] and [59]);

viii) The information relevant to the decision includes information about the reasonably foreseeable consequences of deciding one way or another (Mental Capacity Act 2005 s. 3(4)(a));[24]

ix) The threshold for demonstrating capacity is not an unduly high one (see *CC v KK & STCC* [2012] EWHC 2136 (COP) at [69]).

24 This is addressed in Chapter 4.

3.23 Macdonald J noted[25] that in the case of *Re JB*, the Supreme Court described the impairment/disturbance question in s 2(1) of MCA 2005 as the 'core determinative provision' in assessments of whether P lacks capacity.[26] By contrast, the remaining provisions of MCA 2005, ss 2 and 3 were characterised as mere 'statutory descriptions and explanations' in support of the impairment element in s 2(1).

3.24 Therefore, when the court determines capacity, it asks two questions. The first question is: Is P unable to make a decision for him/herself in relation to the matter? If the answer is yes, the second question is: Is the inability because of an impairment of, or a disturbance in the functioning of, the mind or brain? The Supreme Court in *Re JB* emphasised that the questions must be asked in that order. Any document containing a capacity assessment should be in that order too, as is the national capacity assessment 'Form COP3'.

The first question: Is P unable to make the decision?

3.25 To be able to make a decision, P needs to do four things. This is known as 'the functional test' and is found in MCA 2005, s 3(1). The functional test asks whether P has the ability:

(a) to understand the information relevant to the decision;

(b) to retain that information;

(c) to use or weigh the information as part of the process of making the decision; and

(d) to communicate the decision (whether by talking, using sign language or any other means).

3.26 The Court of Appeal has held that capacity must be determined 'by applying section 3(1) in full and considering each of the four elements of the decision making process that are set out at (a) to (d) of that subsection'.[27] Answering the questions will depend on the facts of the case: 'The extent to which, on the facts of any individual case, there is a need either for a sophisticated, or for a more straightforward, evaluation of any of these four elements will naturally vary from case to case and from topic to topic'.[28] It is inappropriate, therefore, for an assessor to determine that P is unable to understand the relevant information, then leave the rest of the assessment form blank.

3.27 The four limbs of s 3(1) are now examined in turn.

25 *North Bristol NHS Trust v R* (n 23), para 46.
26 *A Local Authority v JB* [2021] UKSC 52, para 65.
27 *IM v LM, AB and Liverpool City Council* [2014] EWCA Civ 37, para 73.
28 Ibid.

(a) To understand the information relevant to the decision

3.28 MCA 2005 s 3(2) states: 'A person is not to be regarded as unable to understand the information relevant to a decision if he is able to understand an explanation of it given to him in a way that is appropriate to his circumstances (using simple language, visual aids or any other means).'

3.29 The assessor must tell P about the nature of the decision to be made, why it must be made, the foreseeable consequences of deciding one way or another and of not making a decision at all. This is dealt with more fully in Chapter 4 which emphasises that P need not volunteer this relevant information. Rather, the assessor must inform P of the relevant information, then explore it.

3.30 P must be able to 'comprehend and weigh the salient details relevant to the decision', but 'it is not always necessary for a person to comprehend all peripheral details', because to do so would place greater demands on P than others of their age, maturity and unchallenged capacity.[29] Peter Jackson J (as he then was) has held that, 'common strategies for dealing with unpalatable dilemmas – for example indecision, avoidance or vacillation – are not to be confused with incapacity. We should not ask more of people whose capacity is questioned than of those whose capacity is undoubted'.[30] Lord Stephens made a similar point in the Supreme Court: 'To require a potentially incapacitous person to be capable of envisaging more consequences than persons of full capacity would derogate from personal autonomy'.[31]

3.31 To 'understand' means the ability to grasp information or concepts. It should not be confused with the ability to appreciate or to apply information to oneself, which is better considered under the third limb of the test: the ability to use or weigh.

(b) To retain the information

3.32 P must retain the information for as long as it takes P to make the decision. If P is unable to retain the information for a short period only, it does not mean P is unable to make the decision.[32] For the purposes of MCA 2005, s 3(1)(b), it does not matter if P has forgotten the information after making the decision.

3.33 A capacity assessment is not a memory test ('What were the three words I told you ten minutes ago?') or a general knowledge quiz ('Who is the prime minister?). However, memory issues may be relevant for the use or weigh limb in subsection (c). For example, in an assessment of P's capacity to decide on care,

29 *LBL v RYJ and VJ* [2010] EWHC 2665 (Fam), paras 24 and 58.
30 *Heart of England NHS Foundation Trust v JB* [2014] EWHC 342 (COP), para 25.
31 *A Local Authority v JB* [2021] UKSC 52, para 75.
32 MCA 2005, s 3(3).

P's inability to remember that they left the gas on at home or walked onto the street at night in their pyjamas may indicate they are unable to use or weigh those pieces of information about whether they need support with preparing meals or staying safe.

(c) To use or weigh the information

3.34 The court has described the use and weigh limb as requiring P to be able to 'actually to engage in the decision-making process itself and to be able to see the various parts of the argument and to relate the one to another', and that 'the really difficult cases' involve a concern that P cannot use and weigh the relevant information.[33]

3.35 The court has held that it is, 'not necessary for a person to use or weigh every detail of the respective options available to them to demonstrate capacity, the salient factors are key'.[34] P may be able to use or weigh some elements sufficiently well to be able to make a capacitous decision. As Hayden J has said, 'It is not necessary to have every piece of the jigsaw to see the overall picture'.[35]

3.36 There are many cases in which the Court of Protection has determined that P lacks capacity to make the relevant decision because P is unable adequately to weigh up the benefits and risks of each option. Research into all reported judgments of the Court of Protection has found that the concept of 'use or weigh' was most frequently linked to:

(a) ability to apply information (including consequences of the decision) to oneself or one's situation, whether due to false beliefs such as delusions or confabulations, lack of insight into one's condition or associated care needs, or other reasons; and

(b) ability to reason, including flexibility of thought in responding to contrary evidence or concerns and comparing advantages and disadvantages of certain outcomes.

3.37 Less frequently, 'use or weigh' was linked to rationales such as the ability to imagine or abstract, the ability to value or care, to think through decisions non-impulsively and to give coherent reasons.[36]

33 *PCT v P AH and the Local Authority* [2011] 1 FLR 287, para 35.
34 *CC v KK and STCC* [2012] EWHC 2136 (COP), para 69.
35 *An NHS Trust and another v WA and another* [2020] EWCOP 37, para 36.
36 Kane NB, Keene AR, Owen GS, Kim SYH, 'Applying decision-making capacity criteria in practice: A content analysis of court judgments' (2021) PLOS ONE 16(2): e0246521. See also https://capacityguide.org.uk (accessed 1 February 2026).

(d) To communicate the decision

3.38 This test is met if P communicates the decision verbally or using sign language or any other means. As long as P can communicate the decision *somehow* – through a grunt, a smile, a thumbs up, a flicker of an eyelid, pressing a button on an assistive device, or pointing to a picture in a communications book – then P can communicate the decision. Whether P's decision matches what the capacity assessor thinks is in P's best interests is irrelevant.

3.39 Only in exceptional circumstances will P be unable to communicate a decision. The MCA Code of Practice[37] gives examples of a person in a coma or having locked-in syndrome.[38] If there is any doubt as to P's ability to communicate the decision, it is important that all practical and appropriate efforts to help them communicate are made. This may involve an assessor drawing on the expertise of speech and language therapists, specialists in non-verbal communication or other professionals.[39]

THE RESULT

3.40 P satisfies the four elements of MCA 2005 s 3(1) if P is able to understand the relevant information, retain it, use and weigh it, and communicate a decision. If they are unable to do one or more of those functions, they are deemed 'unable to make the decision'.

(a) If P is *able* to make a decision, there is no need to answer the second (causal) question as the Court of Protection has no jurisdiction to make a best interests decision in relation to a decision that P has capacity to make.

(b) If P is *unable* to make the decision, the assessor or court must answer the second question, below.

The second question: Is P unable to make the decision 'because of' an impairment or disturbance?

3.41 The second question is whether the inability found in one or more of those four elements of the functional test of MCA 2005, s 3(1) is 'because of an impairment of, or a disturbance in the functioning of, the mind or brain' pursuant to MCA 2005, s 2(1). The Supreme Court has held there must be a 'clear causative nexus between P's inability to make a decision for himself in relation to the matter and an impairment of, or a disturbance in the functioning of, P's mind or brain'.[40]

3.42 This question involves two parts.

37 Department for Constitutional Affairs, *Mental Capacity Act 2005 Code of Practice* (TSO, 2007).
38 Ibid, para 4.23.
39 Ibid, para 4.24.
40 *A Local Authority v JB* [2021] UKSC 52, para 78.

3.43 *Part one* of the question determines whether P has 'an impairment of, or disturbance in the functioning of, the mind or brain' pursuant to MCA 2005, s 2 (I will use 'impairment' as shorthand). A formal diagnosis and a precise formulation of P's underlying condition or conditions are not required to determine that P has an impairment to satisfy s 2.[41]

3.44 If there is medical evidence that P has a mental disorder that constitutes an impairment under MCA 2005, s 2, but P denies it, the assessor cannot use P's lack of insight into that impairment to determine that P lacks capacity to make the decision. Theis J has held that insight is a clinical concept, whereas decision-making is a legal concept, and that lack of insight into mental disorder 'may be relevant to, but not determinative of' whether [P] has an impairment in MCA terms.[42]

3.45 *Part two* of the question determines whether the impairment has caused P to be unable to make the decision. MCA 2005, s 2(1) provides that the inability must be 'because of' the impairment. That is a causal question and will not be satisfied by vague suggestions that the inability is 'referable to' or 'significantly relates to' the impairment.[43]

3.46 In a coercive control case, the court may wish to know whether P's inability to use or weigh the relevant information is because of (for example) frontal lobe dementia, or because of the impact of coercive or controlling behaviour of another person, or perhaps both in combination. Determining whether the inability to make the decision is 'because of' an impairment will require evidence (and may require a psychiatric or psychological expertise) and a careful analysis of the facts.

3.47 In a coercive control case, a letter of instruction to a capacity assessor could direct the assessor in terms such as the following:

> The assessor shall provide an opinion if P is unable to make the decision, whether that is due to an impairment of, or disturbance in the functioning of, the mind or brain pursuant to the MCA 2005, and, if the assessor considers that P has capacity to make any relevant decision, and is in a position to express an opinion, a view as to whether P is vulnerable to influence or coercion by reason of her dementia or for any other reason.

The book considers the question of vulnerability in Chapter 6.

3.48 In directing an assessor to answer the question in this way, the court is obtaining appropriate capacity evidence. In such cases, it is common for the

41 *North Bristol NHS Trust v R* [2023] EWCOP 5, para 48.
42 *CT v London Borough of Lambeth & Anor* (n 1), para 60.
43 *PC (by her litigation friend the Official Solicitor) and another v City of York Council* [2013] EWCA Civ 478, para 58.

controlling person to protest that that the court is inappropriately delegating the fact-finding task to the assessor, but this is not the case.

3.49 The authors of capacityguide.org.uk suggest that where coercive control is suspected, an assessor could usefully explore the following factors when determining whether the real problem is P's impairment or the influence of another person:

(a) P being unable to preserve their independence or free will due to influence;

(b) P having had their perspective and future thinking restricted by the influence;

(c) P being suggestible to the influence of others in a general sense;

(d) P being vulnerable because they are extremely dependent on that specific relationship; and

(e) P rejecting facts about the alleged influencer that are relevant to the risk of them taking that decision, such as a previous conviction for sexual assault.

INTERIM AND FINAL DECLARATIONS OF CAPACITY

3.50 If, on the balance of probabilities, the Court of Protection determines that P lacks capacity to make the relevant decision, the court can make a declaration pursuant to MCA 2005, s 15. The wording of the court order will be, for example,

> **IT IS DECLARED PURSUANT TO SECTION 15 OF THE MENTAL CAPACITY ACT 2005 THAT:**
>
> P lacks capacity to:
>
> (a) conduct these proceedings;
>
> (b) make decisions about residence;
>
> (c) make decisions about care; and
>
> (d) make decisions about contact with others.

3.51 Although the statute does not use the word 'final', many Court of Protection judgments describe s 15 declarations in those terms, notwithstanding that capacity can change over time. For example, a person may have a progressive degenerative disorder whereby they have capacity today but will lack capacity in a year, or the person may have a cyclical mental illness or respond positively to education or medication, such that capacity can be regained. It is possible for the court to come to a different conclusion on capacity at a later date, and many capacity declarations made under MCA 2005, s 15 are not, in fact, final.

3.52 Rule 10.10(b) of the Court of Protection Rules 2017 (COPR 2017) permits the court to grant, among other things, an interim capacity declaration. The court will do so when there is reason to believe that P lacks capacity to make a certain decision, and where the court must make an urgent best interests decisions pursuant to MCA 2005, s 48. This might include appointing a litigation friend to act for P in proceedings. Interim remedies are further considered in Chapter 9.

OBTAINING CAPACITY EVIDENCE

3.53 Capacity evidence is required for the Court of Protection to determine P's capacity with reference to MCA 2005, s 2. Most applications to the Court of Protection are made on a Form COP1, alongside which the applicant must file a capacity assessment on a Form COP3.[44]

3.54 A capacity assessment is usually completed by a social worker or a medical professional. An informal ranking of professionals has emerged in the Court of Protection wherein psychiatrists are considered the best assessors, followed by psychologists, and then social workers. There is no empirical basis for this, and in the context of mental health law, the Upper Tribunal has observed that psychiatrists are no better placed to assess capacity than psychiatric nurses or social workers.[45]

3.55 As noted above, capacity evidence filed with the application may not be robust enough for the court to make a declaration of capacity under MCA 2005, s 15, so the court makes an interim capacity declaration in order to make urgent best interests decisions under MCA 2005, s 48, together with directions about obtaining further and better capacity evidence. There are four ways in which the court can obtain capacity evidence, which are set out below.

A party

3.56 First, the court can direct the relevant public body (either a local authority, an NHS trust in England or a Health Board in Wales) to file capacity evidence. This is usually done by a social worker with relevant post-graduate training on assessing capacity or a mental health professional. This is the easiest, quickest and most cost-effective way to obtain capacity evidence: one of the parties is in control of the evidence, and no other party needs to pay for the evidence.

3.57 However, it may be that a social work has conducted a capacity assessment that the court has already determined to be inadequate. The court may agree with submissions on behalf of P and/or P's family members that there is a benefit in obtaining capacity evidence from an assessor other than the local authority, because of the local authority's vested interest in the outcome.

44 Court of Protection forms and guidance available at: https://www.gov.uk/government/collections/court-of-protection-forms (accessed 1 February 2026).

45 *KH and another v Nottinghamshire Healthcare NHS Foundation Trust and another* [2025] UKUT 128 (AAC), para 73.

3.58 P may assert that they have capacity to decide the relevant matter. Their views on their capacity will be relevant. Where the court has made an interim declaration that P lacks capacity and appointed a litigation friend, the litigation friend is expected to file a witness statement exhibiting a note of their attendance on P, setting out P's wishes and feelings, including with respect to the issue of capacity. Representation of P in coercive control cases is discussed further in Chapter 11, below.

A non-party local authority or NHS body

3.59 The court can obtain capacity evidence from a non-party under MCA 2005, s 49(2). This provision gives the Court of Protection the power to require a report to be written, accompanied by a separate order usually called a 'section 49 order'.

3.60 The provision gives the court the power to compel 'a local authority, or an NHS body, to arrange for a report to be made by one of its officers or employees or by such other person (other than the Public Guardian or a Court of Protection Visitor) as the authority, or the NHS body, considers appropriate.'

3.61 A s 49 report comes from a non-party. If the court wants evidence from a local authority or NHS trust that are parties to the proceedings, it can simply direct them in a directions order, without a separate section 49 order.

3.62 The court can direct a s 49 report to be a capacity assessment or a report about any other topic that assists the court in determining the matter.[46] For example, the court could obtain a report from the NHS or a local authority, or any specific professionals employed within or by those organisations such as psychiatrists, psychologists, learning disability nurses, dieticians, occupational therapists or a speech and language therapists. The court can direct a s 49 report to provide the author's opinions on best interests too. The section 49 order will provide for the maker of the report to be given a copy of all relevant documents,[47] and for them to meet with and interview P.[48]

3.63 Following receipt of the report, any party may apply to the court for permission to send written questions to the report's author.[49] The questions must be sent to the court first, and the court will decide whether to require the report's author to answer them.

3.64 Practice Direction 14E on s 49 reports (PD14E) sets out the procedural requirements with a template section 49 order in its annex containing, at para 3, a list of 'common factors' the court may consider when deciding on a section

46 MCA 2005, s 49(5).
47 This is also envisaged in MCA 2005, s 49(7).
48 Sections 49(8) and (9) make provision for the same with respect to special visitors.
49 COPR 2017, r 14.26.

49 order. These include 'where the public body has recent knowledge of P; or it is reasonably expected that they have recent knowledge of P; or should have knowledge due to their statutory responsibilities under housing, social and/or health care legislation'.[50]

3.65 PD14E provides that wherever practicable, before applying for an order requiring a report under s 49, a party to proceedings should use their best endeavours to: (a) make contact with an appropriate person within the relevant local authority or NHS body so they are made aware that an application is to be made, what its purpose is, and the issues or questions which are hoped to be addressed within the report; (b) identify a named person or by reference to their office ('the senior officer') within the relevant local authority or NHS body who will be able to receive the court order on its behalf; and (c) enquire as to the reasonableness and time scales for providing the report, should the court order it.

3.66 The Practice Direction also specifies that the report must have four main sections: (1) details of the author; (2) details of P; (3) matters and material considered in preparing the report; and (4) conclusions reached. The conclusions must (a) identify any issues or questions which were specified in the directions given by the court as being matters in which the court had a particular interest; (b) address clearly such issues or questions; (c) state clearly all conclusions reached by the person who prepared the report; (d) state clearly the recommendations made by the person who prepared the report; and (e) contain a statement of truth.

3.67 In December 2022, the (then) Vice-President of the Court of Protection Hayden J recirculated PD14E noting that NHS mental health directors considered some s 49 requests were 'disproportionate, overly burdensome, and wrongly authorised'. He noted the need for section 49 orders to be 'clearly focused with tight identification of the issues', and that if a more in-depth assessment across a wider range of questions was required, then an independent expert is likely required.[51]

3.68 MCA 2005, s 49 gives judges a broad discretion as to whether to order a s 49 report and the scope of such report.[52] The discretion is not to be regarded as unfettered: the court should elicit information it considers necessary to illuminate the question in focus. The court must have regard to PD14E, but, given the 'highly fact-specific' nature of Court of Protection proceedings, the common factors identified at para 3 of the annex to PD14E (noted above) are permissive and not mandatory.

50 PD14E, para 3(d).
51 Hayden J, Guidance on s 49 orders, 16 December 2022.
52 *Cheshire and Wirral Partnership NHS Foundation Trust v JMC and another* [2023] EWCOP 14.

A Court of Protection Visitor

3.69 The court may obtain capacity evidence from a Court of Protection Visitor.[53] There are two types of Visitor:

(a) a Special Visitor is a medical practitioner who has special knowledge of mental capacity; and

(b) a General Visitor need not be medically qualified, but must have some experience of mental capacity.

3.70 The Lord Chancellor appoints Visitors.[54] The Office of the Public Guardian (OPG) administers a panel of Visitors who work throughout England and Wales. They mainly work as contractors, although the OPG employs a small number directly. The Public Guardian can direct a Visitor to visit P and report on matters as required.[55] One of the roles of the Public Guardian is to supervise deputies and investigate concerns about the actions of a deputy or attorney: in coercive control cases this may be relevant if there are concerns that the deputy or attorney is exhibiting coercive or controlling behaviour towards P.

3.71 The Court of Protection pays for a Visitor's report and, if needed, funds the Visitor attending court to answer questions. The procedural requirements set out in PD14E apply also to s 49 reports written by Visitors.

An independent expert

3.72 The fourth way in which the court may obtain further capacity evidence is set out in rule 15 COPR 2017 which empowers the court to permit the parties to appoint an expert independent to prepare or give evidence in the proceedings. Rule 15.3 requires the court to give permission to file or adduce an independent expert only if two tests are met:

(1) independent expert evidence must be 'necessary to assist the court to resolve the issues in the proceedings' (necessity is a high standard); and

(2) such evidence cannot otherwise be provided by a rule 1.2 representative (which is appropriate in straightforward, usually uncontested applications, but not in cases involving allegations of coercive control) or in a s 49 report.

3.73 Where there are concerns of coercive control, a party may wish to obtain an independent report on P's capacity to conduct proceedings and make subject matter decisions (see Chapter 4) and instruct a second expert, a psychologist with direct expertise in coercive control (see Chapters 5 and 7 which examine the case law).

53 MCA 2005, s 49(3).
54 MCA 2005, s 61.
55 MCA 2005, s 58(1)(d).

3.74 The person said to have exhibited coercive and controlling behaviour may wish to file evidence from an expert in support of their case. Before instructing the expert, they must obtain the court's permission. They cannot simply send court documents to someone other than a party, as this will likely to breach the transparency order (a reporting restriction order) that prohibits identifying P and sharing their information. If the court gives permission to instruct an expert, the court will want to ensure that the expert has all the relevant documents, rather than a cherry-picked selection. The instructing parties should provide an expert with any material that is likely to have an impact on their views, conclusions and recommendations.[56]

3.75 The duty of any expert – whether a single joint expert (ie, an expert instructed by all parties) or an expert instructed by only one party – is 'to help the court on the matters within the expert's expertise'.[57] The duty of an expert towards the court 'overrides any obligation to the person from whom the expert has received instructions or by whom the expert is paid'.[58]

3.76 The views and conclusions of experts do not dictate the outcome of the case, and the court may prefer the evidence of professionals who have known P over a longer period of time.[59] Hayden J has noted that '[e]vidence of clinicians, experts, social workers, care specialists etc is always to be regarded as individual features of a broader forensic landscape in to which must be factored the lay evidence. One expert or clinician is unlikely ever to provide the entire answer to the case […]'.[60]

SUMMARY

3.77 This chapter has considered the approach of the Court of Protection in determining capacity. It detailed three statutory principles relevant to capacity: the presumption of capacity, the need to take all reasonable practicable steps to support P to make their own decision, and that unwise decisions are not an indication of incapacity. It then described how capacity is assessed by professionals and determined by the court. First, the assessor formulates the subject-matter of the decision being assessed, identifies the information relevant to that decision (these are matters that are considered further in the next chapter), and determines whether P is unable to make the decision by applying the four elements of the functional test, the ability to understand, retain, use/weigh and communicate a decision. Second, if P is unable to make the decision, the assessor determines whether the inability is because of an impairment of, or a disturbance in the functioning of, the mind or brain.

56 *London Borough of Southwark v NP & Ors* [2019] EWCOP 48, para 31(vi).
57 COPR 2017, r 15.4(1).
58 COPR 2017, r.15.4(2).
59 For example, see *PH v A Local Authority and others* [2011] EWHC 1704 (Fam), para 58.
60 *London Borough of Southwark v NP & Ors* (n 56), para 31(vii).

3.78 The chapter then considered the powers of the court in relation to capacity declarations. These include making urgent best interests decisions on the basis that the court has reason to believe that P lacks capacity to make the relevant decision, while giving directions to obtain further and better capacity evidence. The chapter presented the four ways that the court can obtain better capacity evidence, including s 49 reports, Court of Protection Visitors, and independent experts.

CHAPTER 4

Decision-making domains

'The assessment is not a general knowledge test.'[1]

INTRODUCTION

4.01 The previous chapter noted that the Mental Capacity Act 2005 (MCA 2005), s 3(1) contains the first question that a capacity assessor must answer – namely, whether P is able to understand, retain, use and weigh the information relevant to the decision. This chapter explains what the relevant information means in capacity domains that are frequently assessed in coercive control cases. The section headed 'Preliminary points' (at para 4.03) provides guidance to assessors, including the need to tailor the information to P, and to inform P of the relevant information as well as the reasonably foreseeable consequences of deciding one way or another.

4.02 The section headed 'Decision-making areas' (at para 4.22) sets out from the case law the relevant information in 11 decision-making areas: (1) conducting proceedings; (2) deciding about residence; (3) deciding about care; (4) deciding about contact with others; (5) deciding about disclosure of information to others; (6) managing property and financial affairs; (7) deciding on internet and social media use; (8) executing and revoking a lasting power of attorney; (9) engaging in sexual relations; (10) deciding to marry; and (11) testamentary capacity (making a will).

PRELIMINARY POINTS

4.03 Capacity assessors should have in mind five matters when assessing capacity. They should: (1) clearly determine the matter on which a decision is required; (2) tailor the relevant information to P; (3) tell P that information (rather than asking P what it is); (4) explore with P the reasonably foreseeable consequences of deciding one way or the other; and (5) avoid decision-making silos.

1 *Re B* [2019] EWCA Civ 913.

Articulating the matter

4.04 Before carrying out the assessment, the capacity assessor should clearly articulate the precise matter on which a decision is required.[2] If the matter is in proceedings, so too should the Court of Protection. Each matter should have its own assessment rather than combining them. For example, instead of assessing whether P has capacity to decide where to live and receive care under a tenancy; there should be three separate assessments about residence, care and entering into a tenancy.

4.05 An example of the precision required by the Court of Protection in articulating the relevant decision can be found in an appeal in 2023. The first instance judge said the capacity question was: 'Is [P] to be discharged from hospital (in which case she can only go to the bungalow)?'. This had two components: discharge from hospital and return to the bungalow. The appeal judge permitted the appeal on the basis that the lower court had elided two questions, causing 'a degree of confusion as to the relevant question. Did it relate to (i) hospital discharge, or (ii) living arrangements or (iii) a combination of the two?'[3]

Tailoring the relevant information

4.06 Without a clear understanding of the relevant information, the assessor cannot provide an opinion about P's ability to understand, retain, use or weigh it, and the Court of Protection cannot determine whether P has or lacks capacity to make that decision.

4.07 Capacity assessments must be specific to the decision being made, so the assessor must be clear as to 'the precise matter upon which the person's decision is required'. The 'information relevant to the decision', must be identified 'within the specific factual context of the case'.[4] The relevant information should be documented in the capacity assessment.

4.08 The Court of Appeal has held that, 'The assessment is not a general knowledge test. Rather it is an assessment of whether the person being assessed has the ability to understand those matters when explained to him or her and to retain the information for a period of time and to use or weigh it in deciding [the matter]'.[5]

4.09 This chapter provides guidance from case law where judges have suggested relevant information in a series of decision-making domains. Such

2 *A Local Authority v JB* [2021] UKSC 52, paras 68–69.
3 *Wiltshire County Council v RB (by her litigation friend the Official Solicitor) and others* [2023] EWCOP 26, para 25.
4 *A Local Authority v JB* (n 2), paras 68–70.
5 *Re B* (n 1), para 57.

guidance should be 'treated and applied as no more than guidance to be expanded or contracted or otherwise adapted to the facts of the particular case'.[6] The expectation is that:

> the assessment must be unique to P, and to P's specific circumstances. Thus, previous case law, suggesting that any particular type of decision must be assessed in a prescriptive way, must be approached with considerable caution.[7]

4.10 A capacity assessor should prepare carefully for the assessment by writing down the relevant information they will put to, and discuss with, P. Similarly, a letter of instruction to a capacity assessor could set out the relevant information rather than leaving the assessor to formulate the relevant information.

Putting the relevant information to P

4.11 The assessor must tell P what the relevant information is. P 'is not required to identify relevant information him/herself'.[8]

4.12 Paragraph 4.16 of the MCA Code of Practice states, 'It is important not to assess someone's understanding before they have been given relevant information about a decision. Every effort must be made to provide information in a way that is most appropriate to help the person understand'.

4.13 Lawyers commonly see capacity assessments in which the assessor has asked P, 'What are your care needs?' which the person may not be able to answer, rather than putting to P their assessed care needs. To avoid this error, assessors should provide sufficient evidence in the assessment that they have given P the relevant information in relation to each decision, and of their discussions with P about that information.[9]

Reasonably foreseeable consequences

4.14 The MCA 2005 contains only one indication about the relevant information that an assessor must put to, and discuss with, P. Section 3(4) of MCA 2005 states that, 'The information relevant to a decision includes information about the reasonably foreseeable consequences of — (a) deciding one way or another, or (b) failing to make the decision.' As such, assessors must always put to P the reasonably foreseeable consequences of deciding one way or the other.

6 *Re B* (n 1), paras 44 and 62.
7 *Warrington Borough Council v Y & Ors* [2023] EWCOP 27, para 26.
8 *Re B* (n 1), para 60(9).
9 *AMDC v AG & Anor* [2020] EWCOP 58, para 24.

4.15 Assessors should consider whether others would be affected by P's decisions. The Supreme Court in 2021 recognised that:

> consequences are not limited to the 'reasonably foreseeable consequences' for P, but can extend to consequences for others. This again illustrates that the information relevant to the decision must be identified within the factual context of each case.[10]

4.16 There is a practical limit on what needs to be envisaged as 'reasonably foreseeable consequences' in MCA 2005, s 3(4), because 'requir[ing] a potentially incapacitous person to be capable of envisaging more consequences than persons of full capacity would derogate from personal autonomy'.[11]

4.17 The relevant information is at the core of the capacity assessment. Theis J has noted that the information 'will be different in each case but will include the nature of the decisions, the reason why the decision is needed, and the likely effects of deciding one way or another, or making no decision at all'.[12]

Avoiding silos

4.18 MacDonald J has said that, 'there may be an overlap between the various different decisions to be made'.[13] It follows that in complex cases (and I suggest all coercive control cases are) and where multiple decision-making domains are in play (as is usual in coercive control cases), the court may require an omnibus assessment of P's capacity across several decision-making areas. Capacity should not be assessed in self-contained silos without regard to the overlap between them.

4.19 For example, Court of Protection practitioners often see residence and care elided into one capacity assessment. This may be explained by the volume of cases concerning deprivation of liberty safeguards (DoLS) and the way that the 'mental capacity requirement' per para 15 of Sch A1 to the MCA 2005 is assessed. For a standard authorisation depriving P of their liberty to be granted, the assessment should conclude that P 'lacks capacity in relation to the question whether or not he should be accommodated in the relevant hospital or care home for the purpose of being given the relevant care or treatment.'[14] Baker J has held that the relevant information should take account of P's 'concrete situation' and extends to some information about the context in which the deprivation is being imposed'.[15] The mental capacity requirement therefore potentially elides four

10 *A Local Authority v JB* (n 2), para 73.
11 *A Local Authority v JB* (n 2), para 75.
12 *CT v London Borough of Lambeth & Anor* [2025] EWCOP 6 (T3), para 60(8).
13 *A Local Authority v RS (Capacity)* [2020] EWCOP 29, para 33.
14 Schedule A1 to MCA 2005, para 15. Baker J identified relevant information in a hospital case in *A Primary Care Trust v LDV & Ors* [2013] EWHC 272 (Fam), paras 37–39.
15 *A Primary Care Trust v LDV & Ors* [2013] EWHC 272 (Fam), paras 37–39.

domains: (1) residence; (2) care; (3) treatment; and (4) the context in which the deprivation of liberty is imposed, including specific restrictions in place.

4.20 Outside the DoLS regime, residence and care are two distinct decisions which must be assessed separately. However, the domains are often linked, as HHJ Hilder, the senior judge of the Court of Protection, has explained:

> It does not follow from such approach, however, that residence and care are decisions which are made in separate 'silos'. There are differences in the information relevant to making each decision but there is also overlap. Again, comparison of Theis J's two lists immediately illustrates the point – item (8) in respect of a decision about residence is 'what sort of care [P] would receive in each placement in broad terms' (para. 64). The judge noted that the 'Overlap does not however imply that a decision in respect of residence somehow incorporates a decision in respect of care …'[16]

4.21 An example of a siloed approach is the case *Re ZZ*, where allowing an appeal, Theis J held that the first instance judge was wrong to have determined P had capacity to decide on residence and lacked capacity to decide on care.[17] Her reasoning was that the judge (a) did not properly analyse P's wish to live with his girlfriend, (b) did not consider the care that P would receive and P's view that he did not need the care and support that was being provided, and (c) risked approaching the matter in a silo, with implications for coherent care planning.

DECISION-MAKING AREAS

4.22 This chapter now sets out the relevant information in the common decision-making areas that arise in coercive and controlling behaviour cases: (1) conducting proceedings; (2) deciding about residence; (3) deciding about care; (4) deciding about contact with others; (5) deciding about disclosure of information to others; (6) managing property and financial affairs; (7) deciding on internet and social media use; (8) executing and revoking a lasting power of attorney; (9) engaging in sexual relations; (10) deciding to marry; and (11) testamentary capacity (making a will).

Conducting proceedings

4.23 P's capacity to conduct the legal proceedings (also known as 'litigation capacity') may be relevant in coercive control cases. The controlling person may coerce or encourage P to 'choose' a solicitor who the controlling person has selected and may try to influence. The controlling person could select a solicitor

16 *London Borough of Tower Hamlets v A (By Her Litigation Friend the Official Solicitor) and KF* [2020] EWCOP 21, para 65.

17 *Local Authority A v ZZ (By His Litigation Friend the Official Solicitor)* [2024] EWCOP 21, at para 82.

unfamiliar with Court of Protection matters; a solicitor less aware of coercive and controlling behaviours; tell the solicitor that P does not pick up the telephone so the solicitor should contact the controlling person instead' or cherry-pick what documents are sent to the solicitor giving them an perpetrator-friendly picture of the case.

4.24 Several Court of Protection judges have said that it is unlikely, but possible, for a P to have subject matter capacity and lack litigation capacity. In 2004, Munby J said:

> Whilst it is not difficult to think of situations where someone has subject-matter capacity whilst lacking litigation capacity, and such cases may not be that rare, I suspect that cases where someone has litigation capacity whilst lacking subject-matter capacity are likely to be very much more infrequent, indeed pretty rare. Indeed, I would go so far as to say that only in unusual circumstances will it be possible to conclude that someone who lacks subject-matter capacity can nonetheless have litigation capacity.[18]

4.25 More recently, Mostyn J commented on the close relationship between substantive capacity and litigation capacity in medical treatment cases:

> I would go further and say that it is virtually impossible to conceive of circumstances where someone lacks capacity to make a decision about medical treatment, but yet has capacity to make decisions about the manifold steps or stances needed to be addressed in litigation about that very same subject matter. It seems to me to be completely illogical to say that someone is incapable of making a decision about medical treatment, but is capable of making a decision about what to submit to a judge who is making that very determination.[19]

4.26 The leading authority on capacity to conduct proceedings is the 2003 Court of Appeal case of *Masterman-Lister*,[20] which was cited with approval by the Supreme Court in *Dunhill v Burgin*.[21] The test is whether the party is capable of understanding, with the assistance of such proper explanation from legal advisors and experts in other disciplines as the case may require, the issues on which his consent or decision is likely to be necessary in the course of those proceedings. This requires the ability to recognise a problem, obtain, receive and understand relevant information (including advice), the ability to weigh the information (including that derived from advice) in the balance in reaching a decision, and the ability to communicate a decision.

18 *Sheffield City Council v (1) E (2) S* [2004] EWHC 2808 (Fam), para 49.
19 *An NHS Trust v P* [2021] 4 WLR 69, para 33. See also *Re Q* [2022] EWCOP 6, para 22.
20 *Masterman-Lister v Brutton & Co; Masterman-Lister v Jewell* [2002] EWCA Civ 1889.
21 *Dunhill (a protected party by her litigation friend Tasker) v Burgin* [2014] UKSC 18, [2014] COPLR 199.

4.27 It has also been held that P needs a basic understanding of the nature of the claim, of the legal issues involved and the circumstances giving rise to the claim.[22] MacDonald J has held that capacity to conduct legal proceedings is:

> not being simply a question of providing instruction to a lawyer and then sitting back and observing the litigation, but rather a dynamic transactional process, both prior to and in court, with information to be recalled, instructions to be given, advice to be received and decisions to be taken, potentially on a number of occasions over the span of the proceedings as they develop.[23]

4.28 Mostyn J has also held:

> Conducting litigation is not simply a question of providing instructions to a lawyer and then sitting back and watching the case unfold. Litigation is a heavy-duty, dynamic transactional process, both prior to and in court, with information to be recalled, instructions to be given, advice to be received and decisions to be taken, on many occasions, on a number of issues, over the span of the proceedings as they develop.[24]

4.29 In another case, a circuit judge conducted a detailed review of how litigation capacity should be considered and approached.[25] The judge noted that the presumption of capacity was not included in the MCA 2005 to obviate examination of whether a party to proceedings lacked capacity, and that it could not have been Parliament's intention to place a vulnerable person in danger of their lack of capacity being overlooked at the expense of their rights by a slack reliance on the presumption.

4.30 That case was a family law matter where there had been a failure to assess or determine whether the child's mother had capacity to conduct the proceedings, despite her known personality disorder and alcohol misuse which had historically led to her making wrong decisions for the child. The judge reviewed the case law, which in her view contained some internal tensions, but suggested the following as obviously impermissible when litigation capacity is in issue:

(a) failure to grasp the nettle fully and early;

(b) ignoring information or evidence that a party may lack capacity;

(c) purporting to 'adopt' the presumption of capacity in circumstances where capacity has been questioned;

22 *D v R (The Deputy of S) & Anor* [2010] EWCOP 2405, para 43.
23 *TB v KB and LH (Capacity to Conduct Proceedings)* [2019] EWCOP 14.
24 *Re P* [2021] EWCOP 27, para 27.
25 *Z v Kent County Council and Others* [2018] EWFC B65.

(d) making directions addressing the capacity issue, but discharging them or failing to comply with them and thereby leaving the issue inadequately addressed;

(e) failing to obtain evidence (expert or otherwise) relevant to capacity;

(f) use of 'unless' orders;

(g) similarly, using personal service or 'warning notices' on that party;

(h) relying on non-engagement by that party either with assessments or the proceedings;

(i) proceeding with any substantive directions, let alone making final orders, in the absence of adequate enquiry and proper determination of the capacity issue; and

(j) treating a party as having provided consent to any step, let alone a grave and possibly irrevocable final step, where capacity has been questioned but the issue not determined.

4.31 Court of Protection practitioners should be aware of these issues, and raise relevant matters about P's capacity to conduct proceedings and bring them to the court's attention to enable the court to make appropriate orders.

4.32 If the court determines (including on an interim basis: see 'Interim and final declarations of capacity' at para 3.50) that P lacks capacity to conduct proceedings, it will appoint a litigation friend for P. This may be the Official Solicitor or some other person.[26] In coercive control cases, the controlling person sometimes applies for appointment as P's litigation friend, but such application is unlikely to succeed.

Deciding about residence

4.33 Residence means the place where P lives. It does not imply residential care. In the much-cited case of *Re LBX*, Theis J determined that the relevant information when assessing P's capacity to decide on residence was:

(a) what the options are, including information about what sort of properties they are and the facilities they have;

(b) in broad terms, what sort of area the properties are in (and any specific known risks beyond the usual risks faced by people living in an area if any such specific risks exist);

(c) the difference between living somewhere and visiting it;

(d) what activities P would be able to do if they lived in each place;

26 See COPR 2017 r 17.4.

(e) whether and how P would be able to see family and friends if living in each place;

(f) the need to pay money to live there and to pay bills, that there would be an agreement about use of the property;

(g) who P would be living with at each placement;

(h) what sort of care P would receive in each placement in broad terms; and

(i) the impact on contact with others.[27]

4.34 Irrelevant matters which the assessor should not consider include the costs of the placement, value for money, the legal nature of the tenancy or licence, and any long-term consequences of a residence decision on P's family, friends or others. Including such matters would set the bar too high, beyond the 'reasonably foreseeable consequences' required by MCA 2005, s 3(4).[28]

Deciding about care

4.35 In *Re LBX*, Theis J said the information likely to be relevant when determining P's capacity to decide on care was:

(a) what areas P needs support with;

(b) what sort of support P needs;

(c) who will be providing P with support;

(d) what would happen if P did not have any support or refused it; and

(e) carers might not always treat people properly and that complaints can be brought.[29]

4.36 It is unnecessary for P to be able to understand (and retain, use/weigh etc) the funding of care or the arrangements for monitoring and appointing care staff. As such, assessors need not put this information to P.

4.37 A circuit judge has suggested that further irrelevant factors, when assessing P's capacity to decide on care, include why having a support worker is important to P to access the community; the importance of structure and routine in P's day; the importance of regular access to the local community to build and maintain his confidence in daily life and independence and to avoid a deterioration in his anxiety; and, to the same ends, the importance of developing relationships with others outside his close family. The judge said these were, 'nebulous value judgments', and treating them as relevant information had wrongly led to 'the

27 *LBX v K* [2013] EWHC 3230 (Fam), para 43.
28 Ibid, para 44.
29 Ibid, para 48. This list was approved by the Court of Appeal in *Re B* (n 1).

tail of welfare beginning to wag the dog of capacity'[30] – a phrase evoking Peter Jackson J's canine metaphor.[31]

4.38 In coercive control cases, a difficulty may arise if the perpetrator is impeding P's care needs from being assessed or met. A local authority may have a duty to meet P's eligible needs under the Care Act 2014 (in Wales, the Social Services and Well-being (Wales) Act 2014). The eligible outcomes of that Act are set out in reg 2(2) of the Care and Support (Eligibility Criteria) Regulations 2015 (SI 2015/313):

(a) managing and maintaining nutrition;

(b) maintaining personal hygiene;

(c) managing toilet needs;

(d) being appropriately clothed;

(e) being able to make use of P's home safely;

(f) maintaining a habitable home environment;

(g) developing and maintaining family or other personal relationships;

(h) accessing and engaging in work, training, education or volunteering;

(i) making use of necessary facilities or services in the local community, including public transport and recreational facilities or services; and

(j) carrying out any caring responsibilities the adult has for a child.

In Wales, the outcomes are different: see the Care and Support (Eligibility) (Wales) Regulations 2015 (WSI 2015/1578). The outcomes may be salient detail within the *Re LBX* relevant information (see para 4.35 above).

4.39 Examples of how perpetrators may impede these outcomes are set out in the 'Statutory guidance: Controlling or coercive behaviour: statutory guidance framework' (see Chapter 2). These include dictating what P wears, what they eat, when they sleep, and who they meet and talk to. The perpetrator could create rules they expect P to obey, use child arrangements and maintenance to control P, prevent P from accessing leisure activities, or isolate P from family and/or friends.

4.40 The statutory guidance continues that the perpetrator could isolate the victim from 'professionals who may be trying to support them'. In the health or social care contexts, the perpetrator may block assessments of P's needs for care and support,[32] or of P's capacity to make relevant decisions. This can make it

30 *A Local Authority v GP (Capacity – Care, Support and Education)* [2020] EWCOP 56, paras 25–26.
31 *Heart of England NHS Foundation Trust v JB* [2014] EWHC 342 (COP).
32 Care Act 2014, s 9 places a duty on a local authority to assess a person's needs for care and support.

difficult for health and social care professionals to understand P's presentation, needs and decision-making capacity.

4.41 Where social workers cannot assess P's needs for care and support and (a) P lacks capacity to refuse to participate in an assessment and the local authority considers it is in P's best interests to be assessed or (b) P 'is experiencing, or at risk of, abuse or neglect', the local authority must apply s 11(2) of the Care Act 2014 and carry out the needs assessment. The Explanatory Notes to the Care Act 2014 use slightly differently wording: 'if the adult is at risk of harm or financial abuse'.[33] The Statutory Guidance to that Act states that psychological abuse includes humiliation, blaming, controlling behaviour, coercion, harassment, cyber bullying, isolation, and unreasonable and unjustified withdrawal of services or support networks.

4.42 The Statutory Guidance states that: 'Where the adult who is or is at risk of abuse or neglect has capacity and is still refusing an assessment, local authorities must undertake an assessment so far as possible and document this. They should continue to keep in contact with the adult and carry out an assessment if the adult changes their mind, and asks them to do so'.[34] The guidance is silent on the steps the social worker should take where an adult refuses to participate in an assessment because of the influence or control of another person.

4.43 Only one reported Court of Protection case has considered the relevant information for assessing P's capacity to refuse a Care Act assessment, but it did not involve allegations of coercive control. In *Re GP*,[35] the court determined the relevant information as: (a) a local authority has a statutory duty to meet a person's eligible care needs, which may be to prevent or delay the development of needs for care and support or reducing needs that already exist; (b) the assessor may speak to other adults or professionals involved in P's care, and P may refuse to consent to this; and (c) the local authority will assess how P's wellbeing can be promoted and whether meeting these needs will help P achieve his desired outcomes.

Deciding about contact with others

4.44 As the nub of coercive control cases is the influence of another person (or persons), it is important to establish whether P has capacity to make decisions about contact with others. In the context of coercive control, assessments of this decision-making area can be challenging.

33 Explanatory Notes to the Care Act 2014, para 105(b).
34 Para 6.20.
35 n 30, para 20.

4.45 Contact is person-specific, which is an important consideration in coercive control cases.[36] The assessor may be asked to assess P's capacity to make decisions about contact with the allegedly controlling person, and then separately assess P's capacity to make decisions about contact with others. If the assessment concludes that P has capacity to decide on contact with the perpetrator of coercive control, the local authority can make an application for orders to regulate contact under the inherent jurisdiction: see Chapters 6 and 7.

4.46 Information relevant to decisions about contact with others includes the following:

(a) who the others are and in broad terms the nature of P's relationship with them;[37]

(b) what sort of contact P could have with each of them, including different locations, differing durations, and differing arrangements regarding the presence of a support worker;[38]

(c) the positive and negative aspects of having contact with each person, which 'unless demonstrably false, any assessment should include not only an individual's current experiences but also any negative or unpleasant aspects of past experiences during contact with that individual';[39]

(d) the impact of deciding to have or not to have contact of a particular sort with a particular person;

(e) P's family are in a different category from other contact persons;[40] and

(f) evaluation of present or future risk if the contact person has previous criminal convictions or poses any sort of risk to P. The circumstances surrounding the conviction(s) and P's ability to understand any risks or dangers to which they may be exposed are all relevant factors.[41]

4.47 P's own evaluation will only be irrelevant if it is based on demonstrably false beliefs. Abstract notions of contact are irrelevant (eg, the nature of friendship; the importance of family ties; the long-term possible effects of contact decisions; any risks not in issue for P)[42] and should not be taken into account when assessing P's capacity to decide on contact with others.

4.48 In the case of *Re EOA*,[43] P was under the coercive control of family members who were members of a cult. The judge held that it was appropriate to consider P's capacity with them separately from his capacity to have contact with

36 *PC (by her litigation friend the Official Solicitor) and others v City of York Council* [2013] EWCA Civ 478.
37 *Re LBX* (n 27), para 45.
38 Ibid.
39 *WU v BU* [2021] EWCOP 54, para 41(iv).
40 *Re LBX* (n 27), para 46.
41 *Re BU* (n 39), para 41.
42 *Re LBX* (n 27), para 47.
43 *Re EOA* [2021] EWCOP 20.

others. The judge found that P 'does not understand the risk they pose to him and is unable to weigh that in any decisions about contact with him. This rigidity of thinking arises from his autism although may also be impacted by indoctrination. He thus lacks capacity to make decisions in relation to those family members.'[44]

4.49 Finally, if P has made a health and welfare lasting power of attorney (LPA) in favour of the controlling person, or a Court of Protection appointed deputy is in place,[45] neither appointment confers power to prohibit P from having contact with others.

Deciding about disclosure of information to others

4.50 A person displaying coercive and controlling behaviour may want information from or about P, such as health records. This enables the controlling person to, for example, arrange medical appointments or control medication.

4.51 In an unreported case in 2024, a Court of Protection judge permitted the parties to publish the relevant information given to the expert who assessed P's capacity to consent to professionals sharing information about her health and care provision with her family.[46] The relevant information was as follows:

(a) what sort of information might be shared by professionals;

(b) the benefits of sharing this sort of information with her family, including support with appointments, monitoring of care provision, support to engage with services and medication and so on; and

(c) the risks of not sharing this information with her family, including the risk of deterioration, the reported risk of death due to substance abuse, the risk of non-engagement with services. P would need to be able to recall and weigh up past events where her family have, and have not been provided with information, and the impact of those decisions on P.

Managing property and financial affairs

4.52 In *Masterman-Lister*,[47] a case predating the MCA 2005, the Court of Appeal suggested that the following information is relevant to assessing a person's capacity to manage their property and financial affairs:

(a) the extent of P's property and financial affairs, their income and capital (including savings and the value of any property), their expenditure, and liabilities, financial needs and responsibilities;

44 Ibid, para 50.
45 See MCA 2005, s 20(2)(a).
46 See 39 Essex Chambers, 'Mental capacity guidance note: relevant information for different categories of decision'.
47 n 20.

(b) whether there are likely to be any changes in those financial circumstances in the foreseeable future, the skill and specialised knowledge and time it takes to manage those affairs properly; and

(c) whether P would be likely to seek, understand and act on appropriate advice where needed in view of the complexity of their affairs.

4.53 In an early Court of Protection decision, the court held that, '… the general concept of managing affairs is an ongoing act and, therefore, quite unlike the specific act of making a will or making an enduring power of attorney. The management of affairs relates to a continuous state of affairs whose demands may be unpredictable and may occasionally be urgent'.[48]

4.54 In 2023, the Court of Protection distinguished between P's capacity to 'manage his relatively straightforward financial affairs' (eg, to manage a weekly budget) and their capacity 'to deal with the more complex part of his property and affairs' (eg, invested assets, or the sustainability of their assets in light of income and expenditure).[49]

4.55 Assessors should adapt the framework above to P's specific financial circumstances. For example, P may have a weekly allowance, receive a welfare benefit and regularly pay a dog walker, but also have a multi-million-pound portfolio and must make mortgage payments on their bungalow. As P's capacity to manage their property and affairs is fact-sensitive and related to the value and complexity of the assets, the assessor may find that P has capacity to manage the weekly allowance, but lacks capacity to manage their portfolio.

4.56 A person who has capacity to manage their property and financial affairs may still be subject to coercive control by another. In such cases, the local authority may consider an application under the inherent jurisdiction.

Deciding on internet and social media use

4.57 In 2019, Cobb J provided guidance on the information relevant to making a decision about using the internet and social media:[50]

(a) Information and images (including videos) which you share on the internet or through social media could be shared more widely, including with people you don't know, without you knowing or being able to stop it. Sharing includes sending on an email, offering on a file sharing platform, uploading to a site that other people have access to, and possessing with a view to distribute.

48 Mr Justice Hedley in *Re X* [2012] EWCOP 2400, para 41.
49 *A Local Authority A v ZZ* [2023] EWCOP 61, para 39.
50 *Re A (Capacity: Social Media and Internet Use: Best Interests)* [2019] EWCOP 2, para 28.

(b) It is possible to limit the sharing of personal information or images (and videos) by using 'privacy and location settings' on some internet and social media sites. The precise details or mechanisms of the privacy settings need to be understood but P should be capable of understanding that they exist, and be able to decide (with support) whether to apply them.

(c) If you place material or images (including videos) on social media sites which are rude or offensive, or share those images, other people might be upset or offended. The words 'rude or offensive' may be easily understood by those with learning disabilities as including not only the insulting and abusive, but also the sexually explicit, indecent or pornographic.

(d) Some people you meet or communicate with ('talk to') online, who you don't otherwise know, may not be who they say they are ('they may disguise, or lie about, themselves'); someone who calls themselves a 'friend' on social media may not be friendly.

(e) Some people you meet or communicate with ('talk to') on the internet or through social media, who you don't otherwise know, may pose a risk to you; they may lie to you, or exploit or take advantage of you sexually, financially, emotionally and/or physically; they may want to cause you harm.

(f) If you look at or share extremely rude or offensive images, messages or videos online you may get into trouble with the police, because you may have committed a crime. The judge clarified that this was not intended to represent a statement of the criminal law, but was designed to reflect the importance, which a capacitous person would understand, of not searching for such material, as it may have criminal content, and/or steering away from such material if accidentally encountered, rather than investigating further and/or disseminating such material.

4.58 Cobb J stated that internet and social media use is distinct from other forms of contact, which is discussed above (see 'Deciding about contact with others', at para 4.44).

4.59 A case involving both contact and internet and social media use is *Re EOA*,[51] in which Williams J held that Mr EOA lacked capacity to make decisions about contact with family members inside a cult in which Mr EOA was involved, with family members outside the cult, and with strangers. Different reasoning was used in respect of each group. On internet and social media, Williams J held that Mr EOA also lacked capacity because:

> the use of internet and social media is merely one vehicle by which EOA might seek or have contact with family members who pose a risk to him and in respect of whom he lacks capacity to make decisions as to contact. Social media and the internet today are the modern equivalent of a telephone directory or a letter of a previous era: they are simply a means of

51 *Re EOA* (n 43), para 53.

gathering information or communicating and in this case where there are clearly identified individuals whom EOA lacks capacity to make decisions in relation to contact seems to me that this should be recognised.

4.60 Lacking capacity to decide on contact is not an indicator that P will also lack capacity to decide on internet and social media. Williams J observed that the statutory scheme and jurisprudence required a 'tailored and decision specific approach where that is appropriate on the facts'. In that particular case, Williams J included in his contact declarations express remarks on using the internet and social media to contact family, and made an interim order that, in respect of contacting others, practical steps should be taken to enable P to make decisions about internet and social media use.

Executing and revoking a lasting power of attorney

4.61 The family of P or the local authority may be concerned that P has made an LPA under duress or undue influence. An LPA is a powerful weapon for a controlling person, as it gives them formal power to take decisions about P.

4.62 The LPA is the document that specifies that P (the 'donor') has assigned another person (the 'attorney' or 'donee') to take decisions for P. There are two types of LPA: (1) an LPA in relation to health and welfare allows the attorney to make decisions on P's behalf, but only if P lacks capacity to make such decisions; and (2) an LPA in relation to property and financial affairs[52] allows attorneys to take financial decisions on P's behalf: P can indicate in the LPA that the instrument is to come into effect immediately, while P retains capacity to make those decisions.

4.63 If there is a suspicion that the attorney has pressured P into signing an LPA, another person (eg, a social worker) could suggest that P's capacity to execute or revoke an LPA should be assessed. The information relevant to capacity to execute and to revoke an LPA is subtly different.

4.64 In 2017, a tier 1 judge of the Court of Protection held that the relevant information in relation to revoking an LPA is:

(a) who the attorneys are;

(b) what authority they have;

(c) why it is necessary or expedient to revoke the power;

(d) the foreseeable consequences of revoking the power; and

(e) the reasons for the original decision to appoint the attorneys.[53]

52 Property and affairs is often shortened to 'P&A'. It includes all P's intangible and tangible assets (including pets).

53 *SAD & Anor v SED* [2017] EWCOP 3, at para 10.

4.65 In 2022, Poole J held that the relevant information in relation to executing an LPA is:

(a) the effect of the LPA;

(b) who the attorneys are;

(c) the scope of the attorneys' powers and taking into consideration that the MCA 2005 restricts the exercise of their powers;

(d) when the attorneys can exercise those powers, including the need for the LPA to be executed before it is effective;

(e) the scope of the assets the attorneys can deal with under the LPA;

(f) the power of the donor to revoke the LPA when they have capacity to do so; and

(g) the pros and cons of executing the particular LPA and of not doing so.[54]

Engaging in sexual relations

4.66 In coercive control cases, the controlling person may be in a sexual relationship with P, or want to be. If P has a cognitive impairment, their capacity to engage in sexual relations may require assessment. Unlike decisions about contact with others (see 'Deciding about contact with others', at para 4.44 above), capacity to engage in sexual relations is not person-specific. The assessment is about whether P has capacity to engage in sexual relations: with whom is irrelevant.

4.67 The relevant information is:

(a) the mechanics of the sexual act and its character (what sex actually is, depending on the type of sex P may be having);

(b) for heterosexual couples, a reasonably foreseeable consequence of sexual intercourse is pregnancy;

(c) health risks of sexual transmitted infections, and reducing risks by using a condom;

(d) P must consent (P has the right to say no); and

(e) the fact that the sexual partner(s) must have the ability to consent to the sexual activity and must consent before and throughout the sexual activity (sex without consent is rape or sexual assault).[55]

54 *Public Guardian v RI* [2022] EWCOP 22.
55 *Re JB* (n 2).

Deciding to marry

4.68 In 2004 in a pre-MCA 2005 case, the High Court determined that capacity to marry is act-specific, rather than a focus on a particular intended spouse.[56] Nine years later, the Court of Appeal endorsed this approach: 'capacity to marry is to be assessed in general and as a matter of principle, and not by reference to any particular prospective marriage'.[57]

4.69 The relevant information includes the broad nature of the marriage contract, the duties and responsibilities that normally attach to marriage, including that there may be financial consequences, and that spouses have a particular status and connection with regard to each other. In 2021, the court held that 'The contract of marriage is a very simple one, which does not take a high degree of intelligence to comprehend'.[58] Irrelevant for the purposes of capacity are the wisdom of marriage and a detailed understanding of financial remedy law.

4.70 If P wants to marry in order to have children, capacity to engage in sexual relations will be a prerequisite to capacity to marry.[59] However, the court has held that, 'because capacity is always issue-specific, capacity to marry, and capacity to choose to engage in sexual relations, are legally distinct. They may not necessarily produce the same answer, although typically they will'.[60]

4.71 Interestingly, in the United States, there is a line of cases framing marriage as a protective factor; a form of support that can protect a person from vulnerability and expand their individual capacity.[61] These concepts have not yet been discussed in the case law of England and Wales.

Testamentary capacity

4.72 The leading authority from 1870 has been repeatedly affirmed in modern case law.[62] The test requires that, when making a will, the testator must:

(a) understand the nature of the act and its effects (ie, that they are making a will and the effect of their wishes being carried out after death);

(b) understand the extent of the property of which they are disposing (though not every detail or value, but a general awareness);

56 n 18.
57 *PC, NC v City of York Council* [2013] EWCA Civ 478, para 23. See also *Stockport Metropolitan Borough Council v EKK (Rev1)* [2025] EWCOP 42.
58 *NB v MI* [2021] EWHC 224 (Fam), para 26. See also *Stockport Metropolitan Borough Council v EKK (Rev1)* [2025] EWCOP 42.
59 *Re ZZ* (n 49), para 86.
60 *NB v MI* [2021] EWHC 224 (Fam), para 14.
61 See Sarah Lorr, 'The capacity to marry', Columbia L. Rev, forthcoming 2026.
62 *Banks v Goodfellow* (1870) LR 5 QB 549.

(c) comprehend and appreciate the claims to which they ought to give effect, including recognising those whom they are including or excluding from the will; and

(d) not be subject to any disorder of the mind that poisons their affections, perverts their sense of right, prevents the exercise of their natural faculties, or involves an insane delusion influencing the will's dispositions in a way that would not have occurred if the mind had been sound.

4.73 While testamentary capacity can be challenged in the Court of Protection while P is still alive, there are several posthumous cases in the Chancery Division about the validity of the will where relatives argue that the will is invalid due to undue influence. In one such case, it was held that, 'Coercion is pressure that overpowers the volition without convincing the testator's judgment. It is to be distinguished from mere persuasion, appeals to ties of affection or pity for future destitution, all of which are legitimate. Pressure which causes a testator to succumb for the sake of a quiet life, if carried to an extent that overbears the testator's free judgment discretion or wishes, is enough to amount to coercion in this sense'.[63]

CONCLUSIONS

4.74 This chapter has explored 11 decision-making domains within the context of coercive control. It has emphasised the importance of clearly articulating the decision and tailoring relevant information to P's circumstances, as mandated by the MCA 2005. It has set out the need for those assessing capacity to inform P of the relevant information as well as the reasonably foreseeable consequences of deciding one way or another.

4.75 It has highlighted the need to avoid decision-making silos and to ensure that capacity assessments are specific to each decision-making area. The chapter has also underscored the role of capacity assessors in providing relevant information, and explored the challenges posed by coercive control in accurately assessing an individual's capacity. Ultimately, the chapter reflects on the need for a fact-specific, nuanced and tailored approach to the assessment of capacity.

63 *Re Edwards (deceased)* [2007] EWHC 1119 (Ch), para 47.

CHAPTER 5

Coercive control cases in the Court of Protection

'Salad and one potato a day'[1]

INTRODUCTION

5.01 This chapter provides an overview of coercive control cases in the Court of Protection, drawing from the small number of Court of Protection cases published in the National Archive. A selection of paradigm examples is provided in four themes: The section headed 'Learning disabilities' (at para 5.02) considers three cases where the victim/survivor was vulnerable to coercive control because of learning disabilities. The section headed 'Elder abuse' (at para 5.19) looks at two cases: Ms BU who was targeted by a criminal offender, and Ms LC who developed dementia and whose daughter abused her and sought to took advantage of her. The section headed 'Mental illness' (at para 5.52) looks at a case about mental illness where the victim was coercively controlled even while deprived of her liberty in a mental health unit. Finally, under the section heading 'Brain injury' (at para 5.57), is the case of Ms PB who had a brain injury and whose husband's controlling behaviour was so extreme that it jeopardised her care home placement.

LEARNING DISABILITIES

5.02 This section addresses a trio of cases concerning victims/survivors of coercive control with learning disabilities.

1 *A County Council v LW & Anor* [2020] EWCOP 50.

Miss KP lived with her sex-offender stepfather

5.03 An example of the Court of Protection making a protective order to prevent P from being controlled by an offender is the case of *Re KP*.[2] There, 18-year-old Miss KP had learning disabilities and autism and lived with her mother and her mother's partner Mr D who was a registered sex offender and may previously have assaulted Miss KP. The court found that Miss KP was unable to accept the risk Mr D posed to her 'because she does not have the ability to engage with the idea that D and her mother may not be right about this issue.'

5.04 The judge found that Mr D was 'the dominant figure in this household' and due to the poor cognitive functioning of both Miss KP and her mother, Mr D could mould and shape how they saw the world. However, Miss KP wanted to stay in her mother's home, and all attempts to keep her away from there in the past had not created a sustainable environment for her.

5.05 The court made directions designed to increase Miss KP's safety. The judge directed that the social worker should meet Miss KP on her own once a week to check her safety and feelings. Happily, two days after the hearing, Miss KP decided for herself to leave her mother's house and she temporarily moved in with her boyfriend at his parent's house. There, she made disclosures which suggested that Mr D may have been grooming her towards a sexual relationship with him or someone else.

Ms KF wanted to see her violent partner one more time

5.06 Ms KF was a 34-year-old woman with learning disabilities.[3] The relationship with her boyfriend Mr KW involved intimate partner violence: he coerced Ms KF into sexual activities with other men, leading to severe physical harm requiring hospitalisation. He also exploited her financially and dominated her decision-making. Social services had relocated Ms KF to a care home for her safety.

5.07 The court was asked to urgently determine if it was in Ms KF's best interests to have unsupervised contact with Mr KW, including overnight stays where consensual sex was expected. The urgency stemmed from two factors: Mr KW was soon to be sentenced for assault occasioning actual bodily harm against Ms KF, and she had terminal cancer with a prognosis of less than 18 months to live so would likely die before Mr KW's release from prison.

2 *A Local Authority v KP (Acting by the Official Solicitor as her litigation friend) and another* [2023] EWHC 3102 (Fam).

3 *Hull City Council v KF* [2022] EWCOP 33. On determining capacity by avoiding silos, see para 4.18, above.

5.08 Ms KF expressed a desire to spend private time with Mr KW, asserting her right to make personal decisions. The dilemma was whether to allow contact with someone who had harmed her, especially as she neared the end of her life and was clear about her wishes. Poole J, said that it was difficult, 'to see how a person who lacks capacity to decide to have contact with a specific person could have capacity to decide to engage in sexual relations with that person. Sexual intimacy is a form of contact with another or others'. The judge agreed with experts that Ms KF lacked capacity to decide on contact with Mr KW, given his history of violence and the foreseeable risk of harm. He determined also that Ms KF lacked capacity to consent to sexual relations. The decision aimed to ensure coherence across capacity domains, allowing carers to make practical arrangements. If the couple engaged in sex during unsupervised contact, it would constitute rape, as Ms KF could not legally consent.

5.09 The judge also considered Mr KW's potential volatility before imprisonment posed further risk to Ms KF. Ensuring her safety was deemed impossible, and expecting support workers to intervene in a hotel setting was unreasonable. The court allowed a final private meeting where the couple could 'kiss and cuddle', hoping it would be meaningful, as it might be their last encounter.

Mrs A was being pressured to become pregnant

5.10 Mrs A had learning disabilities, and had previously had two children, both of whom had been removed.[4] She then married a man who also had learning disabilities, but not as significant as hers. Mrs A attended a college: Mr A accompanied her there and handled the college fees. He spoke to her like a child. Mrs A had disclosed to a college tutor that her husband forbade her from speaking to social workers. She said that he hit and kicked her and that she was unhappy at home. She showed college staff small marks and bruises caused by her husband. Almost every day, Mrs A would cry or tell staff about a domestic incident. Once, Mrs A was 'just crying and crying' and said that she never wanted to go back to her husband. Mrs A said she did not want another child, but that Mr A had told her he would only continue their relationship if she had a baby.

5.11 Some months later, the couple sent a letter to social services: '… my wife and myself are getting tired of you visiting … We no longer wish to receive any of your services and somebody interferences in our sex life and injections which has nothing to do with you, only with my wife and myself. My wife and myself are capable of living independently life and shall be visiting solicitors again if necessary we apply to court for a court adduction to keep you away …'.

4 *Re A (Capacity: Refusal of Contraception)* [2010] EWHC 1549 (Fam).

5.12 The local authority filed a Court of Protection application for declarations on capacity to decide on Ms A's residence, care, and contact with her husband. Capacity to decide on contraception was later added as an issue. A psychiatrist and social worker attended the marital home to assess capacity, but Mr A ordered them out. On their way out, the psychiatrist asked Mrs A whether her husband had hit her and frightened her. She nodded in reply.

5.13 At the final hearing, the social worker said that when asked a question, Mrs A often looked at Mr A to see what his response was, sometimes would not answer until he did, and tended to go along with whatever he said.

5.14 A psychologist who gave evidence considered that Mr A felt ignored and marginalised, but his resistance to support made cooperation difficult and strained relations. When domestic violence allegations arose, safeguarding rules prevented officials from engaging with him directly. Tensions worsened after court proceedings were initiated and there were unresolved issues about contraception. Mr A was not included in decision-making about Mrs A, deepening his resentment and feelings of intrusion. His rigid views on marriage and responsibility for Mrs A fuelled misunderstanding, creating a destructive cycle with the local authority until communication broke down entirely.

5.15 During proceedings, Mrs A denied that she had made complaints of domestic violence. The judge noted that she had previously complained to college staff, staff at her place of voluntary work, and social workers, and that she was tearful and distressed, and at college she once cried repeatedly. The court found that domestic violence had occurred. This illustrates a common thread in coercive control cases, namely that the abuser and (often but not always) the victim/survivor too denies the abuse.

5.16 The court found Mrs A lacked capacity to decide on contraception, noting the 'completely unequal dynamic in the relationship between Mr and Mrs A [such] that her decision not to continue taking contraception is not the product of her own free will'. However, the court did not make best interests decision about contraception because of the futility of doing so: if Mrs A consented to contraception, there was no need for the court to order it, and if she did not consent, the court would not contemplate forced contraception. Instead, if Mrs A became pregnant, the local authority would conduct a pre-birth assessment of Mr and Mrs A's joint parenting abilities and take appropriate steps.

5.17 In the witness box, Mr A expressed a willingness to allow Mrs A free contact with professionals who could advise her in a disability-appropriate way about contraceptive issues, so long as he was not excluded but involved either concurrently or separately. Given his stance, the judge considered it unnecessary to make injunctions stopping him from preventing his wife from attending meetings, and felt that he should have an opportunity to honour his assurances given to the court to enable Mrs A to gain capacity to make decisions about contraception.

5.18 As for the causative nexus (discussed at para 3.41 in Chapter 3), the judge found that Mrs A was 'unable to weigh up the pros and cons of contraception because of the coercive pressure under which she has been placed both intentionally and unconsciously by Mr A'. It is not obvious from the judgment how this relates to an impairment that caused an inability to use or weigh.

ELDER ABUSE

Ms BU

5.19 Ms BU was a 70-year-old woman of considerable wealth who was preyed on and exploited by a criminal offender.[5] The case draws out themes of power and dominance over older women with cognitive impairments, and contains insights into the psychological grip of a trauma bond, explored in Chapter 10.

5.20 The conundrum that faced Roberts J was whether it was in Ms BU's best interests to return to live with the abusive and controlling Mr NC, as she wished, having had no contact with him for a year.

5.21 Mr NC described himself as a private investigator, a personal carer, an art gallery owner and a self-employed builder. The judge noted that he had 'a somewhat checkered background' with periods of imprisonment. He was 53 at the time of the hearing, but was in his mid-to late-forties when he struck up a friendship with Ms BU.

5.22 During the covid pandemic when there was a lower demand for building work, Ms BU had underwritten Mr NC's company's entire wages bill and paid for materials, equipment and hire costs. Ms BU gifted him a vehicle, as a 'thank you for looking after her', as he put it. Ms BU's family became suspicious when she asked them how she could lend someone several thousand pounds.

5.23 Two years later, the family remained concerned. They asked Ms BU why she associated with Mr NC, given his requests for money to which she said that Mr NC was useful 'because he knows all of the burglars' and 'you have to keep on with these people, so nothing happens to you'. By the following year, Mr NC had become even more entwined in Ms BU's life, taking her to medical appointments and controlling the food she ate. Ms BU was diagnosed with moderate small vessel disease in keeping with vascular dementia. Mr NC moved into Ms BU's home, and his control over her increased. She paid him

5 *WU v BU* [2021] EWCOP 54.

£300 per week. He took her to a solicitor to change her will: he had prepared a codicil under which he would be a beneficiary and would control her property portfolio.

5.24 The family discovered that Mr NC had previous convictions for blackmail and the sentencing judge had described his criminal behaviour as 'a thoroughly cynical unpleasant wicked offence. It was planned, and planned carefully'. The family went to the police, and several women came forward saying they had also been victims of Mr NC's behaviour.

5.25 In May 2020, Mr NC was arrested. Acting with commendable speed, the local authority made an application to the Court of Protection. The court promptly made a declaration that Ms BU lacked capacity to make decisions to manage her property and financial affairs, and appointed a deputy.

5.26 Meanwhile, the police had bailed Mr NC and one of the bail conditions was that he should have no form of contact with Ms BU. He breached this by contacting Ms BU over 40 times. He was re-arrested for perverting the course of justice and when police searched Mr NC's home, they found evidence of five property transactions involving Ms BU. It appeared she only knew about one of them.

5.27 It is common in coercive and controlling behaviour cases for the abuser to say the victim/survivor has capacity, because the abuser wants to retain control. Indeed, Mr NC's position was that Ms BU had capacity to make decisions about contact: his case was that her family worked against her to prevent what she wanted, which was him. While Roberts J did not use the word 'gaslighting', this case serves as an example of the phenomenon that occurs in abusive relationships. Gaslighting is a covert type of emotional abuse where the abuser misleads the person, creating a false narrative and making them question their judgments and reality – in this case, seeking to shift the blame to Ms BU's family. This may cause the victim/survivor to doubt their perceptions of the world and wonder whether they are losing their sanity.

5.28 A psychiatrist said Ms BU had a long-lasting cognitive disability, present from childhood, which interfered with her ability to manage her life independently and she was incapable of fully analysing or understanding the information which the police had disclosed to her about Mr NC's criminal past, or its relevance for her situation.

5.29 A clinical psychologist with expertise in coercive and controlling behaviour was instructed as a court-appointed expert to consider Ms BU's capacity and advise upon the extent to which she had been subjected, by Mr NC or her family members, to any form of victimisation as a result of coercive control or undue influence.

5.30 The expert said that Ms BU lacked capacity in the assessed domains, which left her, 'particularly vulnerable to coercive tactics and undue forms of influence' because of the 'psychological enmeshment' between the two of them: Ms BU had become completely dependent upon and dominated psychologically by Mr NC, such that Ms BU's ability to make independent decisions was either severely limited or completely blocked.

5.31 The psychologist said that Ms BU has shifted her dependency from her family to Mr NC whom she viewed as liberating. 'It is this total faith in NC which is, however, a manifestation of an unhealthy and totalistic identity and dominating influence which, even if not intentionally coercive (on NC's part), in practice renders BU unable to distinguish between good and bad decisions, in thrall as she is to the man that has saved her from herself and from those she blames for the lack of fulfilment in her life over the decades.' This dynamic created a risk of undue influence and coercive control. Mr NC was like a 'boisterous kid in the playground who does not know his own strength (relative to others)' and did not realise his influence over Ms BU, but he retained responsibility for the power imbalance and its resultant psychological injury.

5.32 The expert identified that Ms BU's submission to Mr NC was a hallmark of undue influence and coercive behaviour. In relation to the proposed codicil to Ms BU's will and Mr NC's other plans for Ms BU's assets, he saw a clear pattern:

> whereby BU is almost entirely uncritical, unthinking and at times unknowing regarding the detailed plans involving her assets which NC has outlined and which are purportedly her plans, as well as his. In this context I regard it as significant that when she was asked about the plans reflected in the proposed codicil to her new Will, BU denied that there were any discussions between them about these arrangements.

5.33 The expert considered this 'clear and prima facie evidence of undue influence and a form of financial abuse as set out and defined in s 76 of the Serious Crime Act 2015 and an aspect of controlling and coercive behaviour' (at para 2.43 in Chapter 2). He described the enmeshed relationship between Ms BU and Mr NC as a 'trauma bond', and – perhaps paradoxically – the more Ms BU's family challenged her relationship with Mr NC, the more it reinforced the bond between the two of them.

5.34 The Official Solicitor characterised Mr NC as 'a confidence trickster whose long-term lifestyle appears to have involved repeatedly inveigling money from vulnerable people through coercive control and, at least on three occasions, blackmail'.

5.35 The judge determined that Ms BU was 'deprived of autonomous decision-making' because of 'corrosive and coercive nature of the control' that she found NC to have exercised over Ms BU, rendering her unable to exercise her individual free will in the context of any ongoing relationship with Mr NC.

5.36 The court found that Ms BU 'craves his companionship which she perceives as relieving the intense loneliness and isolation which she has obviously felt outside the loving relationships she previously had with her extended family.' The 'trauma bond between Ms BU and Mr NC binds them together even in absentia', underlying an insight from the trauma literature (see Chapter 10). Roberts J held that, Mr NC had engaged in a 'deliberate and calculated attempt to subvert any independent decision-making on BU's part', and that he manipulated her 'with deliberate intent to secure for himself a financial benefit.'

5.37 As Ms BU lacked capacity to make decisions about contact with Mr NC, the court made best interests decisions. There were two options: permit continuation of contact (which would be difficult to police) or make a no contact order coupled with an injunction against Mr NC. The Official Solicitor said that Ms BU could not move forward with her life with Mr NC in it, and supported the imposition of a no contact order, to be reviewed at a later stage following therapy. As the local authority could not offer such therapy, the court could do no more than record that it is in BU's best interests to be offered such therapy.

5.38 The judge decided that contact with Mr NC was not in Ms BU's best interests, and regarded it as 'essential that steps are taken at the earliest opportunity to address and reverse the current estrangement between BU and her family, and this is unlikely to happen whilst NC's corrosive influence over her persists'. The judge made an injunction against Mr NC prohibiting him from seeking any form of contact with Ms BU (injunctions are considered in Chapter 8).

5.39 The judge also made a forced marriage protection order (FMPO), which are considered in Chapter 8. The judge noted there were, 'no sufficiently protective factors which could be put in place to reduce or eliminate the potential risks of a forced marriage'. To avoid disproportionately interfering with Ms BU's rights to private and family life, the FMPO was limited to 12 months when it would be reviewed.

5.40 The Court of Protection deals with an increasing number of cases of older people who have lived together in abusive relationships for long periods of time. In such relationships, the victim/survivor may develop a degenerative condition that causes them to lose capacity to make decisions about residence, care and/or contact with others. Chapter 1 considered the case of Mary who lived for decades with her violent and controlling husband. However, the abuser is not always the victim's partner, as the next case illustrates.

Ms LC

5.41 Ms LC was 96 years old.[6] She previously lived at home, often with her daughter living there too, but social services had removed her from her home and at the time of the hearing was in a care home. Her daughter had spondylosis and mental health problems, and Ms LC used to provide care to her. In 2002, after the daughter had allegedly pushed over her mother, relationships within the family became fraught. Ms LC spent time living with her niece, her son and her daughter, and the family made regular allegations that the daughter was violent towards her.

5.42 In January 2008, when the daughter was living with her mother, Ms LC was taken to the emergency department of the local hospital. The daughter told medics that a wound sustained when her mother had banged her leg the previous week had 'burst', and the district nurse had suggested going to the emergency department. It was subsequently discovered that the daughter, who had been a nurse some two decades previously, had carried out amateur surgery on her mother's leg before taking her to hospital. The daughter gave evidence to the court that she had cleaned the wound when she saw it bleeding, and had therefore cut away dead tissue. In hospital, the wound was so serious that Ms LC required a skin graft.

5.43 At that time, Ms LC was deemed to have capacity to decide on residence and care, and she returned to live with her daughter. In mid-February 2008, a district nurse saw the daughter rip a dressing off the wound. The nurse reported this to the local authority as physical abuse. In May 2008, a care package was increased from two to four carer visits per day. Ms LC complained to a carer that her daughter had hit her, and the carer saw bruises.

5.44 In June 2008, police were called to the daughter's property, where they found Ms LC locked in the house, banging on a window and shouting for help. The police telephoned the daughter, who hung up before they could speak to her. The police broke into the house and made a safeguarding referral. The local authority thought it was fine for Ms LC to stay in the care of her daughter and asked the care agency to monitor the situation.

5.45 Around a year later, a district nurse raised the alarm because Ms LC had a gash on her head and bruising to her face. She told a carer that her daughter had beaten her up and pleaded with the carer not to leave her alone. In hospital, she was assessed as having dementia and lacking capacity to make decisions about

6 *HBCC v LC* [2010] EWHC 1527 (Fam).

where to live, but she was allowed to go back to the daughter's home. She was subsequently found to have bruises on her legs and arms. Ms LC then moved to a care home where she remained, deprived of her liberty but apparently content.

5.46 The Court of Protection had to establish the facts of what had happened, then use those facts to determine where it would be in P's best interests to live and receive care. The court began by holding a fact-finding hearing (see Chapter 8). The daughter accused the emergency department doctor of assaulting her, which the judge noted was one of a number of examples of the daughter's paranoia.

5.47 The court heard evidence from a psychologist expert who said that Ms LC had dementia and due to that, lacked capacity to conduct proceedings or make decisions about residence, care, and contact with others. The daughter's view was that her mother had capacity in those areas (again, this is a common feature in these cases). The court accepted the expert's evidence and made declarations to that effect.

5.48 The local authority had alleged that the daughter frequently left her mother alone and locked in the house, had hit her mother, that she was routinely verbally abusive, was domineering, had subjected her mother to rough handling, and that she was incapable of accepting advice or working with health professionals. The court found those allegations proved.

5.49 Given that Ms LC's needs required 24-hour care which were best met in a care home environment, and that if she returned to live with her daughter she would be vulnerable to abuse, the court decided it was in Ms LC's best interests to remain in the care home.

5.50 When giving evidence, the daughter removed her glasses and started talking in a heavy French accent. The judge found much of the daughter's evidence 'frankly bizarre' and that the daughter had 'significant, deep-seated psychological and psychiatric problems'. As for contact, the daughter had conversations that upset Ms LC and the care home had instituted supervised contact once a week which had improved matters, and the daughter was showing more tolerance of her mother's disorientation. However, the daughter persisted in telling her mother that she was kept in the care home against her will and that she had been put there by social services and her son. The court decided that supervised contact was in Ms LC's best interests. Finally, the court directed that the daughter should not be involved in administering her mother's finances.

5.51 The judgment noted another common feature of these cases, which is that the controlling person blames everyone but themselves. In Ms LC's case, the daughter made 'incessant complaints about those with whom she comes into contact', including making wild and unsubstantiated accusations against the barrister instructed by the Official Solicitor. Complaints against lawyers is an occupational hazard in this area of law: see Chapters 11 to 13 on legal representation of the parties.

MENTAL ILLNESS

Ms LW

5.52 Ms LW was a 60-year-old woman with bipolar affective disorder.[7] She was coercively controlled by her partner, Mr MG. He had moved into her house and they lived together for 18 months before Ms LW was admitted to a mental health unit. She spent three years there before the matter came to court.

5.53 When they lived together, Mr MG controlled all aspects of Ms LW's life. He 'alienated LW from her family and from any other support, leading to her becoming ever more dependent on him'. He restricted her food intake to such an extent that she became emaciated: 'Salad and one potato a day were all that she was allowed'.

5.54 During her admission to hospital, Mr MG made Ms LW recite 'prayers [which] have a veneer of Roman Catholic liturgy but veer off into content which is fantasy and distortion'. The prayers had to be recited extensively, often daily, in a particular order. This made Ms LW agitated and anxious. During the admission, there was extensive telephone contact, supervised by staff who were put in an 'invidious position of sitting and listening to exchanges which were manipulative, controlling and injurious to LW's welfare without always fully appreciating its impact on her'. Ms LW was regularly anxious before and after these telephone conversations.

5.55 The parties agreed that Ms LW should be discharged from the mental health unit. The judge agreed with the clinical team to cease contact altogether. To prevent a mental health deterioration caused by such an overwhelming change, before being discharged Ms LW had eight weeks of support to come to terms with the absence of Mr MG in her life. The judge could have confidence in his decision because when contact was previously severed Ms LW's mental health and wellbeing improved. Fortunately, Ms LW was disappointed in Mr MG's inaction in facilitating her return to him, and she had begun gently to question his reliability and commitment to her.

5.56 The clinicians said that Ms LW had become so dependent on Mr MG because of 'her false perception that MG has been able to meet her needs'. It was Mr MG's influence 'over LW's fragile personality that compromises her capacity to weigh and evaluate the questions relating to her care and where she should live. This is compounded by her inability to understand her own mental health needs'. This case is an example of how coercive control and mental health intersect to cause the victim to become vulnerable to abuse.

7 *A County Council v LW & Anor* (n 1).

BRAIN INJURY

Mrs PB

5.57 A person's cognitive functioning, and their decision-making capacity, may change suddenly. In March 2018, Mrs PB had a severe brain haemorrhage that caused lasting injury, including impaired cognitive functioning, right sided weakness and spatial neglect.[8] After treatment in hospital, she was discharged to a care home. Unusually, it was not a local authority that made an application to the Court of Protection, but the husband of P. Mr MB wanted more contact with his wife in the care home and also wanted her to live in the marital home. It was agreed that she lacked capacity to conduct proceedings and make decisions about contact with others. The court had to decide where it was in Mrs PB's best interests to live.

5.58 While Mrs PB was in hospital, there were safeguarding referrals about Mr MB's conduct, including his 'combative approach' to the medical professionals. It was alleged that he inappropriately touched Ms PB in a sexual manner. Due to the Covid infection risk, his visits were restricted, and from April 2020 limited to twice weekly video calls.

5.59 Given his overbearing treatment of the medical professionals and his interference with their ability to provide care to Mrs PB and other residents, the court had previously restricted contact, including by way of an injunction that prohibited Mr MB from having direct contact with his wife, from entering or approaching the care home, and severely restricting communication with care home staff.

5.60 Mr MB had completely fallen out with his adult children because he had isolated their mother and prevented her from leading the life she wanted to. He had forbidden Mrs PB from meeting up with her sister. Commenting on Mr MB's fractured relationships with other people, the judge noted an attitude in the abuser that practitioners commonly see in coercive control cases:

> he cannot see how the current situation has arisen and blames everybody else for it. He cannot see that it is to a very large extent of his own making. When asked about trying to build bridges with his children, he said that was a matter for him to deal with as and when he thought appropriate.

5.61 The court held a fact-finding hearing (see Chapter 8) and found, among other things, a pattern of controlling and coercive behaviour before and after

8 *MB v PB* [2022] EWCOP 14.

Mrs PB's admission to the care home. The court found that Mr MB sought to interfere in the provision of care by refusing to accept what professionals told him and insisting that he knew best about the care Mrs PB should receive. The court further found that Mr MB sought to limit and control the contact that Mrs PB had with other members of the family.

5.62 Mrs PB required specialist nursing care 24-hours a day which could not be provided at home: that was clear to all parties and the judge, but not to Mr MB. As there was no other specialist care home locally that could meet Mrs PB's needs, it was overwhelmingly important to protect the sustainability of the current care home. The threat to the placement came from Mr MB, who interfered with the care and was overbearing to the care home staff. The judge put it simply: 'If the choice is between MB's contact with PB and the maintenance of the home, the latter must prevail'.

5.63 The judge thought that a trial resumption of face-to-face contact should start in a pod in the grounds of the care home that had been purchased to facilitate contact during the Covid-19 pandemic. The judge did not make a best interests decision that contact should resume, but expressed 'a strong desire that its practicality should be explored with a hope that a trial might take place in which P's reaction may be observed'.

5.64 A review hearing took place in November 2022, and we know what happened to Mrs PB thanks to a blog by the Open Justice Court of Protection Project.[9] It had not been possible to arrange face-to-face contact, so if Mr MB could identify and fund a suitable care agency, supervised contact could take place in the care home garden. In the meantime, telephone contact between the married couple would continue.

CONCLUSIONS

5.65 Several Court of Protection cases examined in this chapter involve victims/survivors of coercive control whose cognitive impairments have remained static for many years. These include Mrs A who had a learning disability and whose husband permitted her to have no agency over her life, Ms KF who had a learning disability and had suffered sexual violence by the man with whom she wanted to meet before he went to prison, and Ms BU who had had cognitive impairment since childhood and was targeted by a criminal blackmailer. In all those cases, there is a question as to whether the abusers chose their victims because the cognitive impairment made it easier for them to entrap and control.

9 'Coercive and controlling behaviour continuing after brain injury: Matters of finance and contact', 30 November 2022.

5.66 In other cases, the coercive and controlling relationship predated the loss of the victim's capacity to make decisions about care and contact with others. These include Jessica and her overpowering mother, and Mary and her violent husband – both in Chapter 1, Ms LC and her controlling daughter, and Ms PB and her controlling husband in this chapter, and Mrs CA in Chapter 7.[10] In those cases, the victim/survivor becomes less able to fend for themselves and less able to fight back against the controlling and coercive behaviour because of their disability and incapacity. In many of these cases, the controlling person lacked insight into their behaviours, and this led to the court authorising a radical decrease of the contact that the controlling person was permitted to have with the victim/survivor.

5.67 The cases in this chapter are all reported cases, which means they are published in the National Archive. However, most Court of Protection cases are unreported, because (i) most cases conclude by consent and do not require a judgment, and (ii) coercive control cases are mostly dealt with by judges at tier 1 (district judges) and tier 2 (circuit judges) who publish fewer judgments than judges at tier 3 (High Court judges). Coercive control cases where there were no published judgments include:

(a) the court determining that it is in the victim/survivor's best interests to live somewhere other than the family home because of the ongoing risk of harm that the controlling person poses, and authorising the local authority to remove the victim/survivor from their home, and take them to a place of safety (such as a care home) on an interim basis while the court determines capacity and best interests;

(b) two Ps – where both the victim/survivor and perpetrator lack capacity to conduct proceedings and to decide on residence and care;

(c) online coercive and controlling behaviour by a person known to the victim/survivor, revealing the interplay between contact, the internet and coercive and controlling behaviour;

(d) coercive and controlling behaviour online by a perpetrator who may not be a person at all, but an artificial intelligence 'bot' which scams the unsuspecting victim; and

(e) coercive and controlling behaviour by a person outside the jurisdiction, resulting in an application to the court for seizure of the victim/survivor's passport to prevent them travelling, until the matter has been properly risk assessed.

5.68 The cases in this chapter illustrate the range of coercive control cases that have been decided in the Court of Protection. When a person lacks capacity to decide on contact with others, the court usually makes best interests decisions to limit contact with the perpetrator, sometimes with the possibility of unsupervised

10 *Re CA* is considered in Chapter 7 on the inherent jurisdiction because Mrs CA had capacity to decide on contact with others.

contact resuming later. If P lacks capacity in other domains, the coercive and controlling behaviour may be relevant to decisions the court makes in P's best interests, including about residence, care, property and financial affairs, and contact with others.

5.69 As noted in Chapter 3, the Court of Protection deals with cases where the person is 16 or over and lacks subject matter capacity. The next chapter introduces the law and practice of the inherent jurisdiction of the High Court. There, the court can make a decision in respect of an adult who has decision-making capacity pursuant to the Mental Capacity Act 2005, but who is unable to make a free choice due to – among other things – the coercive control of another person.

CHAPTER 6

Law and procedure under the inherent jurisdiction

'You might not be happy with my life choices but it's my life'[1]

INTRODUCTION

6.01 The previous two chapters examined the Court of Protection's powers under the Mental Capacity Act 2005 (MCA 2005) to determine capacity and to make best interests decisions for a person who lacks decision-making capacity. In each of the cases reviewed in the previous chapter, the Court of Protection found that the person (P) lacked capacity to make specific decisions and took into account coercive control as one of the 'relevant circumstances' in MCA 2005, s 4(2) when making a best interests decision.

6.02 Under the MCA 2005, the decision-maker – being the Court of Protection when proceedings are issued – must consider P's past and present wishes and feelings, and P's beliefs and values, when determining best interests. In the cases reviewed in Chapter 5, the court's approach to P's autonomy involved protective intervention. By applying the statutory best interests framework, the court sought to shield P from further harm while giving appropriate weight to P's expressed wishes and values.[2]

6.03 This chapter examines the High Court's inherent jurisdiction for adults. This is a common law jurisdiction, outside any statutory scheme, which was reinvigorated by a High Court authority in 2008. The inherent jurisdiction exists to fill gaps in the MCA 2005 and social care legislation through which a vulnerable adult might otherwise fall and suffer harm. This book does not trace the historical development of the jurisdiction, nor does it address the use of the inherent jurisdiction in relation to children. Its focus is practical: how can a public body[3] use this area of law as a 'safety net' for a vulnerable adult?

1 *Re P (Vulnerable Adult: Withdrawal of Application)* [2024] EWHC 1882 (Fam).
2 MCA 2005, s 4(2), (6).
3 Usually, adult social services at a local authority, but sometimes an NHS body.

6.04 Unlike cases brought in the Court of Protection, the inherent jurisdiction is engaged where the adult *has* capacity to make the relevant decision. This might seem unsettling. The idea of a High Court judge making orders about a capacitous adult may provoke an immediate objection: why should the law in a democratic society override a person's human rights, autonomy and potentially their dignity? Is not one's home one's castle? Can a person not do as they wish so long as they do not harm others? And is it not a central tenet of the law that a capacitous person is free to make unwise decisions?

6.05 On the other hand, the feeling might be one of relief that there is a back-up provision in law to permit the court's intervention not to ride roughshod over rights, but to *prevent* violations of a person's rights and to *uphold* their autonomy and dignity.

6.06 It might be asked why existing statutory protections are not sufficient – for example, non-molestation orders, forced marriage protection orders, civil injunctions or domestic abuse protection orders. The answer is twofold. First, the statutory powers underpinning those orders are tightly defined and limited, as Chapter 9 explains. Secondly, the traumatic effects of coercive control can cause a person to be disabled from seeking help or asserting choice, as discussed in Chapter 10. A non-molestation order has limited benefit as it requires the adult to apply or to be a party to existing 'family proceedings' outside of whose ambit Court of Protection proceedings lie, and the adult may not recognise that they are a victim of coercive control: Ms BU's case in Chapter 5 illustrates this challenge.

6.07 Chapters 5 and 7 examine the case law and, in doing so, refer to substantive orders made in respect of adults. For present purposes, it is important to appreciate the breadth of orders the High Court may make, whether or not the adult agrees with those orders. Free from the constraints of a rigid statutory scheme, the High Court can fashion protective relief creatively to prevent serious harm. For instance, the court may:

(a) remove barriers that prevent professionals from accessing the adult to check their welfare and to undertake needs assessments or capacity assessments;

(b) prohibit contact between the abuser and the adult (entirely or through specified channels), whether temporarily or permanently, even if the adult wishes to maintain contact;

(c) impose restrictions on contact as necessary to protect the adult from harm, notwithstanding the adult's opposition to those restrictions;

(d) direct that the adult be removed from their home, even if they wish to remain there, where this is necessary to secure their safety;

(e) authorise the retention of the adult's passport to prevent travel outside the jurisdiction; or

(f) grant injunctions against the abuser, breach of which may amount to contempt of court, punishable by imprisonment, a fine, and/or sequestration of assets.

This list is not exhaustive.

6.08 While the next chapter reviews illustrative cases from the inherent jurisdiction œuvre concerning forced marriage, intimate partner coercive control, and controlling behaviour within families, this chapter first examines the legal principles governing the inherent jurisdiction as well the key procedural features that distinguish these applications from proceedings in the Court of Protection.

PRINCIPLES OF THE INHERENT JURISDICTION

The foundational cases

6.09 The inherent jurisdiction is an area of law not governed by any statute. It is a residual common law power that is a branch of the Royal Prerogative exercised by His Majesty's Judges. In 1990, the House of Lords Judicial Committee (the precursor to the Supreme Court) dealt with the case of *Re F*, where Lord Donaldson explained,

> … the common law is the great safety net which lies behind all statute law and is capable of filling gaps left by that law, if and in so far as those gaps have to be filled in the interests of society as a whole. This process of using the common law to fill gaps is one of the most important duties of the judges. It is not a legislative function or process – that is an alternative solution the initiation of which is the sole prerogative of Parliament. It is an essentially judicial process and, as such, it has to be undertaken in accordance with principle.[4]

6.10 It has subsequently been claimed that the inherent jurisdiction (rather than the common law) is the great safety net of the law,[5] but the inherent jurisdiction is just one of many common law tools that fill statutory gaps.

6.11 The purpose of the inherent jurisdiction is 'to facilitate the process of unencumbered decision-making by those who [the court has] determined have capacity free of external pressure or physical restraint in making those decisions'.[6] That pithy explanation draws out the core of inherent jurisdiction cases, which is that the adult is under pressure by another person (or persons) which renders their decisions non-voluntary. The inherent jurisdiction is there to protect the *true* autonomy of a person by removing the overbearing influence of another. The

4 *Re F (Mental Patient: Sterilisation)* [1990] 2 AC 1.

5 See, for example, the permission decision in *A Local Authority v BF* [2018] EWCA Civ 2962, at para 22(1).

6 Macur J in *LBL v RYJ and VJ* [2010] EWHC 2665 (Fam).

hope in inherent jurisdiction cases is that in time (and perhaps thanks to court-directed measures) the adult will be free to make a voluntary decision, and the protective safety net of the court can safely be reeled in.

6.12 The Court of Appeal endorsed this approach in its 2012 case of *Re DL* to which many subsequent cases refer.[7] In that case, a married couple aged 85 and 90 lived with their son Mr DL, who was in his fifties. The parents had capacity to make relevant decisions. Mr DL physically assaulted and threatened his parents, prevented them from leaving the house, and controlled who could visit them, including health and social care professionals. Mr DL apparently tried to persuade his father to transfer the marital house into his name, and have his mother moved into a care home against her wishes. An independent social worker formed the view that that the parents were deprived of capacity to make decisions themselves because of the undue influence of their son.

6.13 Mr DL argued that the court had no jurisdiction to deal with the matter, and appealed. Dismissing the appeal, the Court of Appeal said the inherent jurisdiction was 'a jurisdictional hinterland' that survived the entry into force of the MCA 2005 and continued to exist outside its borders.[8] The ruling was that while decisions under the MCA 2005 are made in respect of a person who *lacks* capacity to make the relevant decision, the inherent jurisdiction remained available in relation to a vulnerable adult who *has* decision-making capacity under the MCA 2005 but who is nevertheless disabled from making a decision due to the coercive control or undue influence of another.

6.14 The Court of Appeal confirmed that the jurisdiction is a restorative one which 'is in part aimed at enhancing or liberating the autonomy of a vulnerable adult whose autonomy has been compromised' by another.[9]

6.15 With reference to Chapter 2 which explained the phenomenon of coercive control, how can a controlling person render their victim 'vulnerable'? And what can the inherent jurisdiction offer that vulnerable adult?

The vulnerable adult

6.16 The court can make an order under the inherent jurisdiction if it determines that the adult is 'vulnerable'. The concept was developed in the judgment by Munby J (as he then was), in the 2005 case of *Re SA*.[10] This is an authority to which many subsequent cases refer in glowing terms. The Court of Appeal in *Re DL* noted that, 'it is not easy to define and delineate this group of vulnerable adults', and gave its 'unreserved endorsement' to Munby J's definition

7 *A Local Authority v DL* [2012] EWCA Civ 253, at paras 52 and 70.
8 Ibid, para 1.
9 Ibid, para 54.
10 *Re SA (Vulnerable Adult with Capacity: Marriage)* [2005] EWHC 2942 (Fam).

in *Re SA*.[11] In 2018, Baker LJ said that 'any analysis of the jurisprudence is heavily indebted to the insights and labours' and 'learning and insight' of Munby J.[12]

6.17 What did Munby J say in *Re SA* that has attracted such praise, and has – as this chapter will explore – caused controversy? The case concerned Miss SA, who had just turned 18. She was deaf and communicated using British Sign Language which her Pakistani parents did not speak. She was assessed as having capacity to marry in MCA 2005 terms, although the psychologist said that her communication difficulties meant that, 'it would be extremely easy to mislead [Miss SA] and in that sense she would be both suggestible and vulnerable'.[13]

6.18 Miss SA had limited intellectual functioning. She wanted to marry a man in Pakistan, but could not grasp that if he did not have immigration status to return to the UK, she would not be able to live with him in the UK as she wanted. The court found that Miss SA lacked capacity in MCA 2005 terms to conduct the proceedings but had capacity to make other decisions. As a child, she had been made a ward of court which expired on her eighteenth birthday. Miss SA was part of a Muslim family, and the judge was concerned that her family may remove her from the UK or that she would enter into an unsuitable marriage. Munby J exercised the inherent jurisdiction 'so that a young woman who remains just as vulnerable now she is an adult as she did when she was still a child should not suddenly be deprived of the protection which the court has hitherto felt it necessary to afford her and which I believe is still very much required in her best interests'.[14]

6.19 The judge invented a way to carry the protections that Miss SA had enjoyed as a child into her adulthood, making Miss SA an *ersatz* adult ward of court. Moulding the law to achieve his protective outcome led Munby J to define a 'vulnerable person' for whom the inherent jurisdiction would come to the rescue in the following terms:

> In the context of the inherent jurisdiction I would treat as a vulnerable adult someone who, whether or not mentally incapacitated, and whether or not suffering from any mental illness or mental disorder, is or may be unable to take care of him or herself, or unable to protect him or herself against significant harm or exploitation, or who is deaf, blind or dumb, or who is substantially handicapped by illness, injury or congenital deformity. This, I emphasise, is not and is not intended to be a definition. It is descriptive, not definitive; indicative rather than prescriptive.[15]

11 *Re DL* (n 7), para 68.
12 *A Local Authority v BF* [2018] EWCA Civ 2962, paras 22 and 23.
13 *Re SA* (n 10), para 9.
14 Ibid, para 2.
15 Ibid, para 80.

6.20 This list includes people who have capacity and those who lack capacity and has been the subject of much criticism.[16] Hayden J has said, 'I do not consider, even for a moment, that Munby J's descriptive indications were intended to imply that all those who are blind are necessarily vulnerable and fall within the potential reach of the court's inherent jurisdictional powers'.[17] It is clear that Munby J meant that blindness or deafness were, in fact, indicators of vulnerability: this is a logical conclusion of the finding that Miss SA *had* capacity to make decisions about marriage, and wanting to find a way to protect her from herself. If the case were heard today, the Court of Protection may determine that Miss SA *lacked* the relevant capacity.

6.21 The Court of Appeal agreed with Munby J's view that a statute would struggle to cover the myriad imaginable instances that a vulnerable person may find themselves in need of the protection of the inherent jurisdiction: 'the ability of the common law to develop and adapt its jurisdiction, on a case by case basis, as may be required, may meet this need more readily'.[18]

6.22 With some prescience given that *Re SA* was decided a full decade before the Serious Crime Act 2015 introduced the criminal offence of coercive and controlling behaviour into law and the subsequent statutory guidance was issued (see Chapter 2), Munby J suggested the following parameters of vulnerability in the inherent jurisdiction:

> 77. It would be unwise, and indeed inappropriate, for me even to attempt to define who might fall into this group in relation to whom the court can properly exercise its inherent jurisdiction. I disavow any such intention. It suffices for present purposes to say that, in my judgment, the authorities to which I have referred demonstrate that the inherent jurisdiction can be exercised in relation to a vulnerable adult who, even if not incapacitated by mental disorder or mental illness, is, or is reasonably believed to be, either (i) under constraint or (ii) subject to coercion or undue influence or (iii) for some other reason deprived of the capacity to make the relevant decision, or disabled from making a free choice, or incapacitated or disabled from giving or expressing a real and genuine consent.
>
> 78. I should elaborate this a little:

i) Constraint: It does not matter for this purpose whether the constraint amounts to actual incarceration. The jurisdiction is exercisable whenever a vulnerable adult is confined, controlled or under restraint, even if the restraint is only of the kind referred to by Eastham J in *Re C (Mental Patient: Contact)* [1993] 1 FLR 940. It is

16 For example, see David Lock QC, 'Decision making, mental capacity and undue influence: do hard cases make bad – or least fuzzy-edged law?' 2020 *Fam Law* 1624.
17 *Southend-on-Sea Borough Council v Meyers* [2019] EWHC 399 (Fam), [para 33.
18 *Re DL* (n 7), para 64.

enough that there is some significant curtailment of the freedom to do those things which in this country free men and women are entitled to do.

ii) Coercion or undue influence: What I have in mind here are the kind of vitiating circumstances referred to by the Court of Appeal in *In re T (Adult: Refusal of Treatment)* [1993] Fam 95, where a vulnerable adult's capacity or will to decide has been sapped and overborne by the improper influence of another [emphasis added]. In this connection I would only add, with reference to the observations of Sir James Hannen P in *Wingrove v Wingrove* (1885) 11 PD 81, of the Court of Appeal in *In re T (Adult: Refusal of Treatment)* … and of Hedley J in *In re Z (Local Authority: Duty)* [2004] EWHC 2817 (Fam), [2005] 1 WLR 959, that where the influence is that of a parent or other close and dominating relative, and where the arguments and persuasion are based upon personal affection or duty, religious beliefs, powerful social or cultural conventions, or asserted social, familial or domestic obligations, the influence may, as Butler-Sloss LJ put it, be subtle, insidious, pervasive and powerful. In such cases, moreover, very little pressure may suffice to bring about the desired result.

iii) Other disabling circumstances: What I have in mind here are the many other circumstances that may so reduce a vulnerable adult's understanding and reasoning powers as to prevent him forming or expressing a real and genuine consent, for example, the effects of deception, misinformation, physical disability, illness, weakness (physical, mental or moral), tiredness, shock, fatigue, depression, pain or drugs. No doubt there are others.

6.23 The third category of other disabling circumstances may apply when the state is at risk of breaching an adult's right to life (Article 2 European Convention on Human Rights (ECHR)) or freedom from torture or other forms of ill-treatment (Article 3 ECHR). As will be discussed in Chapter 7, the court can claim jurisdiction over adults who have capacity where they are experiencing a legal wrong.

6.24 In *Re SA*, Munby J emphasised that he was *not* suggesting that facts must fit into one of the above three categories. Rather, an adult is 'entitled to the protection of the inherent jurisdiction if he or she is, or is reasonably believed to be, incapacitated from making the relevant decision by reason of such things as constraint, coercion, undue influence or other vitiating factors'.[19]

6.25 He suggested that powers under the inherent jurisdiction are limitless: 'Just as there are, in theory, no limits to the court's powers when exercising the wardship jurisdiction I suspect that there are, in theory, few if any limits to the court's powers when exercising the inherent jurisdiction in relation to adults'.[20]

19 *Re SA* (n 10), para 79.
20 Ibid, para 84.

6.26 It is settled law that there is no limit on the circumstances in which the High Court has the power to exercise its inherent jurisdiction if the court is satisfied that the adult is vulnerable to the coercion, control or undue influence by another person or persons, which disables the adult from making a voluntary decision.[21] That, however, does not give a judge 'open season to expand the use of the inherent jurisdiction'.[22] In *Re DL*, Davis LJ observed that the inherent jurisdiction is not available to curtail strange decisions or odd behaviour:

> It is, of course, of the essence of humanity that adults are entitled to be eccentric, entitled to be unorthodox, entitled to be obstinate, entitled to be irrational. Many are. But the decided authorities show that there can be no power of public intervention simply because an adult proposes to make a decision, or to tolerate a state of affairs, which most would consider neither wise nor sensible. There has to be much more than simply that for any intervention to be justified: and any such intervention will indeed need to be justified as necessary and proportionate. I am sure local authorities, as much as the courts, appreciate that. It is at all events neither possible nor appropriate exhaustively to define 'vulnerability' for this purpose. Cases which are close to the line can safely be left to be dealt with under the inherent jurisdiction by the judges of the Family Division on the particular facts and circumstances arising in each instance.[23]

6.27 *Re SA* has been the subject of much criticism, including from Munby J himself, who subsequently regretted the 'unfortunately ambiguous use of the word vulnerable'.[24] As noted in Chapter 1, criticism has come also from Lady Hale, the former President of the Supreme Court, who has berated the imprecision of the term 'vulnerable'.[25] Other criticism has come from practitioners such as David Lock KC who has analysed the cases Munby J used in support of his conclusion that a jurisdiction existed for the High Court to make decisions about the lives of vulnerable individuals with capacity, finding that they do not constitute authority that the court has jurisdiction to make decisions for vulnerable adults who have capacity;[26] and pointing out that until *Re SA*, the term 'vulnerable adult' was used in relation to an incapacitous person.[27]

21 *Re DL* (n 7), para 64.
22 *Spencer v Spencer and others* [2018] EWCA Civ 100, para 46.
23 *Re DL* (n 7), para 76.
24 Sir James Munby, 'Whither the inherent jurisdiction? How did we get here? Where are we now? Where are we going? Part II' [2021] *Family Law* 365.
25 Lady Hale, Foreword to Rob George, *Wards of Court and the Inherent Jurisdiction* (Hart, 2024).
26 David Lock QC (as he then was), 'Decision-making, Mental capacity and undue influence: Action by public bodies to explore the grey areas between capacity and incapacity' [2015] *Judicial Review* 42.
27 See Butler-Sloss P (as she then was) in *Re A Local Authority (Inquiry: Restraint on Publication)* [2003] EWHC 2746 (Fam), para 10.

Permitted versus undue influence

6.28 In the 2023 case of *Re RK*, Cobb J (as he then was) explored the line between ordinary influence and undue influence by citing a 1992 Court of Appeal case which, in turn, cited:

> … the much earlier judgment in *Hall v Hall* [1868] Vol. 1 P. & D. 481 at page 482, to the effect that persuasion, appeals to the affections or ties of kindred do not amount to undue influence. On the other hand, 'pressure of whatever character', whether acting on the fears or the hopes, 'if so exerted as to overpower the volition without convincing the judgment', would be so. Threats or interference with 'the free play' of individual's judgment, discretion or wishes to the point that it is 'overborne' will constitute undue influence, even though no force is either used or threatened.[28]

6.29 The nature and intensity of influence is highly fact-specific, so the court will evaluate the evidence and apply the law in each case.

Avoiding the protective imperative

6.30 In exercising powers under the inherent jurisdiction, the court must attach due weight to the adult's wishes and feelings. In doing so, it will be careful to avoid the 'protective imperative'. In *Re CC*, Baker J (as he then was) explained that,

> … in cases of vulnerable adults, there is a risk that all professionals involved with treating and helping that person – including, of course, a judge in the Court of Protection – may feel drawn towards an outcome that is more protective of the adult and thus, in certain circumstances, fail to carry out an assessment of capacity that is detached and objective. On the other hand, the court must be equally careful not to be influenced by sympathy for a person's wholly understandable wish to return home.[29]

HUMAN RIGHTS CONSIDERATIONS

6.31 Before invoking the inherent jurisdiction, the court will consider the adult's rights under the ECHR, which is given legal effect by the Human Rights Act 1998. This section deals with three provisions: Article 3 ECHR which protects against torture and other forms of ill-treatment; Article 8 ECHR which protects against unnecessary or disproportionate interference with a person's

28 *Re RK (Capacity; Contact; Inherent Jurisdiction)* [2023] EWCOP 37 at para 110, referring to *Re T* [1992] EWCA Civ 18.
29 *CC v KK* [2012] EWHC 2136 (COP), para 25.

respect for private and family life, home and correspondence; and the right to liberty under Article 5 ECHR.

Article 3 ECHR

6.32 The European Court of Human Rights (ECtHR) has held that, 'the State authorities have a responsibility to take measures for the protection of an individual whose physical or psychological integrity is at risk from the criminal acts of a family member or partner'.[30] Therefore, where the abuse is very serious and reaches the minimum level of severity of such a breach, a victim of coercive control may be at risk of a breach of their right to freedom from torture, inhuman or degrading treatment or punishment, protected by Article 3 ECHR.

6.33 The case of *Re P*[31] contains a useful summary of the relevant law, and is examined further in the next chapter. There, the High Court reiterated that the threshold of severity required to engage Article 3 ECHR is relative and depends on the particular circumstances of the case, such as the nature and context of the treatment, its duration, its physical and mental effects and, in some circumstances, the age, sex and state of health of the victim.[32] The court held that,

> [t]he person's vulnerability is a key factor in the determination. Domestic abuse, which can include economic and emotional abuse often takes place within personal relationships or closed circuits where women make up an overwhelming majority of the victims. The need for active State involvement to provide victims of domestic abuse with effective protection and safeguards is well established. Special vigilance is required as vulnerable individuals are entitled to State protection in the form of effective deterrence, against such serious breaches of personal integrity.[33]

6.34 The key message for a local authority is that it should act in a proactive manner where a vulnerable adult is at risk of an Article 3 ECHR violation due to coercive control or other forms of abuse. Chapter 12 considers the representation of local authorities in coercive control cases, including the imperative for public bodies to avoid delay.

Article 8 ECHR

6.35 An interference with a person's right to respect for private and family life, or their home and correspondence will engage their Article 8 rights. The

30 *Tunikova and Others v Russia* (55974/16, 14 March 2022), para 103.

31 *Re P (Vulnerable Adult: Withdrawal of Application)* [2024] EWHC 1882 (Fam). Article 3 is also considered in forced marriage cases: see in particular *Re K (Forced Marriage: Passport Order)* [2020] EWCA Civ 190.

32 *AE v Bulgaria* (53891/20, 3 May 2023), paras 84–88.

33 *Re P* (n 31) para 30.

ECtHR has held that, 'The essential object of Article 8 is to protect the individual against arbitrary interference by the public authorities'.[34]

6.36 Protection of an adult's autonomy against arbitrary state interference is a central concern in coercive control cases. The scope of Article 8 includes a person's health and social care provision, where they live, their contact with others, their access to the internet and social media, and sending/receiving any sort of correspondence. The court carefully guards against unnecessary interferences with privacy and family life. For example, the UK Supreme Court has described a married couple being prevented from living together as a 'colossal interference' with Article 8.[35]

6.37 An interference with rights protected by Article 8 will be lawful only if it is considered as a pursuit of a legitimate aim under Article 8(2). This includes, for example, the protection of the person's health. The ECtHR has established that any measure interfering with private life must be accompanied by adequate procedural safeguards. These include the right of the affected individual to participate effectively in the decision-making process, to have access to relevant information, and to have a genuine opportunity to present their case and challenge the evidence against them. The absence of such procedural protections can render the process arbitrary and amount to a violation of Article 8 rights.[36]

6.38 The Family Division has held that, 'the greater the interference the more closely less intrusive means will need to be scrutinised'.[37] The dual lenses through which judicial scrutiny is applied are necessity and proportionality.[38]

6.39 For an interference to be necessary, it must correspond to a pressing social need and must remain proportionate to the legitimate aim pursued.[39]

6.40 The court will test whether an interference is proportionate by asking four questions:

(a) is the objective sufficiently important to justify limiting a fundamental right?;

(b) are the measures which have been designed to meet it rationally connected to it?;

(c) are they no more than are necessary to accomplish it?; and

(d) do they strike a fair balance between the rights of the individual and the interests of the community?[40]

34 *Hokkanen v Finland*, Application No. 19823/92, judgment 23 September 1994, para 55.

35 *R (Quila) v Secretary of State for the Home Department* [2011] UKSC 45, para 32. For application under the inherent jurisdiction, see *London Borough of Croydon v KR & Anor* [2019] EWHC 2498 (Fam) at para 48.

36 *Shtukaturov v Russia* (2012) 54 EHRR 27.

37 *London Borough of Croydon v KR* [2019] EWHC 2498 (Fam), para 51.

38 See *Re DL* (n 7), McFarlane LJ at para 86, and Davis LJ at para 76.

39 *Dudgeon v the United Kingdom* (1983) 5 EHRR 573, paras 51–53.

40 *R (on the application of Ali) v Secretary of State for the Home Department* [2015] UKSC 68, para 29.

6.41 An example of the balancing of human rights concerns as to the duration of an interference is the 2020 case of *Re K*. There, the Court of Appeal held that listing a review hearing four years after the making of an forced marriage protection order struck an appropriate balance between protecting the adult from a potential breach of her Article 3 rights (to be free from ill-treatment) and her competing rights under Article 8 (autonomy to make decisions).[41] The principle to be applied in these cases is that where the evidence establishes a reasonable possibility that conduct sufficient to breach Article 3 might occur, the court should take such measures as are necessary to protect a potential victim from that risk, while limiting any interference with Article 8 rights to what is necessary to protect the Article 3 rights.

Article 5 ECHR

6.42 The inherent jurisdiction can authorise the deprivation of an adult's liberty if it is compatible with Article 5(1) ECHR. This provision states: 'Everyone has the right to liberty and security of person. No one shall be deprived of his liberty save in the following cases and in accordance with a procedure prescribed by law.' The article then specifies several carve-outs, the most relevant to this book being paragraph (e) which, in language that was drafted in the late 1940s, states, 'the lawful detention of persons for the prevention of the spreading of infectious diseases, of persons of unsound mind, alcoholics or drug addicts or vagrants …'.

6.43 Article 5(4) provides that a person deprived of their liberty is 'entitled to take proceedings by which the lawfulness of his detention shall be decided speedily by a court and his release ordered if the detention is not lawful.' In England and Wales, a person deprived of their liberty under the Mental Health Act 1983 may make an application to the First-tier Tribunal (Mental Health). A person deprived of their liberty under the MCA 2005 may challenge that deprivation of liberty by making an application to the Court of Protection.[42]

6.44 The 1979 case of *Winterwerp v The Netherlands* is the grandparent of European Court of Human Rights mental health cases. There the Court held that:

> … except in emergency cases, the individual concerned should not be deprived of his liberty unless he has been reliably shown to be of 'unsound mind'. The very nature of what has to be established before the competent national authority – that is, a true mental disorder – calls for objective medical expertise. Further, the mental disorder must be of a kind or degree

41 *Re K* (n 31), para 77. Another worked through example is *London Borough of Croydon v KR* [2019] EWHC 2498 (Fam).

42 At the time of writing, this is the 'Deprivation of Liberty Safeguards' regime under Schedule A1 to the MCA 2005, where an application can be made under MCA 2005, s 21A. This is to be replaced by the 'Liberty Protection Safeguards' in Schedule AA1, where an application can be made under s 21ZA.

> warranting compulsory confinement. What is more, the validity of continued confinement depends upon the persistence of such a disorder …[43]

6.45 Therefore, in an emergency, it is lawful to deprive an adult of their liberty in the absence of evidence of mental disorder without infringing Article 5 ECHR. Is it possible to use the inherent jurisdiction to authorise a deprivation of liberty?

6.46 Mr Meyers was 97 years old and had been removed from his bungalow where he lived in squalid conditions with his son Mr KF, and placed in a care home on an interim basis while capacity assessments were undertaken. Those assessments concluded that he had capacity to decide on residence and care. For reasons irrelevant for present purposes, there was an application for permission to appeal, which Baker LJ dismissed in December 2018 in a case called *Re BF*.[44] The matter was remitted back to the Court of Protection where Hayden J handed down a judgment in February 2019, by which time anonymity was lifted and Mr BF was known by his name, Mr Meyers.[45]

6.47 Hayden J found that Mr KF was 'needy, irrational, frequently out of control as well as manifestly emotionally dependent on a father who, despite the alarming history of this case, he obviously loves'.[46] Mr KF's influence on his father was 'insidious and pervasive' and triggered the father's 'sense of duty, guilt, love and responsibility.' Because of the coercive relationship,

> the two men have become so enmeshed that the autonomy of each has been compromised. In reality, KF exerts an influence over his father which is malign in its effect if not in its intention. The consequence is to disable Mr Meyers from making a truly informed decision which impacts directly on his health and survival.[47]

6.48 Hayden J described Mr Meyers' decisions as 'foolhardy'. He noted that the inherent jurisdiction should be used sparingly and that, '[h]owever well motivated the State may be in seeking, paternalistically, to protect people from their own unwise decisions, it is a dangerous course which has the potential to threaten fundamental rights and freedoms'.[48]

6.49 Nevertheless, Hayden J held that the state had an obligation to protect Mr Meyers' life and made an order preventing Mr Meyers from living with his son, either in the bungalow or elsewhere. The judge explained that this did not amount to a deprivation of liberty because, 'the ambition here is not to confine Mr Meyers to the Care Home, but to protect him from the grave danger that living in the bungalow with his son has already been demonstrated to represent'.

43 *Winterwerp v The Netherlands*, Application No. 6301/73, [1979] ECHR 4, (1979) 2 EHRR 387.
44 See *Re BF* (n 5), at para 34.
45 *Southend-on-Sea Borough Council v Meyers* [2019] EWHC 399 (Fam).
46 Ibid, para 41.
47 Ibid, para 41.
48 Ibid, para 42.

It was 'his choices, not his liberty' that was being restricted.[49] The court therefore cornered a capacitous adult into making a particular decision by removing all other available choices: 'It is fair to say that this decision is very much an outlier'.[50]

6.50 In a case decided in 2019, Cobb J (as he then was) held that inherent jurisdiction cannot be used to authorise the deprivation of liberty of a person where, even in an emergency, there was no reason to believe that they had a mental disorder.[51] He relied in part on the observation of McFarlane LJ in *Re DL* that the inherent jurisdiction should be used for 'facilitative, rather than dictatorial' reasons.[52] In the same year, Gwynneth Knowles J held that the inherent jurisdiction could be used to plug the gap created by an earlier Court of Appeal decision that rendered the First-tier Tribunal (Mental Health) powerless to order the conditional discharge of a restricted patient detained under the Mental Health Act 1983 if to do so would deprive the patient of his liberty in the community.[53]

6.51 Baker LJ's decision in *Re BF* was a permission decision so it carries no precedential weight. However, it is interesting to note what was said about deprivation of liberty of a person who has capacity and is not 'of unsound mind'. The judge appeared to have suggested that keeping Mr Meyers in the care home while the local authority carried out 'very careful planning' to put in place domiciliary support would be consistent with Article 5 ECHR.[54] It is hard to see a difference between keeping a person in a care home against their will and depriving them of their liberty.

6.52 In October 2020, the Court of Appeal considered deprivation of liberty in the case of *Re Mazhar*.[55] This was an appeal against an order made under the inherent jurisdiction that authorised an adult's removal to hospital. The court did not need to determine whether the inherent jurisdiction could authorise a deprivation of liberty, so it declined to do so. Giving judgment for the court was Baker LJ again. He expressed:

> uncertainty as to whether it is permissible in urgent situations to depart from the *Winterwerp* criteria, in particular the requirement for medical evidence. The qualification in *Winterwerp* itself ('except in emergency cases') suggests that some limited departure may be permissible, although

49 Ibid, para 59.
50 *London Borough of Islington v EF* [2022] EWHC 803 (Fam), para 42.
51 *Wakefield MBC v DN and MN* [2019] EWHC 2306 (Fam), [2019] COPLR 525. Cobb J also handed down the following case on the same day (5 September 2019): *Redcar and Cleveland Borough Council v PR and others* [2019] EWHC 2305 (Fam), in which he said *obiter* at para 40, that in emergency cases *Winterwerp* could be relied on by the inherent jurisdiction, which can be used to authorise a deprivation of liberty in the absence of reliable evidence of a mental disorder.
52 *Re DL* (n 7), at para 67.
53 *Hertfordshire County Council v AB* [2018] EWHC 3103 (Fam).
54 *A Local Authority v BF* (n 5), para 35.
55 *Mazhar v Birmingham Community Healthcare Foundation NHS Trust and others* [2020] EWCA Civ 1377.

more recent decisions of the European Court have not repeated that qualification.[56]

6.53 Munby LJ has pointed out[57] that the two authorities that Baker LJ relied on in his judgment in *Re BF* did not suggest that the inherent jurisdiction could authorise a deprivation of liberty, as both concerned adults who *lacked* capacity[58] – the point being that these are cases that the Court of Protection can deal with, a court that has the power to authorise a deprivation of liberty.

6.54 In November 2021, Lieven J sitting in the Family Division had occasion to comment *obiter* on the scope of the inherent jurisdiction in the case of *Re EG*.[59] She said that the right to liberty under Article 5 ECHR and the common law is 'jealously protected and should only be removed in carefully understood and constrained circumstances', consistent with ECtHR jurisprudence.[60] In May 2023, Mostyn J held, again *obiter*, that the inherent jurisdiction could not authorise the forcible removal from their home of a capacitous yet extremely vulnerable adult who was being victimised and exploited by their family or carers, noting that the gap in the law should be filled 'not by judicial legislation, but by parliamentary legislation'.[61]

6.55 There is little case law to suggest that an order under the inherent jurisdiction could lawfully authorise the deprivation of liberty of a vulnerable adult who *has* capacity to decide on residence or care and who is not 'of unsound mind'. Hayden J's workaround in *Re Meyers* notwithstanding, an applicant local authority should tread carefully when making an application under the inherent jurisdiction for an order that would result in the adult being deprived of their liberty.

Deprivation of liberty in practice

6.56 Where a person is assessed as being at risk from another person, the local authority may have insufficient evidence about the person's capacity to decide on residence, care or contact with others to make an application to be to the Court of Protection. If the local authority believes the adult to be under influence or constraint in *Re SA* terms, the local authority could make an application under the inherent jurisdiction for an order that:

56 Ibid, para 52.
57 Sir James Munby (n 24).
58 *Re PS (Incapacitated or Vulnerable Adult)* [2007] EWHC 623 (Fam); and *A NHS Trust v A* [2013] EWHC 2442 (COP), [2013] COPLR 605. This case was decided on 9 March 2007, and the Court of Protection was established under the MCA 2005 and began operating on 1 October 2007.
59 *Cumbria, Northumberland Tyne & Wear NHS Foundation Trust & Anor v EG* [2021] EWHC 2990 (Fam).
60 Lieven J cited the ECtHR judgment in *Ilnseher v Germany*, Application No. 10211/12, [2019] MHLR 278. At para 129 the Court stated, 'the permissible grounds for deprivation of liberty listed in article 5(1) are to be interpreted narrowly. A mental condition has to be of a certain severity in order to be considered as a "true" mental disorder for the purposes of sub-paragraph (e)'.
61 *A Local Authority v LD and another* [2023] EWHC 1258 (Fam), paras 40-42.

(a) directs the controlling person to remove themself from P's home for a few hours so that social workers have access to P to carry out assessments of needs for care, and to carry out relevant capacity assessments and then develop a strategy for next steps; or

(b) authorises the temporary removal of the adult from their home and transfer to a place of safety (eg, a care home) for assessment.

6.57 These are draconian powers, and the court will need a proper evidential basis for making such orders. How then, are such applications made?

PROCEDURE

Civil Procedure Rules

6.58 Inherent jurisdiction cases are governed not by the Court of Protection Rules 2017 or by the Family Procedure Rules, but by the Civil Procedure Rules 1998 (CPR). The CPR should be followed in respect of forms, evidence, costs and appeals. The party making the application in the Court of Protection is the 'applicant', but under the CPR is known as the 'claimant'. Similarly, under the CPR, a 'respondent' is technically a 'defendant'. Despite this, several judgments under the inherent jurisdiction use the terms applicant and respondent.

6.59 The CPR are ill-suited to the sort of inquisitorial exercise required in inherent jurisdiction cases, so judges and lawyers commonly craft orders to mould the requirements of the CPR to meet the needs of the case and make orders more akin to norms in the Court of Protection. For example, (a) disclosure is commonly directed to be sent to the adult's representatives in the first instance; (b) it is common practice in inherent jurisdiction cases, as it is in the Court of Protection, for the court to permit the instruction of a single joint expert, but not in civil litigation; and (c) there is no provision in the CPR for the appointment of a litigation fiend unless the adult lacks capacity in MCA 2005 terms but an appointment is regularly made in inherent jurisdiction cases anyway.[62] It is hoped that the judiciary will create a CPR Practice Direction governing procedure under the inherent jurisdiction.

Form of application

6.60 An application under the inherent jurisdiction is made by issuing a Part 8 Claim Form. The applicant must pay the court fee and provide supporting evidence.

62 See for example, *Re P (Vulnerable Adult: Withdrawal of Application* [2024] EWHC 1882 (Fam), para 13.

Level of judiciary

6.61 Only judges of the Family Division of the High Court can hear inherent jurisdiction cases. This includes deputy High Court judges.[63] Therefore when a parallel application is made under the Court of Protection, a High Court judge will hear both applications sitting also as a tier 3 judge of the Court of Protection.

Funding

6.62 Legal aid is available to parties in inherent jurisdiction proceedings, and is subject to both a means and merits test.[64] Funding of the victim/survivor's legal representation is considered in Chapter 11.

Transfer from/to the Court of Protection

6.63 If the matter is already in the Court of Protection, that court can transfer the case to a High Court judge of the Family Division and the court may dispense with the need to issue a separate application form. A matter can also be transferred from the Family Division to the Court of Protection if the person lacks capacity to make relevant decisions.

Determining capacity or undue influence

6.64 At the outset of an application it may be unclear whether the adult has capacity in MCA 2005 terms to conduct proceedings, or whether they are compromised from acting because of the coercive control or undue influence of another. The court can make a *Harbin v Masterman*[65] order inviting the Official Solicitor to investigate the adult's capacity, and their true wishes, to ascertain whether they are operating under the influence of another in relation to the subject-matter decisions (which might include the contact that the adult has with that other person).[66] This will need to be paid for, and at the initial stages of an application the only source of funding is likely to be the local authority.

63 These include a practising barrister or solicitor who sits as part-time judge of the High Court, or a salaried judge who is permitted to sit as a judge of the High Court pursuant to s 9 of the Senior Courts Act 1981.

64 Legal Aid, Sentencing and Punishment of Offenders Act 2012, Sch 1, para 9.

65 [1896] 1 Ch 351.

66 See for example *In Re L (Vulnerable Adults with Capacity: Court's Jurisdiction)* [2010] EWHC 2675 (Fam) where the wording of the order was, 'The Official Solicitor, if he so consents, shall be appointed to visit ML and GRL to investigate their true wishes and to ascertain whether they are operating under the influence of DL in relation to the contact that they have with him.' *Harbin v Masterman* orders were discussed in *Re L (Vulnerable Adults with Capacity: Court's Jurisdiction)* [2011] EWHC 1022 (Fam) (which on appeal became *A Local Authority v DL* [2012] EWCA Civ 253); and *Re P (Vulnerable Adult: Withdrawal of Application* [2024] EWHC 1882 (Fam) at para 10. See also Official Solicitor's Practice Note 'Appointment as litigation friend in personal welfare proceedings in the Court of Protection', 3 February 2021, para 30.

6.65 It is common for the controlling person to object to the victim/survivor of coercive control undergoing a capacity assessment. Where there is credible evidence of coercive control, the court will need to make robust case management orders to ensure the evidence can be gathered, so that the court can make appropriate findings of facts and orders either in the Court of Protection or under the inherent jurisdiction.

Litigation friend

6.66 The CPR permits the appointment of a litigation friend for a party only where that person lacks capacity to conduct proceedings in MCA 2005 terms (see in Chapter 4 at para 4.23). In mixed Court of Protection and inherent jurisdiction cases (where the adult has capacity to make some decisions but not others), the Official Solicitor is routinely appointed as litigation friend.[67]

Without notice applications

6.67 The applicant (usually a local authority) may wish to make the application without notice to other parties.[68] Sometimes, telling the victim/survivor and/or the controlling person about the application will jeopardise the victim/survivor's safety, or may encourage them to flee without care and support. In some cases, there is a risk that the controlling person will abduct the victim/survivor.

6.68 In the Court of Appeal case of *Re Mazhar,* considered above at para 6.52, Baker LJ provided a checklist for legal representatives to follow when considering a without notice application:

(1) save in exceptional circumstances and for clear reasons, orders under the inherent jurisdiction in respect of vulnerable adults should not be made without notice to the individual;

(2) a party who applies for an order under the inherent jurisdiction in respect of vulnerable adults without notice to another party must provide the court with their reasons for taking that course;

(3) where an order under the inherent jurisdiction in respect of vulnerable adults is made without notice, that fact should be recorded in the order, together with a recital summarising the reasons;

67 Examples considered in Chapter 7 include *Re TT (Injunctive Relief) (by his litigation friend the Official Solicitor)* [2022] EWHC 2185 (Fam), and *In the Matter of CA (Fact Finding – Capacity – Inherent Jurisdiction – Injunctive Relief)* [2024] EWCOP 64 (T3).

68 Still in use is the Latin phrase *ex parte* (or *ex p*), which means without notice.

(4) a party who seeks to invoke the inherent jurisdiction with regard to vulnerable adults must provide the court with their reasons for taking that course and identify the circumstances which it is contended empower the court to make the order;

(5) where the court is being asked to exercise the inherent jurisdiction with regard to vulnerable adults, that fact should be recorded in the order along with a recital of the reasons for invoking jurisdiction;

(6) an order made under the inherent jurisdiction in respect of vulnerable adults should include a recital of the basis on which the court has found, or has reason to believe, the circumstances are such as to empower the court to make the order; and

(7) finally, if an order is made out of hours, it is essential that the matter should return to court at the earliest opportunity.[69]

Interim orders

6.69 Interim orders are considered in Chapter 9.

CONCLUSIONS

6.70 This chapter on the principles and procedure of the inherent jurisdiction has elucidated the unique role of the High Court in safeguarding vulnerable adults who have decision-making capacity pursuant to the MCA 2005.

6.71 Where a capacitous person is of 'unsound mind' within the meaning of Article 5(1)(e) ECHR, the inherent jurisdiction can be used to authorise deprivation of liberty, but in practice this remains rare. The domestic courts are bound by the jurisprudence of the ECtHR, and must only impose orders that are necessary and proportionate and always have proper regard to the adult's autonomy.

6.72 Unlike the law applied in the Court of Protection which derives from statute, the inherent jurisdiction is a common law construct, allowing the court to intervene where statutory protections fall short. This area of law is invoked to protect individuals from coercion, undue influence, or other disabling circumstances that compromise their autonomy.

6.73 The chapter has explained that under the inherent jurisdiction, the court can make wide-ranging orders, such as restricting contact with abusers or

69 *Re Mazhar* (n 55), at para 74.

authorising temporary removal from the home, to ensure the individual's safety and autonomy. Remedies are considered further in Chapter 9. The inherent jurisdiction remains a vital, albeit controversial, tool in the legal landscape, balancing the protection of vulnerable adults with respect for their autonomy and human rights. The next chapter reviews coercive control cases where the inherent jurisdiction has been invoked.

CHAPTER 7

Coercive control cases under the inherent jurisdiction

'It's so traumatic that I can't even remember what happened now'[1]

INTRODUCTION

7.01 The previous chapter set out the law and procedure of the inherent jurisdiction with respect to adults, where the court replaces a capacitous adult's decision with its own. The approach is akin to forced marriage cases where, 'In lay terms, the court [...] has jurisdiction, in a particular case, to protect a person from themselves'.[2] A similar approach is taken in cases concerning vexatious litigants.[3]

7.02 This chapter outlines a handful of cases under the inherent jurisdiction to illustrate the sorts of scenarios that the court has considered. It starts with partner control and describes the case of Mrs FH who was not allowed to move back to her abusive husband of many decades (at para 7.03). It then looks briefly at three cases concerning overbearing control by parents – Mr TT whose decisions were made by his mother who knew best (at para 7.11), Ms KP whose home was controlled by a child sex offender (at para 7.15), and then Ms P who wanted to moving back home where her father controlled her every move (at para 7.24). The chapter then considers a case where an adult daughter had an enmeshed relationship with her mother and sought to take all decisions for her (at para 7.25). Finally, it touches on forced relationships (at para 7.51), which include forced marriage and overseas travel.

CONTROL OF A PARTNER

7.03 Mrs FH was 81-year-old woman with Alzheimer's disease, who lived in a care home.[4] She had been diagnosed with colon cancer which had metastasised to the liver. Mrs FH had been subject to coercion and control by her husband Mr

1 *Re CA (Fact Finding – Capacity – Inherent Jurisdiction – Injunctive Relief)* [2024] EWCOP 64 (T3).
2 *Re K (Forced Marriage: Passport Order)* [2020] EWCA Civ 190.
3 For example *Attorney General v Edwards* [2010] EWHC 2160 (Admin) where at para 19 the court held that, 'E needed to be protected from himself so that he could resume what, apart from the litigation, was no doubt a respectable and sensible way of life.'
4 *Wakefield Metropolitan District Council v FH and others* [2024] EWHC 830 (Fam).

MH, who it was said, had manipulated her over years, and been physically and verbally abuse. They were estranged from their wider family.

7.04 The local authority made the application in June 2023 and the court determined that Mrs FH had capacity to conduct litigation, and make decisions about residence and care. The inherent jurisdiction was therefore available to the court.

7.05 Mr MH presented as volatile and quick to lose his temper. He interfered with discussions between Mrs FH and her carers and intervened unhelpfully to frustrate the administration of medication to Mrs FH. Despite injunctions made in June 2023, Mr MH's behaviour had not abated. There was an incident when carers had to intervene to prevent him abusing Mrs FH.

7.06 Mrs FH was admitted to hospital and the case was heard the following day by Cobb J (as he then was). Mrs FH had fallen out of bed, and 'was in a state of very considerable distress'. The judge listened to a recording of a Care Line call, and noted that, 'What was striking about MH's response to that situation was that he appeared to show no empathy or care for her in her situation but, on the contrary, demonstrated high levels of verbal abuse of her, both directly *to* her and *at* her.'

7.07 The local authority made the application to authorise a move back to a care home, without which, it was said, Mrs FH would be returned to an environment in which she would continue to be subject to intolerable and unacceptable coercion and control.

7.08 At the final hearing in March 2024, Mrs FH told the judge how much she loved her husband. She emphasised the longevity of their marriage and their commitment to each other. Notwithstanding that contact took place in the care home and was relatively unobtrusive, with the care staff simply monitoring the interactions between them from a chair by the door, Mrs FH found supervised contact intrusive and unwelcome.

7.09 The agreed position at the final hearing was a continuation of the injunctions. Cobb J therefore injuncted Mr MH: (a) from removing Mrs FH from the care home which would continue until or unless it was discharged; (b) from removing Mrs FH from a hospital should she be admitted to hospital; and (c) from having unsupervised face-to-face contact with his wife. The judge agreed to the continuation of protective injunctive orders as 'a proportionate response to the risks'.

7.10 As noted in Chapter 1, love and coercion are often entangled in coercive control cases. Cobb J said he had, 'no doubt at all about the love which' the married couple had for each other.

CONTROL BY A PARENT

Mr TT and his mother

7.11 *Re TT* was a mixed Court of Protection and inherent jurisdiction case where the court made protective orders in respect of Mr TT, a 46-year-old man of Asian heritage who had a mild learning disability.[5] His mother Mrs ST had done her best caring for him, but did not regard him as an adult who was able to make decisions for himself. She did not believe that he was able to live independently of her, in his own supported living home. A previous judge found that Mrs ST, 'has controlled TT, or sought to coerce TT, throughout his life, as she sees it, for his benefit and she has not made the transition from caring for a child, to supporting an adult to make the best of his life'. She wanted to decide where her son lived and how much time he spent with his girlfriend. She repeatedly chastised him when he returned to his home and not hers. She telephoned Mr TT's girlfriend, telling her not to spend time with him.

7.12 In summarising Mrs ST's evidence, the judge said that Mrs ST took opportunities to frustrate opportunities for Mr TT to exercise his autonomy, that she was 'profoundly mistrustful' of social workers and psychologists. 'She is unswerving in her belief that only she knows TT and what is best for him and can keep him safe. She was invited to consider whether there was anything about her own behaviour that needed to change, but she did not.'

7.13 That description will be familiar to legal practitioners who have dealt with a disabled person's overbearing relatives who have little to no insight of the impact that their behaviour has on the person they clearly love and are trying to protect. In *Re TT*, the judge found that Mrs ST's behaviour fell squarely into Munby J's definition in *Re SA* of a dominating relative because Mrs ST, 'has attempted to control and influence TT's daily life and decisions in almost every respect: where he goes and what he does with his day-to-day life, who he sees and when, and most of all, where he shall live.'

7.14 Mr TT had been assessed as lacking capacity to decide on residence, so the court made an injunction in the Court of Protection against Mrs ST, prohibiting her from preventing her son to live at his home, preventing her from seeking to persuade him not to return to his home, or moving back to the family home. Mr TT had capacity to decide on contact with others, so the court invoked the inherent jurisdiction to injunct Mrs ST from interfering in Mr TT's contact with his girlfriend.

5 *Re TT (injunctive relief)* [2022] EWHC 2185 (Fam).

Ms KP and her cousin/step-father

7.15 The court was faced with an altogether different application when it was asked to make orders to protect Ms KP, a young woman, from harm.[6] Her mother Ms J was in a relationship with Mr D and they had two young children together. Mr D was also Ms KP's cousin, so he was her stepfather too. Ms KP lived in their house with Ms J and Mr D and their two children.

7.16 The background that gave rise to a risk to Ms KP was that Mr D had spent 11 months in prison for possession of indecent images of children and was then recalled to prison for breaching a sexual harm prevention order, all while the three children were under the age of 18. Ms KP and the two other children were taken into care, and she then lived in placements arranged by the local authority.

7.17 A previous family judge had described Mr D as an intelligent man who had chosen to live with a woman who had a much lower level of intelligence, noting he was, 'serious, determined, persistent, manipulative and obsessive'. By the time the inherent jurisdiction application was made in 2023, Ms KP had become an adult and had moved back to her mother and Mr D's home. Mr D did not let Ms KP meet with social workers. He sought either to covertly listen-in or attend when social workers did eventually visit.

7.18 The local authority's application was for an order for Ms KP to move out of the family home, cease contact with Mr D and live in supported accommodation. There were three problems. First, no accommodation had been identified. Second, given that Ms KP lived at Ms J's house, unless the court evicted Mr D from Ms J's house which the court could not do as Mr D was not a party to the proceedings, there was no way to stop contact between Ms KP and Mr D.

7.19 A third and more fundamental problem was that the application should have been made to the Court of Protection. The psychological evidence was that Ms KP had autism and had an extremely low score in a cognitive test such that 99% of the population would score the same or better. The court accepted that this amounted to an impairment of the mind or brain for the purposes of s 2 of the Mental Capacity Act 2005 (MCA 2005). A second psychological report explained how the cognitive impairment and autism affected Ms KP's decision-making:

6 *A Local Authority v KP (Acting by the Official Solicitor as her litigation friend) and another* [2023] EWHC 3102 (Fam).

> Young people with learning difficulties and/or autism also find it hard to understand that people who appear friendly may be manipulating them. This is an aspect of their impaired social imagination. In KP's case, Dr Kliman explained that KP would struggle to understand if someone was seeking to manipulate or exploit her, or that someone might be telling her something that was not true. All that makes someone who has the combination of low intelligence and ASD [autism spectrum disorder] hugely vulnerable to manipulation.[7]

7.20 The psychologist thought that even if Ms KP was to accept that Mr D had been properly convicted of paedophilia offences, she may never be able to accept that he posed a potential danger to her because she had adopted her mother's firm and often expressed belief that Mr D was a danger to no-one.

7.21 The court accepted the expert evidence, finding that Mr D has 'has a considerable ability to mould and shape how both KP and her mother see the world. They are clearly acting under his influence and it is an influence that he is keen to maintain'.[8]

7.22 However, the court noted that since moving back to the family home, Ms KP had not self-harmed, and that there was no evidence that Mr D had done anything or said anything adverse to Ms KP's best interests. There was no alternative accommodation, but even if there were, Ms KP wanted to live in the family home. The real question was what arrangements could be put in place to enable Ms KP to live as safely as possible in Ms J's house with Mr D living there too. The court directed that a social worker should meet Ms KP at a pre-arranged time away from the family home every week, and neither Ms J nor Mr D would attend those meetings or interfere with them.

7.23 Where there is a published judgment following court proceedings, the judgment usually ends with the court's decision and the reader is left wondering what happened next. In this case, the judge added a postscript to the judgment in which he recorded that two days after the hearing, Ms KP decided of her own free will to move out of the family house and temporarily move in with her boyfriend at his parents' house. Ms KP also made a series of disclosures which suggested that Mr D may have been grooming her towards a sexual relationship with him or someone else. The proceedings seemed to have had an effect on her insight into Mr D, as she emailed her social worker saying, 'I'm going to start getting my life together and thank you G [social worker] for opening my eyes wish I could hug you'.

7 Ibid, para. 53.
8 Ibid, para. 74.

Ms P and her father

7.24 The third case in this section on overbearing parents has extraordinary facts, features a local authority that took admirable pre-litigation steps to resolve the matter, and resulted in an unusual outcome. The question for the court was whether 20-year-old Ms P should continue to live with her father, Mr Y, who exercised control over her, including denying her access to necessities such as heating and food.[9]

7.25 Ms P previously lived with her brother, mother and father. The father ruled the roost: the three family members were not allowed to leave the family home unaccompanied by Mr Y. He forbade them from working, or claiming state benefits. Shopping was done as a group and Mr Y controlled the family finances, only allowing £1.50 a day for food for the entire family. Food was rationed and measured out in small amounts and the family diet often consisted of bread and jam or mustard. He limited their time in the shower, and he cut their hair. The mother reported that the children had to wear covert recording equipment at school so that Mr Y could monitor them.

7.26 As a result, the judge said that Ms P, 'had experienced a dysfunctional family life that has left her homeless, isolated from her wider family and her peers, lacking formal education or training, distrustful of authority, and likely to be at risk of harm without support from others which she has consistently refused'.[10]

7.27 In October 2023, Ms P had been compelled to live in a care home, so that she could be apart from her father. With some difficulty, a psychiatrist assessed her and found no mental disorder, but was of the view that Ms P's behaviour and views were a manifestation of the undue influence of her father arising from coercion and control. The psychiatrist thought that if Ms P left the care home, 'there would be a significant risk that P would not have developed the relevant and necessary skills to prevent a return to her father's control and a re-establishment of her prior dependence, enmeshment, and coercion'.[11]

7.28 The case came before Gwynneth Knowles J in July 2024. The question for the court was whether to continue the previous court order mandating Ms P to live in a care home. By the time of the hearing, the local authority thought it would be disproportionate to continue the placement, and that other safeguarding measures were unlikely to be effective in helping Ms P extricate herself from a relationship of control and dependence.

9 *Re P (Vulnerable Adult: Withdrawal of Application)* [2024] EWHC 1882 (Fam).
10 Ibid, para. 1.
11 Ibid, para. 12.

7.29 The social worker's evidence was that moving Ms P into the care home had had limited positive effect. Little progress had been made in Ms P's understanding of the risks arising from her enmeshed relationship with her father or her recognition that she had been subject to controlling, coercive and abusive behaviour. It was thought that no significant progress could be made 'unless contact with her father could be prevented, but the only means by which this could be achieved would be placing P in a locked setting and restricting her access to the internet and social media. In those circumstances, the social worker considered it would be disproportionate to require P to continue living in the placement'.[12]

7.30 During her time at the care home, Ms P had made it clear she wanted nothing to do with the local authority. She wanted to leave the care home and return to her old way of life. She wanted her own accommodation without social workers' interference: 'I want to be left alone to be with my dad. I want to be in a house or a flat … You might not be happy with my life choices but it's my life'.[13]

7.31 The local authority applied to withdraw the application, which the court granted. The local authority had a duty to assess need for care and support pursuant to Care Act 2014.[14] A person with capacity may refuse an assessment, and the court noted that Ms P had capacity to make decisions about residence and care, but was deprived of exercising a free choice because of Mr Y's undue influence.

7.32 The local authority made three proposals which the court said were an appropriate discharge of their statutory obligations to Ms P. First, it would set up a prepaid card with a balance of £500 for Ms P. Second, the local authority would withdraw the claim for state benefits it made on Ms P's behalf, and it would inform the Department for Work and Pensions that Ms P should not be assumed to lack capacity to make any future application for state benefits. Third, a pack of information was made available for Ms P to access help and support should she wish to do so.

7.33 The court determined that: (a) the proposals put forward by the local authority to offer Ms P support and accommodation were an appropriate discharge of its statutory obligations towards her; (b) notwithstanding the risks to Ms P's welfare should she refuse the offers of support from the local authority and return to live with her father, it was not appropriate for the court to make further orders regulating her residence or otherwise constraining her choices; and (c) concluding the proceedings without further or continuing orders did not constitute a breach of Ms P's Article 3 or 8 European Convention on Human Rights (ECHR) rights.

12 Ibid, para. 17.
13 Ibid para, 18.
14 See para 4.41 in Chapter 4, above.

7.34 The court agreed that 'there are, in reality, no good outcomes for [Ms] P'.[15] Despite the array of powers available to the High Court in the exercise of its inherent jurisdiction, making a restrictive order sometimes causes more harm than good. The judge noted her hands were tied: this case 'makes plain the limit of legal intervention to protect a vulnerable adult who has every intention of re-establishing the living arrangements which sparked the proceedings'.

CONTROL OF A PARENT

7.35 The final case in this chapter is an elder abuse case that illustrates the interplay between the MCA 2005 and the inherent jurisdiction. The case concerned a 79-year-old woman Mrs CA.[16] She formerly had a diagnosis of Alzheimer's dementia which the court-appointed psychiatric expert considered was incorrect. His view was that Mrs CA had mild cognitive impairment and memory loss that constituted an impairment in, or disturbance in the functioning of, the mind or brain pursuant to s 2(1) of MCA 2005.

7.36 Mrs CA lived in her own house, and live-in care had been put in place for her protection following the discharge from hospital and allegations of coercive and controlling behaviour by her daughter Ms DA. Mrs CA had signed a lasting power of attorney (LPA) designating Ms DA as attorney for both property and affairs, and health and welfare. The local authority made an application to the Court of Protection seeking declarations of capacity, best interests decisions concerning contact, and revocation of the health and welfare LPA as the daughter had made decisions as health and welfare attorney contrary to Mrs CA's best interests.

7.37 The independent court-appointed psychiatrist had originally concluded that Mrs CA had capacity in all assessed areas (conducting proceedings, residence, care, contact with others, making and revoking an LPA, and managing property and affairs). Upon considering his report, the local authority made a parallel application under the inherent jurisdiction, so that if the court found that Mrs CA *had* capacity to decide on care or to decide on contact with others, it would be open to the judge (who was a judge of the High Court) to determine that Mrs CA was a vulnerable person disabled from exercising autonomous choices because of her daughter, and that it was proportionate and in line with Mrs CA's Article 8 ECHR rights for the court to make orders under the inherent jurisdiction.

15 *Re P* (n 9), para 36.
16 *Re CA (Fact Finding – Capacity – Inherent Jurisdiction – Injunctive Relief)* (n 1).

7.38 In the evening of day one of a two-day capacity hearing, the expert had the opportunity of reviewing care notes. In the morning of day two he told the court that he could not be confident of his conclusions (that Mrs CA had capacity across the board) given what he had read. One of the difficulties in the case had been that the local authority had asked the court to make a series of findings of coercive and controlling behaviour by the daughter, which the daughter strongly disputed. The local authority had suggested the court should first establish the facts, and only then could Mrs CA's capacity be assessed. Those facts would be 'the information relevant to the decision' per s 3(1) of MCA 2005 which the assessor could then evaluate whether P was able to understand, retain, use or weigh, and communicate a decision.[17] The court had initially disagreed with that suggested approach, and in his first assessment of Mrs CA, the psychiatrist had not put to Mrs CA many of the allegations.

7.39 The psychiatrist told the court that his faith in his own conclusions had diminished overnight having read the care records, and that he may inadvertently have come to the wrong conclusions. The judge adjourned the hearing and directed the parties to agree a detailed letter of instruction for the psychiatrist setting out the main allegations so that he could put them to Mrs CA and evaluate her responses. Although Ms DA thought this was unfair because those allegations had not (yet) been proven, the court took the view that it was important for the assessor to put the allegations to Mrs CA for the purposes of gaining information about her capacity to make relevant decisions.

7.40 The court relisted the capacity hearing to be heard on day two of a four-day hearing, day one of which would be the fact-finding hearing. At the fact-finding hearing, the court found all the local authority's 11 consolidated allegations proved. These included that Ms DA had caused upset to her mother while her mother was in hospital, which the daughter noted was because of a conspiracy by the local authority and others which led to complaints being made about her. The judge dismissed the conspiracy theory by saying it would involve too many staff who had no motive to lie.

7.41 The court found that Ms DA made her mother walk around the ward when Mrs CA was reluctant to do so, and shouted at her mother when she thought she was not drinking enough, calling her a 'senile old woman'. The daughter described this as typical banter between them. The daughter denied holding up a wet pad to her mother's face and saying 'Have you pissed yourself again, mum?', which the judge found proved as staff had witnessed it, and it was just the sort of thing Ms DA would say and do.

17 For a discussion of relevant information in capacity assessments, see 'All practicable steps' at para 3.13 in Chapter 3, above.

7.42 Further allegations included setting up a camera and audio system so that the daughter could monitor the carers in her mother's house and command them through the speakers. The court found that the daughter was controlling of the carers and her mother, and that the daughter, 'who has little or no self-control or anger management, would insult the carers looking after her mother'.

7.43 Then there were two allegations of physical abuse, both denied, but found proved. One was that the daughter tried to force-feed her mother pizza, and the other was that she tipped a bowl of lasagne over her mother's head. After the lasagne incident, the daughter was arrested for assault and was on police bail. It was this incident that prompted the local authority to make an application to the Court of Protection.

7.44 Two allegations concerned Mrs CA's ex-husband who was still involved in her life. The first was that while Ms DA was bailed for the assault and bail conditions prohibited her from contacting her mother, the ex-husband went to see Mrs CA and tried to persuade her to tell the carers (including the witness to the alleged assault) that she did not need them any longer. The court found that he did so, probably hoping to ensure that the prosecution of his daughter was dropped. The second allegation was that on two dates he told Mrs CA that if she wanted to see her daughter again, she should contact social services to change the carer who had given a statement about the lasagne assault to the police.

7.45 The court concluded that Ms DA 'fails to make any allowances for her mother's age and frailty. She is hoping that by force of her personality she can keep her mother healthy and able to look after herself. There is no doubt in my mind that mother and daughter love each other deeply and DA has certainly cared for her mother as much as she is able to'. Ms DA had persuaded Mrs CA that she was 'lazy and stubborn and that her failure to look after herself better is her own fault', and that Ms DA 'bullies and forces her mother to do the things that she believes will keep her alive for longer. When she force-feeds her it is because her mother is not eating enough and she has had anorexia. Their relationship of verbal abuse is mutual, but CA is ageing and getting increasingly frail and deserves a different approach from an adult daughter.'

7.46 The judge dismissed Ms DA's unevidenced assertion that the local authority was persecuting her, finding that Mrs CA 'is subject to the undue influence of her daughter in a number of different ways'. Ms DA's personality led her to behave in the manner she had: 'She lacks self-control and in particular she is unable to control her anger at times. CA describes her daughter as bullish and brutish, and I agree with that description. It is a dysfunctional, volatile relationship with a mother and daughter who are enmeshed and depend on each other emotionally'. This was a smothering relationship where boundaries did not exist.

7.47 On capacity, the judge agreed with the expert that Mrs CA lacked capacity to conduct proceedings, lacked capacity to decide on care, lacked capacity to manage her finances.

7.48 As to decisions about contact with others, the expert had put to Mrs CA the facts that the court had found proven and Mrs CA told him, 'It's so traumatic that I can't even remember what happened now, but we've always had arguments'. The judge noted that Mrs CA herself described her daughter as 'brutish' and 'bullish', and that they were 'devoted to each other but have at times a fiery relationship punctuated by abuse'. The court noted that mother and daughter had had a tempestuous relationship for decades, but Ms DA 'had not adapted to her mother's increasing frailty, and she needed to learn to soften her approach to her mother'. The court agreed with the expert that Mrs CA had capacity to enter into and revoke the LPAs.

7.49 As for the inherent jurisdiction, the court noted that Mrs CA had a very poor memory and that she tended to do what her family wanted her to do, even if it was not in her best interests. An example of this was when she went along with the family's suggestion that she should dismiss the carer. This, in the judge's view, was undue influence. The judge noted that Mrs CA was unable to stand up to her daughter when the daughter assaulted her, and that there was a power imbalance between the two of them. Mrs CA described herself to the expert as vulnerable, and the judge agreed. The court directed that to prevent Mrs CA from ongoing harm from her daughter, contact between the two of them should be supervised by the live-in carer. The judge left the LPAs intact, but issued 11 injunctive directions against the daughter to circumscribe her behaviour, and found the use of the inherent jurisdiction as a means to interfere with the family's Article 8 ECHR rights was justified to protect Mrs CA.

7.50 In a later judgment, Arbuthnot J found Ms DA in contempt of court for five breaches of undertakings Ms DA had made to the court and the injunctions noted in the preceding paragraph.[18] The court imposed a fine of £500.

FORCED RELATIONSHIPS

Ms AG

7.51 The final section of this chapter provides three examples of how the inherent jurisdiction can be used to bolster the frameworks of the Care Act 2014

18 [2025] EWCOP 15 (T3). A third judgment in this case concerns an application to vary reporting restrictions: [2025] EWCOP 16 (T3).

and the MCA 2005. The first example is Ms AG who was 24 years old and had a mild learning disability.[19] The local authority made an application under the inherent jurisdiction for protective orders and for a forced marriage protection order for one year to prevent her from travelling to Pakistan to get married. She had undergone a marriage ceremony previously in circumstances which were unclear, so the court could not determine whether Ms AG had been married, and there was some evidence that she had subsequently divorced under Pakistani and Sharia law. The uncertainty was caused by 'the failure of the local authority to properly investigate and analyse the evidence, or keep it under review'.

7.52 Ms AG had then made a (capacitous) decision to move to a shared lives arrangement. She felt unable to tell her parents as they wanted her to live with them. The judge found evidence of parental control and coercion, but it was unclear how the coercion linked to a risk that the parents would force Ms AG into a new marriage.

7.53 The judge accepted the submission of the Official Solicitor, who sought a six-month review of the order, partly because the local authority had failed to undertake the necessary assessments. Under the inherent jurisdiction, the court made a limited term order regulating contact between Ms AG and her parents of one telephone call a day and two periods of face-to-face contact each week.

Ms EF

7.54 A case where the local authority's application for protective orders did not succeed was in the case of Ms EF.[20] She was a vulnerable 18-year-old woman who had capacity to decide to travel to Brazil to continue a romantic relationship with a 29-year-old man Mr GH who the applicant local authority considered had groomed her. The local authority sought a six-month travel ban to prevent Ms EF travelling to see him.

7.55 The court found worrying features, including that the relationship started when she was a child, as well as Mr GH's 'addiction to porn, him downloading child pornography, her mental ill health and vulnerability and him being willing for her to move to Brazil despite the risks to her health'. That said, the court did not find that Mr GH had groomed her and decided that the order sought was dictatorial and unjustified in the circumstances, noting that the inherent jurisdiction should be used sparingly to enhance a vulnerable person's rights under Article 8 ECHR rather than limit them.

19 *Luton Borough Council v G and others* [2024] EWCOP 18.
20 *London Borough of Islington v EF* [2022] EWHC 803 (Fam).

Amina

7.56 The inherent jurisdiction is so far-reaching that it can protect a vulnerable British adult who is not habitually resident in England and Wales. In *Re Al-jeffrey*,[21] the court was concerned with a young woman called Amina. When she was 17, her father (a Saudi national) took Amina from the UK to Saudi Arabia. Four years later, proceedings were commenced in England on her behalf, pursuant to the Forced Marriage (Civil Protection) Act 2007 and the inherent jurisdiction on the basis that Amina was a dual British and Saudi national. On Amina's instructions, those proceedings were dismissed and all orders discharged in April 2013. Despite expressing her earnest wish to return to the UK, Amina's father did not permit her to leave Saudi Arabia.

7.57 When she was 21, Amina applied for relief under the inherent jurisdiction. She said that her father had tricked her into dropping the earlier proceedings, and that he ill-treated her, kept her under constraint in his flat, and prevented her from leaving Saudi Arabia. The father had refused to comply with a court direction to allow Amina unrestricted confidential and secure access to the British consul and to her solicitor. These events, the court held, 'vividly illustrate and underline the degree of continuing control and constraint being exercised'.

7.58 The court considered the peril from which Amina needed to be rescued,[22] finding that Amina was under constraint and had suffered ill-treatment such that she was disabled from functioning as an independent adult. The inherent jurisdiction was engaged, albeit that Amina had not lived or been present in England or Wales since 2012 and was, when the hearing took place in 2016, habitually resident in Saudi Arabia. The judge granted Amina's application and directed her father to permit and facilitate Amina's return to the UK if she so wished and to pay the air fare. Explaining the decision, the judge said the intention was not to force Amina to do anything, but 'to create conditions in which she, as an adult of full capacity, can exercise and implement her own independent free will and freedom of choice'.

CONCLUSIONS

7.59 The cases presented in this chapter illustrate how the court treats 'vulnerability' in the descriptive sense rather than as a precise legal formulation. The phenomenon of coercive control, considered in Chapter 2, sits at the core of the broad descriptor of being stripped of the ability to make a free choice. The court's mission under the inherent jurisdiction, is to rescue the person from a controlling situation, and create the conditions in which the adult can exercise choice, free from the constraints of others.

21 *Amina Al-Jeffery v Mohammed Al-Jeffery* [2016] EWHC 2151 (Fam).

22 This phrase emanates from case law on the inherent jurisdiction for children. See *Re B (A Child) (Habitual Residence: Inherent Jurisdiction)* [2016] UKSC 4, para 60.

7.60 In certain circumstances, it may be appropriate for a court to make interim orders that ensure that the appropriate public bodies are able to carry out necessary investigations and assessments. The use of the inherent jurisdiction to hold the fort while clarity is obtained is important in cases where a perpetrator of coercive control makes such information-gathering impossible.

7.61 The Family Division of the High Court has a wide range of remedies in its inherent jurisdiction arsenal and the cases presented in this chapter have shown how the court's remedies can have a profound impact on both the victim/survivor of coercive control and the perpetrator, and remedies are considered further in Chapter 9. The next chapter considers the court's approach where facts need to be determined before the court makes orders to protect the victim/survivor of coercive control.

CHAPTER 8

Finding facts

'... key to this particular form of domestic abuse is an appreciation that it requires an evaluation of a pattern of behaviour in which the significance of isolated incidents can only truly be understood in the context of a much wider picture'[1]

INTRODUCTION

8.01 Fact-finding hearings are 'relatively rare'[2] in the Court of Protection. They 'require tight judicial control and an unswerving focus both on their scope and ambit as well as on purpose'.[3] This chapter outlines the circumstances in which disputed facts may need to be determined, before the Court of Protection makes best interests decisions (at para 8.02), or the High Court makes protective orders under its inherent jurisdiction (at para 8.12). Fact-finding raises ethical and practical challenges for lawyers in coercive and controlling cases, and these are further considered in Chapters 11 to 13.

FACT-FINDING IN THE COURT OF PROTECTION

Why establish facts?

8.02 The Vice-President of the Court of Protection has held that: 'The facts which are sought to be found must have a direct impact on the welfare decisions that need to be made in respect of P. The fact finding must be 'necessary' for the determination of those welfare decisions'.[4]

8.03 Where a pattern of coercive and/or controlling abusive behaviour is alleged and the determination of that issue is likely to be relevant to the assessment of the risk of future harm and best interests decisions, the matter will need to be determined by the court.[5] An example is the case of *Re PB* which was considered in in Chapter 5, where the factual findings enabled the court to decide that it was

1 Hayden J in *F v M* [2021] EWFC 4, para 60.
2 *Nottinghamshire County Council v SV & Anor* [2025] EWCOP 37 (T3), para 48.
3 *An ICB v G (by her litigation friend the Official Solicitor) and others* [2024] EWCOP 13, para 23.
4 *Nottinghamshire County Council v SV & Anor* (n 2), para 55.
5 *Re H-N and others (Children) (Domestic Abuse: Finding of Fact Hearings)* [2021] EWCA Civ 448, para 53.

in Mrs PB's best interests to remain in the care home and to restrict contact with her husband.[6]

8.04 In coercive control cases, where decisions may involve leaving the victim/survivor in an abusive environment or removing them from their home, Article 8 of the European Convention on Human Rights will be engaged, and absent a urgent interim decision needing to be made, the court typically avoids making such significant decisions without facts that are either agreed or judicially determined.

8.05 It is not uncommon for the controlling person, once accused of controlling behaviour, to ask the court to find facts against the local authority as a quasi counterclaim. Although each case turns on its facts, the Court of Protection is not a supervisory court or a guardian and will likely not permit a party to use court proceedings to conduct a wider investigation.

Facts before capacity

8.06 In *some* cases, capacity can only be assessed after facts are established. For example, it may be appropriate to determine the allegation that P's husband controlled and denied her access to family and friends *before* assessing P's ability to understand, retain and use or weigh that piece of relevant information, which (if it is a fact) the capacity assessor must put to P during the assessment (see Chapter 4 for the information relevant to a capacity assessment).

Determining whether to hold a fact-finding hearing

8.07 The decision to hold a fact-finding hearing is a case management decision and an exercise of power under the Court of Protection Rules 2017 (COPR 2017).[7] The court will seek to give effect to the overriding objective of the COPR 2017 which is to deal with a case justly and at proportionate cost.[8] This means that the court will: deal with the case expeditiously and fairly; properly consider P's interests and position; deal with the case in a way that is proportionate to the nature, importance and complexity of the issues; ensure that the parties are on an equal footing; save expense; allot to the case an appropriate share of the court's resources, while taking account of the need to allot resources to other cases; and enforce compliance with rules, practice directions and orders.[9]

6 *MB v PB (by her litigation friend the Official Solicitor) and others* [2022] EWCOP 14, para 13.

7 These are decisions governed by COPR 2017, r 1.3(3)(f) which places a duty on the court to actively manage a case including by deciding promptly which issues need a full investigation and hearing and which do not and the procedure to be followed in the case; and by virtue of r 3.1.(2)(h) under which the court can direct a separate hearing, for example, to establish facts.

8 COPR 2017, r 1.1.

9 COPR 2017, r 1.1(3).

8.08 There is no threshold requirement in the Mental Capacity Act 2005 (MCA 2005) as to when a fact-finding hearing is necessary. The Court of Appeal in *Re H-N* provided guidance as to the circumstances in which such hearings are appropriate in family law cases involving domestic abuse.[10] The Court of Protection has applied this guidance.[11]

8.09 Adapting the *Re H-N* guidance, in cases where coercive control is alleged in the Court of Protection, and, it is suggested, under the inherent jurisdiction of the High Court – with some flexible bending of the Civil Procedure Rules (CPR) to create an inquisitorial forum (see Chapter 6) – the court is likely to consider the following factors:

(1) **Direct impact on the court's decision-making**: The nature of the allegations and the extent to which findings are relevant in deciding:

  (a) in the Court of Protection: best interests decisions on behalf of P; and

  (b) in the inherent jurisdiction: whether the adult is a vulnerable adult in need of a protective order.

(2) **Purpose**: This is to provide a basis of assessment of risk and therefore the impact of the alleged coercive control on:

  (a) in the Court of Protection: P; and

  (b) in the inherent jurisdiction: the adult who is said to be vulnerable.

(3) **Necessity and proportionality**: This includes whether there is other evidence which provides a sufficient factual basis to proceed and the relevance to the issue before the court if the allegations are proved.

(4) **Practicalities**: This includes the pressures on the court, including the likely cost to public funds, court resources and the diversion from other cases, achieving a fair and just process, practical limits to a party's desire to litigate every issue, the effect of adjourning a case on the administration of justice, and effect of delay on the welfare of:

  (a) in the Court of Protection: P; and

  (b) in the inherent jurisdiction: the adult who is said to be vulnerable.

10 *H-N And Others (Children) (Domestic Abuse: Finding of Fact Hearings)* (n 5). The Court of Appeal handed down its judgment on 30 March 2021, and referred to the decision of Hayden J in the family law coercive control case of *F v M* (n 1) to which the Court of Appeal made reference. Those cases refer to the Family Procedure Rules 2010: Practice Direction 12J – Child Arrangements and Contact Orders: Domestic Abuse and Harm (PD12J). See in particular para 37 of *Re H-N* (n 5). See also *K v K* [2022] EWCA Civ 468.

11 *Re MB* (n 6) and *Nottinghamshire County Council v SV & Anor* (n 2).

Interim findings

8.10 Parties will sometimes request the court to make interim decisions at directions hearings, which are typically listed for one or two hours. This timeframe is usually insufficient for the judge to read in, hear evidence and submissions, consider the case, and hand down a judgment. Typically, parties will agree on an interim solution for the victim/survivor of coercive control on a without prejudice basis, that is, the controlling person makes no admissions of wrongdoing and no findings are recorded in the order.

8.11 Alternatively, if there is no urgent need for an interim decision because the victim/survivor is not at risk of harm, the parties may invite the court to list a longer hearing to determine the facts in the interim. This approach avoids waiting several months for a multi-day hearing to establish facts and make longer-term decisions.[12]

FACT-FINDING IN THE INHERENT JURISDICTION

8.12 In cases under the inherent jurisdiction involving allegations of coercive control, parties often have sharply different views of the facts. The local authority might gather evidence from multiple sources to argue that the adult is vulnerable and in need of protection, in particular where as a result of trauma, the victim/survivor has a fragmented recall of the events (see Chapter 10). Conversely, the controlling person may deny these allegations, claiming they are misconstrued, misunderstood, or simply made up. The victim/survivor might agree with either party or provide different accounts to different people.

8.13 The court will consider the victim/survivor's views, but these are not decisive in determining whether to pursue a fact-finding process. It is crucial to establish that the adult is 'vulnerable' as defined in the *Re SA* case,[13] discussed in Chapter 6. The court will examine documentary evidence and resolve any factual disputes by hearing evidence.

8.14 For instance, before deciding whether a person should stay in a care home or return to their marital home with an apparently controlling partner who is said to have blocked access to carers, the court must determine if (a) the person is vulnerable in *Re SA* terms, (b) the partner was controlling, and (c) the partner prevented carers from entering the home. In such cases, a fact-finding hearing may be held before making an order under the inherent jurisdiction.

12 See *LBX v TT* [2014] EWCOP 24.
13 *Re SA (Vulnerable Adult with Capacity: Marriage)* [2005] EWHC 2942 (Fam).

SCHEDULES OF ALLEGATIONS

8.15 Typically, the party asking the court to find facts will be directed to file a schedule of allegations, sometimes called a Scott Schedule.[14] In abuse cases not involving coercive control, it may be straightforward to list dates, locations, and details of incidents of (for example) violence. However, drafting a schedule for coercive control cases is challenging because coercive control is a *pattern* of behaviour, there may be no violent incidents at all, the time period may span several years or decades, and it is important to establish the *impact* on the victim/survivor. These factors do not easily lend themselves to be enumerated in a list.

8.16 In January 2021, Hayden J published a judgment commenting on the use of schedules in coercive control cases.[15] He held that a focus on specific incidents might be counterproductive when assessing a long-term pattern of behaviour: in coercive control cases, the use of a schedule was 'both ineffective and frequently unsuitable'.

8.17 Two months later, the Court of Appeal commented on schedules in *Re H-N*. The court said that, '[a]busive, coercive and controlling behaviour is likely to have a cumulative impact upon its victims which would not be identified simply by separate and isolated consideration of individual incidents'.[16] The Court of Appeal advised that a trial judge should limit the number of incidents on a schedule to key events. However, this approach can make it difficult to identify a *pattern* of behaviour:

> By reducing and then further reducing its field of focus, the court is said to have robbed itself of a vantage point from which to view the quality of the alleged perpetrator's behaviour as a whole and, importantly, removed consideration of whether there was a *pattern* of coercive and controlling behaviour from its assessment.[17]

8.18 The Court of Appeal did not determine what should replace schedules, but suggested that when faced with a fact-finding conundrum, a judge should start by identifying the form of harm and then examining the granular detail. This could be done by way of a 'narrative statement' focusing on the overall nature of the relationship, whether a person has been harmed, and in what manner. The judge would then be able to decide which facts need determination at a fact-finding hearing.[18]

8.19 Hayden J had occasion to comment on schedules once more in the Court of Protection case of *Re G* in 2024.[19] There, he noted that alternatives to schedules

14 From the House of Lords case, *Scott v Scott* [1913] AC 417.
15 *F v M* (n 1), para 113 post script.
16 *Re H-N* (n 5), para 44. See also *F v M* (n 1), paras 41–49.
17 Ibid, para 45.
18 *F v M* (n 1), para 48.
19 *Re G* [2024] EWCOP 13, para 43.

were elusive. The Official Solicitor suggested that the court should approach its judgment by narrative findings which would be similar to the 'narrative statement' idea mooted by the Court of Appeal in *H-N*: this would allow the court to consider the overall nature of the relationships in focus and identify the real character of the allegations before going on to examine the detail. Hayden J did not replace the micro for the macro, instead saying that he had 'endeavoured to address the overall picture emerging from the broad evidential canvas as well as its individual parts'.[20]

8.20 Judges must decide the best way to identify a pattern of coercive control, and the pros and cons of various approaches will continue to be developed through case law.

FACT-FINDING HEARINGS

8.21 A fact-finding hearing is court hearing during which documentary evidence is read, and evidence is heard from live witnesses, and submissions are then made by (or on behalf of) each party. The court then determines whether the allegations are found proved by issuing a judgment.

Timetabling a fact-finding hearing

8.22 Creating witness templates, or timetables, for fact-finding hearings is challenging. Judges must balance competing interests. The local authority aims to establish enough incidents or behaviours to demonstrate a pattern of coercive control and secure the desired orders. The controlling person may wish to cross-examine witnesses, and this may take up much time, particularly if the person is unrepresented.

8.23 Against this backdrop, the Court of Appeal has advised that the judge should:

> … set a proportionate timetable and to maintain control of the court process where it has been determined that a fact-finding hearing is necessary. It is, however, our expectation that, in cases where an alleged pattern of coercive and/or controlling behaviour falls for determination, and the court has made that issue its primary focus, the need to determine a range of subsidiary date-specific factual allegations will cease to be 'necessary' (unless any particular factual allegation is so serious that it justifies determination irrespective of any alleged pattern of coercive and/or controlling behaviour).[21]

20 Ibid.
21 *Re H-N* (n 5), para 56.

8.24 The court may direct counsel to prepare a witness template that contains judicial reading time, submissions at the end of the evidence, time for the judge to consider their judgment, and then hand it down: either in court (as an *ex tempore* judgment), or some days or weeks later in writing.

Witnesses

Court of Protection

8.25 The Court of Protection can control evidence by giving directions about (i) the issues on which it requires evidence, (ii) the nature of the evidence it needs, and (iii) the way in which the evidence is presented.[22] The COPR 2017 provides that the court can exclude evidence that would otherwise be admissible; allow or limit cross-examination; and admit such evidence, whether written or oral, as it thinks fit. P may provide information in writing, through a solicitor, or orally (this need not be on oath).[23]

8.26 A witness can rely on their written evidence before a final hearing, but any fact which needs to be proved by evidence of a witness can only be proved at a final hearing by that witness's oral evidence. Where a witness is called to give oral evidence, the witness statement or statements stands as that witness' evidence in chief unless the court directs otherwise, for example, to amplify the witness statement or give evidence about a matter that has arisen since the witness statement was made.

8.27 The COPR 2017 provides that the court will only give permission to do this 'if it considers that there is good reason not to confine the evidence of the witness to the contents of the witness statement'.[24] The court may be more flexible with litigants in person, allowing them to summarise their written evidence in the witness box. However, judges will likely maintain strict control over the hearing timetable.

8.28 Witnesses may give evidence via video link,[25] but post-pandemic practice generally requires courtroom presence unless there are exceptional circumstances.

Inherent jurisdiction

8.29 Rules under the inherent jurisdiction are similar. As explained in Chapter 6, cases under the inherent jurisdiction are governed by the CPR. Part 32 CPR outlines evidence rules similar to Part 14 of the COPR 2017. Rule

22 COPR 2017, r 14.2.
23 COPR 2017, r 14.2(e). Participation of a victim/survivor is considered in Chapter 11.
24 COPR 2017, r 14.3(4).
25 COPR 2017, r 14.5.

32.5 CPR goes slightly further than the COPR 2017 by specifying that if a party wishes to rely on a witness statement at trial, they 'must call the witness to give oral evidence unless the court orders otherwise or he puts the statement in as hearsay evidence'.[26]

The hearing itself

8.30 Fact-finding hearings 'require tight judicial control and an unswerving focus both on their scope and ambit as well as on purpose'.[27] The Court of Protection has said that the framework of fact-finding hearings is 'broadly the same' as in the family courts. Baker J (as he then was) has explained:

> First, the burden of proof lies with the local authority. It is the local authority that brings these proceedings and identifies the findings that they invite the court to make. Therefore, the burden of proving the allegations rests with them.
>
> Secondly, the standard of proof is the balance of probabilities: *Re B (Children)* [2008] UKHR 35. If the local authority proves a fact on the balance of probabilities, this court will treat that fact as established and all future decisions concerning M›s future will be based on that finding. Equally, if the local authority fails to prove any allegation, the court will disregard that allegation completely …
>
> In my judgment, the same approach must surely apply in the Court of Protection where the court is carrying out a similar exercise in determining the facts upon which to base decisions as to the best interests of an incapacitated adult.
>
> Thirdly, findings of fact in these cases must be based on evidence. As Munby J (as he then was) observed in *Re A (A Child: Fact-finding hearing: speculation)* [2011] EWCA Civ 12:
>
>> 'It is an elementary proposition that findings of fact must be based on evidence, including inferences that can properly be drawn from the evidence, and not on suspicion or speculation.'
>
> Fourth, the court must take into account all the evidence and, furthermore, consider each piece of evidence in the context of all the other evidence. As Dame Elizabeth Butler-Sloss, President, observed in *Re T* [2004] EWCA Civ 458, [2005] 2 FLR 838, at paragraph 33:
>
>> 'Evidence cannot be evaluated and assessed in separate compartments. A judge in these difficult cases must have regard to the relevance of each piece of evidence to the other evidence and to exercise an overview of

26 CPR 32.5(1). See also Part 33 for provisions on hearsay evidence.
27 *Re G* (n 19), para 23.

the totality of the evidence in order to come to the conclusion whether the case put forward by the local authority has been made out to the appropriate standard of proof.'

Fifth, whilst appropriate attention must be paid to the opinion of medical experts, those opinions need to be considered in the context of all the other evidence. The roles of the court and the experts are distinct. It is the court that is in the position to weigh up expert evidence against the other evidence: *A County Council v. K, D and L* [2005] EWHC 144 Fam, [2005] 2005] 1 FLR 851 per Charles J.

Sixth, in assessing the expert evidence, which involves a multi-disciplinary analysis of the medical information conducted by a group of specialists, each bringing their own expertise to bear on the problem, one important consideration – and of particular relevance in this case – is that the court must be careful to ensure that each expert keeps within the bounds of their own expertise and defers where appropriate to the expertise of others – see the observations of Eleanor King J in *Re S* [2009] EWHC 2115 Fam.

Seventh, the evidence of the parents is of the utmost importance. It is essential that the court forms a clear assessment of their credibility and reliability. They must have the fullest opportunity to take part in the hearing and the court is likely to place considerable weight on the evidence and impressions it forms of them – see *Re W and another (Non-accidental injury)* [2003] FCR 346.

Eighth, it is not uncommon for witnesses in these cases to tell lies, both before and during the hearing. The court must be careful to bear in mind that a witness may lie for many reasons – such as shame, misplaced loyalty, panic, fear and distress – and the fact that a witness has lied about some matters does not mean that he or she has lied about everything – see *R v. Lucas* [1981] QB 720. The assessment of the truthfulness is an important part of my function in this case.'[28]

8.31 This list has been applied in the Court of Protection. In Chapter 7 we considered the case of *Re CA*,[29] where an adult daughter controlled her elderly mother. At paragraph 16, Arbuthnot J added four more principles to Baker J's list above:

(a) Findings can be drawn from the account and demeanour of a party or a witness or an assessment of the family, but the court should bear in mind that memories fade and change with time, sometimes matters are remembered

28 *A Local Authority v M* [2014] EWCOP 33, [2015] COPLR 6, paras 82–90. Baker J's list has been cited with approval more recently in the Court of Protection by Hayden J in *An ICB v G (by her litigation friend the Official Solicitor) and others* [2024] EWCOP 13, where Hayden J said at para 23 that, '[…] fact-finding hearings in the Court of Protection, as in the Family Court, require tight judicial control and an unswerving focus both on their scope and ambit as well as on purpose'.

29 *Re CA (Fact Finding – Capacity – Inherent Jurisdiction – Injunctive Relief)* [2024] EWCOP 64 (T3), considered in Chapter 7.

that were not remembered initially but the court should be careful that it is not imagination that is becoming more active or memory being affected by strong emotion or mental health challenges.

(b) A witness may come to honestly believe something happened or did not happen when it bears either no or little relation to the events that occurred at the time.

(c) In assessing and weighing the impression which the Court forms of all the witnesses, the court must also keep in mind the observations of Macur LJ in *Re M*, that '… any judge appraising witnesses in the emotionally charged atmosphere of a contested family dispute should warn themselves to guard against an assessment solely by virtue of their behaviour in the witness box and to expressly indicate that they have done so.'[30]

(d) Hearsay evidence is admissible but the weight to be given to that evidence is a matter for the Court. The Court will look to see, for example, if it is receiving multiple hearsay or whether the evidence is contemporaneous with the events it describes, whether there was a motive for the witness to falsify their evidence or whether from other evidence it is clear that the hearsay is (or may be) wrong or mistaken. This is a particularly relevant consideration for the Court where a number of allegations are not directly from witnesses but are taken from hospital complaints which were set out in local authority records.[31]

8.32 In *Re CA*, Arbuthnot J expanded on the *Lucas* direction at point 8 in Baker J's list, in para 8.30, above. Arbuthnot J said that the guidance in *R v Lucas* was that, if a person is lying or telling the truth about point A it does not mean that they are lying about or telling the truth about point B.[32] There are many reasons why a person might lie including (as examples given by Lord Lane in *R v Lucas*) an attempt to bolster up a just cause, shame, or an attempt to conceal disgraceful behaviour from their family.[33]

8.33 In 2016 the Court of Appeal commented on the application of the *Lucas* direction in family proceedings. It held that the court needs to go beyond reminding itself of the principle, but must properly apply the principles in *R v*

30 *Re M (Children)* [2013] EWCA Civ 1147, para 12.

31 The COPR 2017 are silent on the issue of hearsay (as was the previous 2007 version). In *London Borough of Enfield v SA* [2010] EWHC 196 (Admin), [2010] COPLR Con Vol 362, McFarlane J held that the Court of Protection has 'power to admit hearsay evidence which originates from a person who is not competent as a witness and which would otherwise be inadmissible …'. The weight to be attached to any evidence will be a matter for specific evaluation in each individual case. Within that evaluation, the fact that the individual from whom the evidence originates is not a competent witness will be an important factor. For anonymous hearsay evidence, see *Re G (Court of Protection: Injunction)* [2022] EWCA Civ 1312, para 93.

32 *R v Lucas* [1982] QB 720 and *R v Middleton* [2000] TLR 293.

33 It is interesting to note that shame features heavily in the trauma literature, considered in Chapter 10, reinforcing the observation that a person exhibiting coercive and controlling behaviour may have experienced trauma themselves.

Lucas.[34] Subsequent to the Court of Appeal's decision, Lieven J has summarised the approach to be taken as follows:

> The Court should first determine if the alleged perpetrator has deliberately lied. Then, if such a finding is made, consider why the party lied. The Court should caution itself that the mere fact an alleged perpetrator tells a lie is not evidence that they are culpable of the incident alleged. The Court should remind itself that a person may lie for many reasons, including 'innocent' explanations in the sense that they do not denote culpability of the incident alleged.[35]

The judgment

8.34 After the hearing, the court will issue a judgment. This may be an *ex tempore* judgment, which is an oral decision spoken into the record, or the court may 'reserve judgment' and provide a written decision at a later date.

8.35 A judgment from a fact-finding hearing follows a formulaic structure. It addresses each allegation in turn, describes the allegation, summarises the evidence provided by the party seeking to prove the allegation (including any oral evidence), summarises the evidence of the person against whom the allegation is made, and states the court's decision on whether the allegation is proved on the balance of probabilities.

8.36 In cases of coercive and controlling behaviour, the judgment is likely to include commentary on whether any individual incidents found proved constitute a pattern of coercive control. The court's determination on this issue may be informed by expert evidence.

CONCLUSIONS

8.37 When making best interests decisions on behalf of P, the Court of Protection 'must consider all the relevant circumstances'.[36] In many coercive control cases, the person accused of such behaviour may deny it or offer alternative explanations. The judge can decide that proceeding on a disputed factual basis is insufficient and may clarify what happened to P, as these are relevant circumstances for future-focused best interests decisions.

8.38 Similarly, a judge in the inherent jurisdiction may seek a firm factual basis before determining whether coercive control happened, whether the adult

34 *Re H-C (Children)* [2016] EWCA Civ 139, para 100 onwards.
35 *Wakefield Metropolitan District Council v R & Others* [2019] EWHC 3581 (Fam), para 109.
36 MCA 2005, s 4(2).

is 'vulnerable' and whether protective orders are necessary and proportionate, including their nature and scope.

8.39 This chapter has explained the mechanics of fact-finding hearings, including the challenges an applicant local authority might face in presenting its case, given judicial comments on the inadequacies of a list of allegations in establishing a pattern of behaviour.

8.40 Once facts are established, the court will make substantive decisions. The next chapter explains the types of decisions available to the court and the remedies it can provide in response to findings of coercive control.

CHAPTER 9

Remedies

'Mai nessun m'avrà! [No one will ever possess me!]'[1]

INTRODUCTION

9.01 This chapter explains the remedies that are available in cases of coercive control. These include best interests decisions in the Court of Protection (at para 9.05) in relation to the list of decision-making matters that were considered in Chapter 4: (a) conducting proceedings (at para 9.10); (b) deciding about residence (at para 9.11); (c) deciding about care (at para 9.13); (d) deciding about contact with others (at para 9.14); (e) deciding about disclosure of information to others (at para 9.18); (f) managing property and financial affairs (at para 9.19); (g) deciding on internet and social media use (at para 9.20); (g) executing and revoking a lasting power of attorney (at para 9.22); (h) engaging in sexual relations (at para 9.25); (i) deciding to marry (at para 9.26); and (j) making a will (at para 9.27).

9.02 We then consider remedies in the inherent jurisdiction (at para 9.28). These are aimed to be facilitative. That is, any restrictions shall remain in place for no longer than necessary for the adult to take decisions for themselves, free from the control or influence of another.

9.03 The chapter then looks at the circumstances in which parties can give an agreement (at para 9.36) or an undertaking (at para 9.37). It sets out the legal test for granting an injunction against the controlling person (at para 9.36), and the implications for breaching such orders. Interim remedies are then considered (at para 9.46): the court may need to make decisions that 'hold the fort', or protect the victim/survivor from imminent harm by, for example, removing them to a place of safety.

9.04 Finally, the chapter summarises ancillary civil remedies that practitioners may need to consider (at para 9.60). These include non-molestation orders, forced marriage protection orders, restraining orders, and domestic abuse protection orders.

1 Giacomo Verdi, *Turandot*.

Best interests decisions in the Court of Protection

9.05 A finding of a coercive control may well be relevant to decisions the court is asked to make in the victim/survivor's best interests. An illustration of how the Court of Protection considers 'all the relevant circumstances' is *Re BU*,[2] considered in Chapter 5.[3] It would have been artificial and narrow for the judge to have put out of her mind the coercion and control that Mr NC had exerted over Ms BU, despite them not having had contact for over a year. The court took into account the severity of the coercive control in deciding that it was in Ms BU's best interests to sever contact with Mr NC.

9.06 For the purposes of the subject matter of this book, it is important to note that the Mental Capacity Act 2005 (MCA 2005) says very little about what best interests actually is. If sets out some basic requirements before the best interests decision-maker (including the Court of Protection) makes a best interests decision.

9.07 Regarding the subject matter of this book, it is important to note that the MCA 2005, s 4 provides limited guidance on what constitutes 'best interests'. It outlines some basic requirements that the decision-maker, including the Court of Protection, must consider before making a best interests decision. These are:

(1) Have regard to whether the purpose for which it is needed can be as effectively achieved in a way that is less restrictive of the person's rights and freedom of action.[4]

(2) Do not determine best interests on the basis of P's age or appearance;[5]

(3) Do not determine best interests based on P's condition or an aspect of their behaviour which might lead others to make unjustified assumptions about what might be in their best interests;[6]

(4) Consider all the relevant circumstances. These include those that the decision-maker was aware of, and those which it would be reasonable to regard as relevant;[7]

(5) Consider the likelihood of P at some time having capacity in relation to the matter in question, and if yes, when.[8]

(6) As far as reasonably practicable, permit and encourage P to participate, or to improve their ability to participate, as fully as possible in any act done for them and any decision affecting them.[9]

2 *WU v BU* [2021] EWCOP 54.
3 MCA 2005, s 4(2).
4 MCA 2005, s 1(6).
5 MCA 2005, s 4(1)(a).
6 MCA 2005, s 4(1)(b).
7 MCA 2005, s 4(2) and (11).
8 MCA 2005, s 4(3).
9 MCA 2005, s 4(4).

(7) Consider, so far as is reasonably ascertainable, P's past and present wishes and feelings including anything they wrote when they had capacity;[10]

(8) Consider, if possible, P's beliefs and values that would likely influence their decision if they had capacity;[11]

(9) Consider the other factors that P would be likely consider if they were able to do so;[12]

(10) Take into account, if it is practicable and appropriate to consult them, the views of anyone who provides care for P, or who is interested in their welfare, or any attorney or deputy.[13]

9.08 If P lacks capacity to make a decision, the court can make that decision on behalf of P, in P's best interests. The court can decide between available options that are available, and has no power to direct a public body (or anyone else) to fund something they do not wish to.[14] This point may be misunderstood by the controlling person who may demand the public body to provide services to P that P does not require.

9.09 Chapter 4 of this book explained how the court determines capacity in several decision-making domains, and we now follow the same list to explore the sorts of best interests decisions the court could make, in the context of coercive control cases.

Conducting proceedings

9.10 If P lacks capacity to conduct proceedings, the court will appoint a litigation friend. This is not a best interests decision, but one of case management, and is considered further in Chapter 11.[15]

Residence

9.11 If P lacks capacity to decide on residence, the Court of Protection can decide where P should, in their best interests, live. If P has been removed from a property where they were subject to coercive control, the court decide (for example) that it is in not in P's best interests to return to their home, or that it is their best interests to move until further order to a place of safety. The court could direct the local authority to develop alternative residence options.

10 MCA 2005, s 4(6)(a).
11 MCA 2005, s 4(6)(b).
12 MCA 2005, s 4(6)(c).
13 MCA 2005, s 4(7).
14 *N v ACCG* [2017] UKSC 22.
15 See rules 17.1 to 17.8 of the Court of Protection Rules 2017.

9.12 The court can make a best interests decision for preliminary steps to be taken to plan P's move to a particular place. Once a transition plan and a care and support plan are in place, the court could authorise the move. If there is at least one viable option for residence, the court could make a more precise best interests decision, for example that, 'It is in P's best interests to reside in Almond Manor care home to receive care.'

Care

9.13 If P lacks capacity to decide on care, the Court of Protection can choose care that is available for P: the court can put itself in P's shoes and decide between options, in the same way as a capacious P with needs under the Care Act 2014 could make that choice.[16] Care covers a range of issues. For example, the local authority may invite the court to make a decision that it is in P's best interests:

(a) for their care needs to be met by a professional carer, not the controlling person;

(b) to be offered meal choices rather than their diet being dictated by the controlling person;

(c) for the controlling person to be prohibited from viewing P in their house via a video/audio system connected to an app because it is unnecessary and an interference with P's right to privacy; or

(d) not to participate in the controlling person's religious or cultural practices, such as trimming pubic hair.[17]

Contact with others

9.14 When a victim/survivor of coercive control lacks capacity to make decisions about contact with the controlling person, the Court of Protection can intervene to regulate contact. This may differ from what the controlling person believes is best for the victim/survivor.

9.15 As discussed in Chapter 5, the court can completely ban contact with certain individuals and if it is just and reasonable to do so, issue an injunction against the controlling person (injunctions are further explored in this chapter). The court has the authority to decide on the frequency, duration, location, and nature of contact. It can require that contact be supervised and can approve contact plans that prevent the contact person from discussing topics that might upset or

16 Choice is a key concept of the Care Act 2014, and the statutory guidance says at para 2.21: 'Giving people choice and control over the support they may need and access to the right information enables people to stay as well as possible, maintain independence and caring roles for longer.' See also para 4.38: 'Local authorities must encourage a range of different approaches to services to ensure people have a genuine choice of different types of service.'

17 See, for example, *Re IH (Observance of Muslim Practice)* [2017] EWCOP 9.

distress the victim/survivor. Additionally, the court can prohibit the controlling person from discussing care delivery with care staff, or criticising them, or telling the victim/survivor that they will come home. If contact is supervised, the court can allow the supervisor to end the contact if the controlling person causes distress to the victim/survivor. The court has extensive powers and often examines the details of contact, as it can provoke inappropriate behaviour from the controlling person.[18]

9.16 The controlling person might attempt to contact P, going as far as harassing care staff or taking gifts to the victim/survivor. Their behaviour during contact might threaten the stability of the placement. Chapter 5 discussed the case of *Re PB*, where the judge prioritised the stability of the care home placement over contact.

9.17 When placing restrictions on contact with others, the court must consider whether the interference with the victim/survivor's Article 8 of the European Convention on Human Rights (ECHR), which protects private and family life, is necessary and proportionate.[19]

Information sharing

9.18 Where the victim/survivor lacks capacity to share information with others, the court may determine what information is shared and with whom. It weighs up the pros and cons of sharing with the controlling person, who may claim entitlement if they have a caring role. If the victim/survivor lives with or is close to the controlling person, these claims may hold some weight. However, if the victim/survivor is in a safe place away from the controlling person, such arguments are less likely to succeed.

Property and financial affairs

9.19 Where the victim/survivor lacks capacity to manage their property and financial affairs, it is unlawful for 'informal' arrangement to continue. If the victim/survivor has few assets (generally less than around £5,000) and is in receipt of state benefits only, then an appointee can be appointed by the Department for Work and Pensions. Where the victim/survivor has more assets or owns property, a deputyship application will need to be made so that a deputy can make decisions about property and financial affairs in the victim/survivor's best interests. The Chancery Division has authority to set aside a document such as a trust deed on grounds of undue influence.[20]

18 *MB v PB* [2022] EWCOP 14.
19 ECHR considerations are considered in Chapter 6.
20 *Humphreys v Humphreys* [2004] EWHC 2201 (Ch).

Internet and social media

9.20 Where the victim/survivor lacks capacity to use the internet and social media, the Court of Protection can approve an internet plan in their best interests. Such a plan is usually written by a local authority, sometimes with the input from a specialist internet security company that might advise restrictions on hardware or software, including the instillation of software on devices that render it impossible for the user to download certain apps or access certain internet sites.

9.21 The content of an internet and social media plan varies from case to case and will need to be individualised to mitigate against the risks specific to the victim/survivor. One of these risks is post-separation contact by the controlling person and managing the risk that the victim/survivor may face, including seeking to control the victim/survivor through digital means (see Chapter 2 on post-separation abuse).

Lasting power of attorney

9.22 The Court of Protection can revoke a lasting power of attorney (LPA) or remove an attorney. This applies both with respect to LPAs governing property and affairs, and LPAs governing health and welfare. In coercive control cases two situations may arise:

(a) If the controlling person has coerced P into signing an LPA and/or naming the controlling person as the attorney, the court can determine whether the requirements for the creation of an LPA have been met.[21] One of these is that 'no fraud or undue pressure is being used to induce the donor to create a lasting power of attorney', which an external person must attest to on the certificate when the donor executes the LPA.[22] If the court determines that fraud or undue pressure was used, the court may direct that an unregistered LPA is not to be registered, or if it is already registered and P lacks capacity to do so, revoke the LPA.[23]

(b) If the attorney has behaved, is behaving, or proposes to behave in a way that contravenes his authority or is not in the donor's best interests, the court has the same powers to prevent registration or revoke the LPA.[24] The evidence that the attorney has behaved contrary to the P's best interests may have to be established by way of a fact-finding hearing (see Chapter 8).

9.23 When revoking an LPA, the Court of Protection must be satisfied that the victim/survivor of coercive control currently lacks capacity to revoke the instrument, otherwise it has no jurisdiction to make the decision on their behalf.[25]

21 MCA 2005, s 22(2)(a).
22 MCA 2005, Sch 1, para 2(e)(ii).
23 MCA 2005, s 22(3)(a) and (4).
24 MCA 2005, s 22(3)(b) and (4).
25 *Re DP (Revocation of Lasting Power of Attorney)* [2014] COPLR 188.

9.24 In *Re CA*, considered in Chapter 7,[26] the controlling daughter was her mother's health and welfare attorney. The court determined Mrs CA had capacity to make and terminate an LPA, so it had no power to revoke the instrument under MCA 2005, s 22. The court had determined that Mrs CA lacked capacity to decide on care, so the controlling daughter could continue to decide on care in a way (given the findings of physical and emotional abuse) that was controlling and harmful. The court left the LPA intact but made an injunctive order against the daughter, circumscribing her ability to make welfare decisions that were contrary to Mrs CA's best interests.

Engaging in sexual relations

9.25 If P lacks capacity to engage in sexual relations, proxy consent is not possible and no best interests decision may be made.[27] The local authority will have to develop a care plan that prevents the person from having sex.

Marrying

9.26 Similarly, if P lacks capacity to marry, no one else can consent to marry on their behalf and best interests decision may be made.[28] In appropriate circumstances, the court may consider making a forced marriage protection order (see para 9.65, below).

Making a will

9.27 Where the Court of Protection finds that P lacks testamentary capacity (the capacity to make a will) the Court of Protection has no power to annul a will written under the coercion or undue influence of another. A person other than P may make an application for a statutory will. To grant the application the court must be satisfied that making the statutory will is in P's best interests.[29] The power to make a statutory will cannot be delegated to an attorney or deputy.

ORDERS UNDER THE INHERENT JURISDICTION

Objectives of remedies

9.28 The inherent jurisdiction is said to be facilitative, and its orders are designed to increase the adult's capacity to make voluntary decisions by changing

26 *In the Matter of CA (Fact Finding – Capacity – Inherent Jurisdiction – Injunctive Relief)* [2024] EWCOP 64 (T3). This case was considered in Chapter 5.
27 MCA 2005, s 27(1)(b).
28 MCA 2005, s 27(1)(a).
29 MCA 2005, s 18(1)(i).

whatever it is that prevents them from making an autonomous choice. In theory, any of the best interests decisions outlined in the previous section can be made under the inherent jurisdiction as its powers are limitless: see Chapter 6.

9.29 In *Re SA* itself, Munby J was invited to make decisions about a woman who was at risk of forced marriage. The judge aimed to create space for Miss SA to exercise free will:

> whatever inquiries are needed to ascertain, when a marriage is proposed or arranged, what SA's true wishes are and to ascertain whether or not she has been able to exercise her free will or is confined, controlled, coerced or under restraint – in short to ascertain the true state of affairs.[30]

Munby J granted injunctions against Miss SA's parents, to 'to protect, support and enhance SA's capacity to control her own life and destiny in the way she would wish'.[31]

9.30 In an inherent jurisdiction case in 2010, Macur J said that the inherent jurisdiction is not there, 'in the case of a capacitous adult to impose a decision upon him/her whether as to welfare or finance', but rather to 'to facilitate the process of unencumbered decision-making by those who they have determined have capacity free of external pressure or physical restraint in making those decisions'.[32]

9.31 The same year, Theis J commented that the 'primary purpose' of the inherent jurisdiction 'is to create a situation where the person concerned can receive outside help free of coercion, to enable him or her to weigh things up and decide freely what he or she wishes to do. That is precisely what Munby J ordered in *SA*.'[33] Dismissing the appeal against Theis J's decision, the Court of Appeal agreed wholeheartedly with her approach. Giving judgment of the court, McFarlane LJ commended the approach described by Macur J as 'entirely on all fours with the re-establishment of the individual's autonomy of decision making in a manner which enhances, rather than breaches, their European Convention Art 8 rights'.[34]

LPAs

9.32 A perpetrator of coercive control can seek to make lawful their control over the victim by forcing them to create an LPA in which they (the perpetrator) are named as attorney. An LPA can therefore be used as a 'technology' of control, to use Evan Stark's phrase (see Chapter 2). There is no reported case where an

30 *Re SA (Vulnerable Adult with Capacity: Marriage)* [2005] EWHC 2942 (Fam), para 126.
31 Ibid, para. 133.
32 *LBL v RYJ and VJ* [2010] EWHC 2665 (COP), para 62.
33 *A Local Authority v DL & Ors* [2011] EWHC 1022 (Fam), para 53(7).
34 *DL v A Local* Authority [2012] EWCA Civ 253, para 67, considered in Chapter 6 of this book.

LPA has been revoked under the inherent jurisdiction in circumstances where a controlling attorney has made decisions about care that are harmful to the victim/survivor, and where the victim/survivor lacks capacity to decide on care but retains capacity to make and revoke an LPA. Given that there is no theoretical limit to the court's powers under the inherent jurisdiction, this would be possible.

Removal from home

9.33 The National Assistance Act 1948, s 47 permitted social services to remove an 'aged, infirm or physically incapacitated' person from her home if she was not receiving adequate care. That legislation was repealed by the Care Act 2014 which contains no power for a local authority representative to enter P's home without her consent (and neither does the Social Services and Well-being (Wales) Act 2014.

9.34 An order can be made under the inherent jurisdiction to remove a capacitous person from their home, if they are deemed 'vulnerable' in *Re SA* terms. However, as noted in Chapter 6, unless the person is 'of unsound mind' pursuant to Article 5 ECHR, the inherent jurisfiction cannot authorise a deprivation of liberty. No purpose is served ordering a vulnerable but capacitous person out of their home, because absent being deprived of liberty somewhere else, they will be able to return to their home. Instead, the court would usually consider making injunctions against the controlling person, for example, directing them to permit social workers to enter the property when making unannounced visits.

9.35 Although decisions under the inherent jurisdiction are supposed to be short term, providing the victim/survivor time and means to regain free choice, they are not always temporary. Chapter 6 considered the case of *Re Meyers*, where the court used the inherent jurisdiction to make long-term orders about the adult's place of residence and the people with whom he could live, against his express wishes.[35]

UNDERTAKINGS AND INJUNCTIONS

Agreements

9.36 A perpetrator of coercive control could agree to restrictions that the court deems appropriate, and such agreement can be recorded in a recital in the court order. For example, a recital could state that the person has agreed 'not to contact P in-person, and shall have telephone contact with P only if P decides to telephone him, such telephone calls always being supervised by a member of care home staff.'

35 *Southend-on-Sea BC v Meyers* [2019] EWHC 399 (Fam).

Undertakings

9.37 A more formal type of agreement or promise is an undertaking. In the Court of Protection and under the inherent jurisdiction, this is given on Form N117. The court may dispense with the need for a written undertaking if the person has given the undertaking orally in court. The person signing the document will undertake to take or refrain from taking actions that are specified on the document. It bears a statement that carries a penal notice requiring the person to sign: 'I understand the undertaking that I have given, and that if I break any of my promises to the Court I may be fined, my assets seized or I may be sent to prison for contempt of court.' An undertaking and an injunction have the same weight. The difference is that the former is agreed, and the latter is imposed.

Injunctions

9.38 An injunction is a direction by the court to a named person ordering them to do a specified act or refraining from doing an act. An injunctive order is usually a separate order and bears a penal notice in the same terms as that described above in respect of undertakings. Breaching an injunction may constitute a contempt of court.

Injunctions against a person other than the victim/survivor

9.39 An injunction should be made against a person who is able to understand the purpose of an injunction and comply with it, so should be made against the controlling person, not against P in the Court of Protection who may lack capacity to abide by the injunction.[36]

Just and convenient

9.40 In the Court of Protection and under the inherent jurisdiction, an injunction may be granted only if the court finds it just and convenient to do so.[37]

9.41 In coercive control cases, an injunction is usually made in support of (or to bolster) a best interests decision (including an interim best interests decision, see from para 9.47, below) in relation to contact between the victim/survivor and the controlling person. The injunction is designed to prevent the court's decisions from being frustrated or undermined. For example, Chapter 5 considered the case of Mrs PB who had a brain injury and whose controlling husband was rude and

36 This is the test both in the Court of Protection: *London Borough of Wandsworth v M & others* [2017] EWHC 2435 (Fam); and under the inherent jurisdiction: the Senior Courts Act 1981, s 37(1) confirms the High Court's power to grant injunctions (interlocutory or final) 'in all cases in which it appears to the court to be just and convenient to do so'.

37 *Re G (Court of Protection: Injunction)* [2022] EWCA Civ 1312.

disruptive towards care home staff, interfering with the provision of care.[38] The court made an injunction prohibiting the husband from having direct contact with Mrs PB or entering the care home, and restricting his communication with care home staff.

9.42 An example of the court deciding that the just and convenient test was *not* met is the sexual control case of Mrs A, considered in Chapter 5, where the controlling husband sought to control Mrs A's contraception. During the hearing, Mr A expressed willingness to allow Mrs A to have free contact with those professionals who had the skills to advise her in an ability-appropriate way about contraceptive issues, provided he was not excluded but involved as well, either concurrently or separately. The judge gave him an opportunity to honour his assurances and did not grant an injunction.[39]

Wording of injunctions

9.43 Judges fashion injunctive relief to the circumstances of each case. The following are two examples of the terms of injunctions. First, Chapter 7 considered the case of Mr TT, a man with learning disabilities who needed protection against his all-controlling mother Ms ST.[40] Within the Court of Protection proceedings in which Mr TT was found to lack capacity to decide on residence, the court made an injunction, such that the mother was not to:

(a) prevent TT from living at 'the placement', save that and solely subject to his wishes, he is at liberty to spend a maximum of two nights per week at his family's home;

(b) allow TT to live at the family home;

(c) seek to persuade or coerce TT into not returning to 'the placement';

(d) take any action to prevent TT returning to 'the placement'; or

(e) seek to persuade or coerce TT once he has returned to 'the placement' into moving back to the family home and/or to reside with ST anywhere, or to move to or reside at any property, premises or otherwise other than 'the placement'.

9.44 There was no evidence that the presumption that Mr TT's capacity to make decisions about contact with others (including his girlfriend Miss Y) was displaced, so the court made injunctions under the inherent jurisdiction, such that the mother was not to:

(a) prevent, restrict, or seek to persuade or coerce Mr TT not to have, or to have less, contact with 'Miss Y';

38 *MB v PB* [2022] EWCOP 14 (n 18).
39 *A Local Authority v Mrs A (by the Official Solicitor)* [2010] EWHC 1549 (Fam), para 80.
40 *Re TT (Injunctive Relief)* [2022] EWHC 2185 (Fam).

(b) contact by any means Miss Y or Miss Y's mother; or

(c) request, demand or take from TT any sum of money by way of 'rent' or contribution to expenses save in circumstances when TT remains overnight at ST's home when his contribution must be limited to a maximum of £5 per night.

9.45 The second example is the Court of Appeal case of *Re DL*, considered in Chapter 6. There, the court explained that Wall P at first instance had made interim injunctions on an *ex parte* basis restraining the controlling son DL from:[41]

(a) assaulting or threatening to assault his father or mother;

(b) preventing the father or mother from having contact with friends and family members;

(c) seeking to persuade or coerce the father into transferring ownership of the current family home;

(d) seeking to persuade or coerce the mother into moving into a care home or nursing home;

(e) engaging in behaviour towards father or mother that is otherwise degrading or coercive, including (but not limited to): stipulating which rooms in the house father or mother can use; preventing father or mother from using household appliances, including the washing-machine; 'punishing' the father or mother, for example, by making the mother write 'lines'; shouting or otherwise behaving in an aggressive or intimidating manner towards them.

(f) giving orders to care staff;

(g) interfering in the provision of care and support to the mother;

(h) refusing access to health and social care professionals; or

(i) behaving in an aggressive and/or confrontational manner to care staff and care managers.

INTERIM REMEDIES

Court of Protection

9.46 MCA 2005, s 48 gives the Court of Protection the power to make a best interests decision where there is 'reason to believe' that P lacks capacity to make a decision. The court may grant interim injunctions, interim declarations and any other interim order it considers appropriate.[42] Such orders are either to maintain/stabilise the status quo, or to change the situation temporarily, to prevent P from being exposed to the risk of harm, until the court has further and better evidence

41 *A Local Authority v DL* (n 31), para 9.
42 Rule 10.10 of the Court of Protection Rules 2017.

to properly determine the matter. The court can make any best interests decision on an interim basis.

Capacity evidence at the start of proceedings

9.47 When an application is made to the Court of Protection, capacity evidence may not be sufficiently 'cogent, clear and carefully analysed'[43] for the court to determine capacity and make a declaration under MCA 2005, s 15. Coercive control cases often begin with gaps in information, for reasons suggested in the following paragraph. The court will try to make sense of the situation and make case management decisions directing further and better capacity evidence. Interim capacity declarations are considered in Chapter 3 (at para 3.50).

9.48 In coercive control cases, three challenges may arise:

(1) The controlling person may have prevented social workers from assessing P's capacity. This sort of control was discussed in Chapter 2. Upon receiving an application, the Court of Protection is likely to find creative ways of ensuring that social workers have unfiltered access to the victim/survivor. The court may decide there are red flags that need investigating, and make orders that create an enabling environment for relevant professionals to carry out assessments. The court could issue an injunction against the controlling person to step out of the way when social workers or other professionals visit, so that they can have access to the victim/survivor. As noted above, the court can make an interim decision that P lacks capacity to conduct proceedings (and the court will appoint a litigation friend) and can make urgent best interests decisions on an interim basis to mitigate the risk of harm to the victim/survivor.

(2) The victim/survivor may have a trauma bond with the controlling person. As such, the victim/survivor may say what they consider the controlling person want them to say, even in the controlling person's absence.[44] The court will need to ensure that an experienced and skilled professional is instructed to assess the victim/survivor's capacity.

(3) The controlling person may say that the victim/survivor *has* capacity to conduct proceedings. This argument is advanced on the misapprehension that if the court declares the victim/survivor has capacity to make relevant decisions, then the controlling person can continue to influence, control and manipulate the victim/survivor. An application under the inherent jurisdiction may thwart the controlling person's hopes of ending proceedings in the Court of Protection on the basis that the victim/survivor has capacity (see Chapter 6).

43 Per Hayden J in *QJ v Local Authority* [2020] EWCOP 7, [2020] 1 WLUK 374, para 23.
44 An example is *WU v BU* (n 2), considered in Chapter 7.

Substantive test

9.49 MCA 2005, s 48 provides the Court of Protection with the power to make interim best interests decisions. There is a three-limb test:

(1) Is there reason to believe that P lacks capacity in relation to the matter? In *Re DP*,[45] Hayden J held:

  (a) the presumption of capacity applies with equal force to s 48 as it does to a declaration pursuant to s 15, but the exercise required is different: to make an urgent best interests decision under s 48, the court must focus on whether the evidence establishes reasonable grounds to believe that P may lack capacity, (in contrast to a s 15 declaration that requires the court to find that P lacks capacity);

  (b) the question of whether there is reason to believe P lacks capacity stimulates an evidential enquiry in which the entire canvas of the available evidence requires to be scrutinised';

  (c) The objective of s 48 is neither restrictive, in the sense that it requires a high level of proof, nor facilitative, in the sense that it is to be regarded as a perfunctory gateway to a protective regime'; and

  (d) in relation to best interests decisions which the court must make on less-than-perfect capacity evidence, '[t]here is a balancing exercise in which the Court is required to confront the tension between supporting autonomous adult decision making and to avoid imperilling the safety and well-being of those persons whom the Act and the judges are charged with protecting'.[46]

(2) The decision must be one that the Court can make: usually a straightforward hurdle to clear.

(3) It is in P's best interests to make the order, or give the directions, without delay. This 'indicates that the section is designed for circumstances of perceived urgency or emergency'.[47]

9.50 If all three limbs are met, the court can make an interim best interests decision.

Inherent jurisdiction

9.51 Rule 25.1(1) CPR provides at paragraph (a) that the court may grant an interim injunction, (b) an interim declaration, and (k) an interim third-party

45 *DP (By His Accredited Legal Representative) v London Borough of Hillingdon* [2020] EWCOP 45, [2020] COPLR 769. Mostyn J interpreted s 48 differently in *A Local Authority v LD and another* [2023] EWHC 1258 (Fam), para 22.
46 *Re DP*, ibid, paras 61 and 62(ix).
47 Ibid, para 59.

disclosure order. Rule 25.1(3) gives the court power to grant interim remedies that are not specified in r 25.1(1). For example, the court could make an interim order in the case of prohibiting the vulnerable adult from leaving the country and against the Passport Office to hold any passport,[48] or make an interim order directing a person not to remove the vulnerable adult from hospital.[49]

9.52 In describing the exercise of the jurisdiction on an interim basis in *Re SA*, Munby J used wording similar to that of MCA 2005, s 48 when he described the inherent jurisdiction as being available when a vulnerable adult 'is, or is reasonably believed' to be under a form of control. Orders can be made on an interim basis while proper enquiries are made, 'and while the court ascertains whether or not an adult is in fact in such a condition as to justify the court's intervention'.[50]

9.53 In Cobb J's view, the phrase 'reasonably believed' should not be read, 'as diluting the test for involvement, or lowering the threshold beyond which it could be appropriate to make an order under the inherent jurisdiction'.[51]

9.54 In a different case, Cobb J held that, 'there is, now, well-recognised access to the inherent jurisdiction for the making of <u>interim</u> orders in cases where there is evidence of vulnerability and a need to protect the vulnerable person'.[52] He gave this advice to applicant public bodies:

> before a local authority makes an application under the court's inherent jurisdiction which is designed to regulate the conduct of the subject by way of injunction, particularly where mental illness or vulnerability is an issue, it should be able to demonstrate (and support with evidence) that it has appropriately considered:
>
> i) whether X is likely to understand the purpose of the injunction;
>
> ii) will receive knowledge of the injunction; and
>
> iii) will appreciate the effect of breach of that injunction.
>
> If the answer to any of these questions is in the negative, the injunction is likely to be ineffectual, and should not be applied for or granted as no consequences can truly flow from the breach.[53]

9.55 A local authority may require access to the victim/survivor:

48 *London Borough of Islington v EF* [2022] EWHC 803 (Fam).
49 *London Borough of Croydon v KR, ST* [2019] EWHC 2498 (Fam), para 12.
50 *Re SA* (n 27), para 47.
51 *Re RK (Capacity; Contact; Inherent Jurisdiction)* [2023] EWCOP 37, at para 111.
52 *Redcar and Cleveland Borough Council v PR and others* [2019] EWHC 2305 (Fam), para 38. See also *Wookey v Wookey; Re S (A Child) (Injunction)* [1991] Fam 121 at p 143.
53 Ibid, para 46.

(1) to carry out an assessment of needs for care and support where the local authority suspects that the adult is experiencing, or is at risk of, abuse or neglect;[54]

(2) to assess capacity to make relevant decisions (see Chapter 4);

(3) to carry out safeguarding enquiries;[55]

(4) to assess the nature and extent of any coercive control; and

(5) to obtain the victim/survivor's wishes and feelings about any of the above.

9.56 In these circumstances,

> … if the evidence indicates a *prima facie* case of vulnerability, and justifies the necessity and proportionality of an order, it is entirely proper for the inherent jurisdiction to be invoked as an interim measure while proper inquiries are made, and while the court ascertains whether or not an adult is in fact in such a condition as to justify the court's intervention.[56]

9.57 The court can make an order recording an agreement or undertaking or by making an injunction against the controlling person,[57] with the intention of removing the obstruction, clearing the path for social workers to have access to the victim of coercive control.

9.58 The purpose of an order under the inherent jurisdiction is to be 'facilitative, rather than dictatorial'.[58] This rather binary approach is inconsistent with the evidence on the effects of trauma, presented in Chapters 10 and 11. Simply removing the victim/survivor from their home, or restricting their contact with the controlling person may not enable the victim/survivor to make voluntary decisions. The reasons are first, that the connection between the victim/survivor and the controlling person can be so deep that influence persists without physical presence. For example, in *Re BU* (Chapter 5), the perpetrator exerted such psychological control that a 'trauma bond' kept them connected, despite no contact for a year.[59] The second reason why removing the victim/survivor from the harmful environment, or restricting their contact with the perpetrator may not be sufficient is that absent therapy, the victim/survivor may not be able to overcome the trauma and may be stuck in the past: again, this is considered in Chapter 10.

54 In England, the Care Act 2014, ss 9 and 11; in Wales, the Social Services and Well-being (Wales) Act 2014, ss 19 and 20.

55 In England, the Care Act 2014, s 42; in Wales, the Social Services and Well-being (Wales) Act 2014, s 126.

56 *Wakefield Metropolitan District Council and another v DN and another* [2019] EWHC 2306 (Fam), para 47.

57 Agreements and undertakings were considered in paras 9.37–38, above.

58 *A Local Authority v DL* (n 31), para 67.

59 *Re BU* (n 2), para 89.

Deprivation of liberty

9.59 The Court of Protection can authorise the deprivation of P's liberty if P lacks capacity to decide on residence or care, and the deprivation is necessary and proportionate to prevent P from coming to harm, and it is in their best interests to be deprived of liberty. Deprivation of liberty under the inherent jurisdiction is dealt with at paragraphs 6.42 to 6.57 in Chapter 6.

REMEDIES AVAILABLE ELSEWHERE

9.60 Finally, and for completeness, six further remedies may be relevant for victims/survivors of coercive control. Some are available in the Court of Protection or under the inherent jurisdiction, and others are not. They are (a) a non-molestation order, (b) an occupation order, (c) a forced marriage protection order, (d) a restraining order, (e) a domestic abuse protection order and (f) a domestic abuse protection notice.

Non-molestation order

9.61 A non-molestation order is available in family law proceedings to protect a person from 'molestation' which is defined broadly to prevent the abuser from acting in a certain way, such as threatening the person, or using or threatening physical violence, intimidating, harassing, pestering or communicating with the specified person.[60] Such order could prevent the abuser from coming within a certain distance of the person, or visiting their home address or workplace. The order can prevent an abuser from instructing or encouraging another person to take any of the above actions. The order may also protect any child.

9.62 The abuser must have an 'association' with the person, as defined by the Family Law Act 1996 to include those who are or were married, civil partners, living together or partners, or people who are relatives and in-laws, or two people who are the parents of a child. An order may be made for a specified period or until further order.

9.63 This chapter has set out the powers of the Court of Protection and under the inherent jurisdiction to issue an injunction, which can be drafted in the same terms as a non-molestation order.

Occupation order

9.64 Section 33 of the Family Law Act 1996 grants the family court the power to make an occupation order with regard to the matrimonial home in

60 Family Law Act 1996, s 42.

which the applicant has a right to occupy. The occupation order can regulate occupation, exclude the respondent (the perpetrator of coercive control), or enforce the applicant's entitlement to remain in occupation. In contrast, the Court of Protection has no power to direct a person to leave a property they are entitled to occupy. If the victim/survivor is at risk of harm from the cohabiting controlling person and the victim/survivor lacks capacity to decide on residence, the Court of Protection may decide it is in the victim/survivor's best interests to live elsewhere, to reduce the risk of harm.

Forced marriage protection order

9.65 A forced marriage is a marriage that takes place without the full and free consent of both parties. The family court may make a forced marriage protection order (FMPO)[61] to protect person A if another person (B) forces A to enter into a marriage (whether with B or another person) without A's free will and full consent. Force can include psychological abuse (or other forms of pressure to destroy person A's free will) or physical abuse, abduction, deprivation of liberty, restraint, harassment, stalking and control of finances.

9.66 The Court of Protection can also make an FMPO. An example is *Re BU* in Chapter 5, where the court found the risk of forced marriage was so great given the total subordination of the victim's free will that the court granted an FMPO for 12 months, thereafter to be reviewed.

Injunction to protect a person from harassment

9.67 Harassment is any course of conduct that the perpetrator knows or ought to know amounts to harassment of that person. A course of conduct involves conduct on at least two occasions in relation to that person. Harassment includes alarming or causing distress. Irritations and annoyances that arise in day-to-day dealings do not amount to harassment.

9.68 Any person who is or may be a victim of harassment may apply to the High Court or the county court for an injunction to restrain the perpetrator from pursuing any conduct amounting to harassment in relation to any person or persons mentioned or described in the order.[62] An application should be made on a Part 8 claim form, and can be made by a person who may be the victim of the conduct in question.

61 Family Law Act 1996, s 63B.
62 The Protection from Harassment Act 1997, s 3A, introduced by the Serious Organised Crime and Police Act 2005, s 125(5).

Domestic abuse protection order

9.69 The Domestic Abuse Act 2021 consolidated a range of orders that were available in domestic abuse cases. It introduced two new civil protection injunctions: a domestic abuse protection order and a domestic abuse protection notice (see below).

9.70 The county court may make a domestic abuse protection order (DAPO),[63] which prohibits person A from doing things described in the order (or requires that person to do things described in the order) for the purpose of preventing person A from being abusive towards person B. This may include prohibiting contact, excluding person A from specified premises, or requiring them to leave shared accommodation.

9.71 Person B must be aged 16 or over and must be 'personally connected' to person A (this being defined in the Domestic Abuse Act 2021 and not repeated here). A DAPO may be made in a wide set of proceedings, including claims for personal injury, nuisance, trespass, contentious probate, money, possession, and property boundary.[64] Breach of a DAPO without reasonable excuse is a criminal offence.

Domestic abuse protection notice

9.72 In England and Wales, a police officer at least the rank of inspector may issue a domestic abuse protection notice (DAPN) to a person if two conditions are met: (1) the officer has reasonable grounds to believe that person A has been abusive towards person B who is aged 16 or over to whom person A is personally connected; and (2) it is necessary to issue the notice to protect person B from domestic abuse or its risk by person A.[65]

9.73 The notice prohibits person A from being abusive and can include conditions such as prohibiting contact or requiring them to leave shared premises. A DAPN cannot be given to a person under 18 and have effect throughout the UK. The process is designed to provide immediate, emergency protection and create breathing space for victims to make informed decisions about their safety and welfare, including that of children involved.

CONCLUSION

9.74 This chapter has discussed the remedies available in cases of coercive control, covering various aspects of the victim/survivor's life such as residence,

63 The Crime and Security Act 2010, ss 27–28 and the Domestic Abuse Act 2021, ss 27–49.
64 The Domestic Abuse Protection Orders (County Court: Relevant Proceedings) Regulations 2024 (SI 2024/253).
65 Domestic Abuse Act 2021, s 22.

care, contact with others, and financial affairs. Remedies under the inherent jurisdiction aim to facilitate the victim's ability to make autonomous decisions by removing undue influence.

9.75 Additionally, the chapter has addressed the use of injunctions to prevent the controlling person from undermining court decisions. Ancillary family and civil remedies, including non-molestation orders and domestic abuse protection orders, were also considered, as they may be used alongside the core legal frameworks that are the focus of this book, to protect the rights and interests of victims/survivors of coercive control.

9.76 In discussing how remedies will be tailored to the specific circumstances of each case, the chapter has begun to explore the traumatic effects of coercive control on victims/survivors. Drawing from literature in sociology and psychology, the next chapter considers trauma in more detail.

CHAPTER 10

The traumatic effects of coercive control

'Trauma is not what happens to you, but what happens *inside* you.'[1]

INTRODUCTION

10.01 The chapter introduces the reader to the traumatic effect of coercive control (at para 10.03), explaining how trauma is distinguished from the ordinary stresses of life. It outlines the range of trauma responses that a victim/survivor of coercive control may display, long after the risk of harm has been removed (at para 10.08). Like all chapters, this chapter uses the term victim/survivor inclusively to respect people's own language preferences.

10.02 The reader will be introduced to a range of mental health conditions that may be caused by coercive control (at para 10.13), and the relevance of diagnoses to the legal process (at para 10.21). The chapter looks at the physical health effects of trauma (at para 10.41). It is suggested that lawyers pay particular attention to ensuring access by a victim/survivor of coercive control to appropriate mental and physical health assessments and therapies (at para 10.30) to have opportunities to heal from their trauma. These matters are often overlooked by local authorities which commonly are the lead public body in abuse cases but are not health providers. The chapter finishes by considering victims/survivors with learning disabilities or who are neurodiverse (at para 10.50): they are at increased risk of abuse and being targeted by exploitative offenders, and at risk of not being listened to or understood, their testimonies dismissed.

COERCIVE CONTROL AND TRAUMA

10.03 Victims/survivors of coercive control have usually endured prolonged experiences that are shameful, frightening, threatening, degrading, and sometimes violent. Taken individually and cumulatively, such experiences can result in complex trauma. It is through this lens of trauma that this chapter proceeds, informing the guidance and practice considerations that follow.

1 Gabor Maté, *The Myth of Normal* (Penguin, 2022), p 24.

10.04 The psychologist Judith Herman has explained the link between coercive control and trauma as follows:

> The methods of establishing control over another person are based upon the systematic, repetitive infliction of psychological trauma. They are the organized techniques of disempowerment and disconnection. Methods of psychological control are designed to instil terror and helplessness and to destroy the victim's sense of self in relation to others.[2]

10.05 In 2023, a systemic review and meta-analysis examined the mental health implications of coercive control. It identified moderate associations with measures of post-traumatic stress disorder (PTSD) and depression symptom severity, when considered across all available studies, with an overall strength of these associations comparable to those involving broader measures of psychological intimate partner violence with both PTSD and depression.[3]

10.06 Trauma differs from the stresses of everyday life. The psychiatrist Gabor Maté has explained that, 'An event is traumatizing, or retraumatizing, only if it renders one *diminished*, which is to say psychically (or physically) *more limited* than before in a way that *persists*'.[4] His observation aligns with coercive control cases in the Court of Protection or under the inherent jurisdiction of the High Court, where victims/survivors often suffer a devaluation of self-esteem, sense of agency, security, and belonging, with trauma undermining their core sense of self. These effects can be even more pronounced in individuals with pre-existing mental health conditions, learning disabilities, cognitive impairments (such as dementia), or neurodiversity.

10.07 This chapter aims to equip lawyers representing traumatised victims of coercive control with insights into the various manifestations of trauma. Drawing from the trauma literature, the next chapter offers practical approaches for trauma-informed lawyering in the Court of Protection and under the inherent jurisdiction.

TRAUMA RESPONSES

10.08 Lawyers need to know about the ways in which trauma can impact a victim/survivor's ability to recall events and tell their lawyer about them. Coercive control cases can drag out over many months, especially if capacity is to be determined, facts are to be found, and best interests decisions are to be made. Over the course of proceedings, the lawyer will meet with their client

2 Judith L. Herman, *Trauma and Recovery* (Basic Books, New York, 2022), p 112.

3 S Lohmann, S Cowlishaw, L Ney, M O'Donnell and K Felmingham, 'The trauma and mental health impacts of coercive control: A systematic review and meta-analysis' (2023) 25(1) *Trauma, Violence, & Abuse* 630–647.

4 Maté (n 1), 24.

many times and will want to keep the client updated and gather their views about evidence that is filed in the course of the litigation.

10.09 Trauma can cause a victim of coercive control to display a range of emotions, behaviours and responses. Fight, flight, freeze, fawn and flop are trauma responses which are protective mechanisms against pain. Trauma psychologist Ahona Guha explains that, whereas we would normally assess a non-immediate threat and choose the most appropriate response, victims of trauma may be unable to control their reactions or engage in conscious emotional processing:

> Sometimes, the mechanisms of fight, flight, or freeze can become personality-driven learned features, such that people will characteristically respond to *any* threat with anger and aggression (fight); or by avoidance of any perceived danger (flee); or by detachment, dissociation, and surrender (freeze).[5]

10.10 When it is impossible to resist abuse (fight) or escape from it (flight), a victim/survivor may experience an autonomic biological protective response that is not consciously controlled, such as entering a freeze state of hypo-arousal, dissociating from the trauma and its memories. This can occur even in a safe setting, such as a meeting with a lawyer, when a client is asked to recall repressed memories of past abuse. It might even be triggered by a word used, a particular colour, how the room is set up, a door banging: these are all things the client may be unaware of, let alone the lawyer.

10.11 Freeze responses can impair verbal communication and may include physical symptoms such as a slowed heart rate or feeling cold, highlighting the need for trauma-informed approaches that allow the client time and safety to respond. Gabor Maté explains that this reaction is because, 'a traumatized nervous system […] never gets to *un*freeze'.[6]

10.12 As well as fight, flight and freeze, trauma victims may experience fawn or flop responses. An animal displays fawn behaviour when it faces a predator and lowers itself to avoid the threat. In coercive control situations, a fawn response is when the victim/survivor seeks to appease or submit to the abuser to avoid harm: this may be shown by the victim/survivor avoiding conflict, not saying no to the abuser (or others), apologising, and pleasing the abuser even if it harms them. A flop response is when the person feels numb, has little emotional or physical energy, or feels they are not in the present moment: they shut down.

5 Ahona Guha, *Reclaim: Understanding Complex Trauma and Those Who Abuse* (Scribe, 2023), p 55.
6 Maté (n 1), 28.

TRAUMATIC MEMORY RECALL

Shutting trauma away

10.13 Victims/survivors of coercive control may struggle to give a coherent account of their experiences. This reflects the profound traumatic impact of coercive control. Trauma alters brain function, including the way traumatic experiences are recalled. As a result, the victim/survivor may be unable to process information, assess situations, determine appropriate responses, or remember anything at all. Chapter 7 explained the case of Mrs CA whose daughter controlled and abused her including by throwing food on her. When the psychiatric expert asked about these incidents, Mrs CA replied, 'It's so traumatic that I can't even remember what happened now'.[7]

10.14 The Holocaust survivor and Nobel Peace Prize laureate Ellie Wiesel observed this phenomenon too. When looking back on the horrors he experienced, he observed: 'while I had many things to say I did not have the words to say them'.[8] These are examples of how trauma hides memories as a protective mechanism.

Collage, not chronology

10.15 However eager the lawyer is to obtain their client's wishes and feelings, therefore, the client may be unable to respond verbally, or at all, because they may block or suppress distressing experiences, and their memory and emotional responses can be impaired. These are subconscious responses, and while they may want to help the lawyer, they just may not (yet) be able to.

10.16 Traumatic memory differs fundamentally from ordinary memory. This is because trauma shatters memory it into fragments – not necessarily into pieces of factual information that can be reassembled like a jigsaw puzzle, but pieces within 'a collage of sensations, emotions, and behaviors'.[9] This explains why expecting a full account of a victim/survivor's experience of coercive control in one meeting is over-ambitious. The victim/survivor may struggle to *re-member*, to reconstruct or to account for abusive or traumatogenic events they have experienced and survived.

10.17 'Traumatic memories are fundamentally different from the stories we tell about the past', explains van der Kolk, because '[t]hey are dissociated: The different sensations that entered the brain at the time of the trauma are not properly

7 *In the Matter of CA (Fact Finding – Capacity – Inherent Jurisdiction – Injunctive Relief)* [2024] EWCOP 64 (T3), para 118.
8 Elie Wiesel, *Night* (Penguin Book, 2008).
9 Peter A Levine, *Trauma and Memory: Brain and Body in a Search for the Living Past* (North Atlantic Books, 2015), p 21.

assembled into a story, a piece of autobiography'.[10] Trauma psychologist Peter Levine describes how trauma memories 'tend to arise as fragmented splinters of inchoate and indigestible sensations, emotions, images, smells, tastes, thoughts, and so on'.[11]

10.18 Neurological studies have shown how 'imprints of traumatic experiences are organized not as coherent logical narratives but in fragmented sensory and emotional traces: images, sounds, and physical sensations.' As a result, when the abuse is put to the victim/survivor, the 'inescapable shock' may cause their recall system to become overwhelmed and break down.[12]

10.19 Given that coercive control is a *pattern* of behaviour that occurs over a potentially lengthy period of time consisting of hundreds or thousands of incidents, comments, put-downs, acts of humiliation etc, it is challenging for a victim to remember each of these chronologically.

Substance abuse

10.20 To manage overwhelming feelings, dampen traumatic memories or cope with daily life, some people may use substances, develop disordered eating, engage in self-harm (from cutting to spending hours playing video games). The psychiatrist Bruce Perry explains that, 'without connection to people who care for you, and support you, it is almost impossible to step away from any form of unhealthy reward and regulation'.[13] This is one of the reasons why it is suggested in this chapter that lawyers pay particular attention to ensuring a victim/survivor has access to specialist therapy, considered at paras 10.30 to 10.40, below.

MENTAL HEALTH: DIAGNOSES

10.21 Coercive control may cause mental health problems including mood disorders such as depression, anxiety disorders, personality disorders, impulse control disorders, eating disorders, or post-traumatic stress disorder (PTSD). While simple PTSD is associated with a one-off traumatic event, it is Complex PTSD (C-PTSD) that is associated with coercive control. These diagnoses are not made out by the nature of abuse, but rather its effects.

10.22 In 2018, the World Health Organization included the diagnosis of C-PTSD into the International Statistical Classification of Diseases and Related

10 Bessel van der Kolk, *The Body Keeps the Score* (Penguin, 2014), p 233.
11 Levine (n 9), 7.
12 Van der Kolk (n 10), 211.
13 Bruce D Perry and Oprah Winfrey, *What Happened to You? Conversations on Trauma, Resilience and Healing* (Flatiron Books, 2021).

Health Problems, 11th edition, ICD-11.[14] That document provides the following definition:

> Complex post traumatic stress disorder (Complex PTSD) is a disorder that may develop following exposure to an event or series of events of an extremely threatening or horrific nature, most commonly prolonged or repetitive events from which escape is difficult or impossible (e.g. torture, slavery, genocide campaigns, prolonged domestic violence, repeated childhood sexual or physical abuse). All diagnostic requirements for PTSD are met. In addition, Complex PTSD is characterised by severe and persistent 1) problems in affect regulation; 2) beliefs about oneself as diminished, defeated or worthless, accompanied by feelings of shame, guilt or failure related to the traumatic event; and 3) difficulties in sustaining relationships and in feeling close to others. These symptoms cause significant impairment in personal, family, social, educational, occupational or other important areas of functioning.

10.23 To find a diagnosis of C-PTSD, the diagnostic requirements of (non-complex) PTSD must be met. Primarily, there must be an event or series of events, which may include prolonged domestic violence or repeated childhood sexual or physical abuse. The three post-event core elements of PTSD must also be met, namely:

(1) re-experiencing the traumatic event or events in the present in the form of vivid intrusive memories, flashbacks, or nightmares, which may occur via one or multiple sensory modalities and is typically accompanied by strong or overwhelming emotions, particularly fear or horror, and strong physical sensations;

(2) avoidance of thoughts and memories of the event or events, or avoidance of activities, situations, or people reminiscent of the event(s); and

(3) persistent perceptions of heightened current threat, for example, as indicated by hypervigilance or an enhanced startle reaction to stimuli such as unexpected noises.

10.24 These symptoms must persist for at least several weeks and cause significant impairment in personal, family, social, educational, occupational or other important areas of functioning.

14 For the ICD-11 website, see https://icd.who.int/en/. For a history of the development of C-PTSD, see M Cloitre, 'ICD-11 complex post-traumatic stress disorder: simplifying diagnosis in trauma populations' (2020) 216(3) *The British Journal of Psychiatry* 129–131.

10.25 The ICD-11 says that a person with C-PTSD will usually have persistent beliefs about self as diminished, defeated or worthless, accompanied by deep and pervasive feelings of shame, guilt or failure related to the stressor. An example given is that a person may feel guilty about not having escaped from or succumbing to the adverse circumstance.

10.26 In addition, the victim/survivor may have persistent difficulties in sustaining relationships and in feeling close to others. The person may consistently avoid, deride or have little interest in relationships and social engagement more generally. Alternatively, there may be occasional intense relationships, but difficulty sustaining them.

10.27 The ICD-11 says that the disturbance needs to result in significant impairment in personal, family, social, educational, occupational or other important areas of functioning. If functioning is maintained, it is only through significant additional effort.

10.28 In closing this section on diagnoses, two points are crucial for lawyers to understand. First, a badge is not an explanation: a diagnosis tells us nothing about the causes of the person's perceptions and experiences. And second, trauma-informed approaches to lawyering do not require the victim/survivor client to have a diagnosis: adjustments should be needs-led.

10.29 Lawyers working on cases of coercive control may suggest to the court that the person experiencing such control be assisted by way of specialist psychological interventions for C-PTSD.

MENTAL HEALTH: THERAPY AND HEALING

10.30 Trauma affects how victims/survivors perceive and interact with the world, impacting their sense of trust, self-worth, safety, and identity. Additionally, the court process itself may be counter-therapeutic and psychologically damaging. Legal proceedings are inherently stressful, but in cases of coercive control, the outcomes may not only be undesirable for the client, but potentially triggering or retraumatising. For example, if the court decides to sever or limit the victim/survivor's contact with the controlling person in their best interests but against their will, this may mimic experiences of powerlessness and loss of control and invoke in the victim/survivor yet more trauma. As discussed in Chapter 2, there are many reasons why a victim/survivor of coercive control might express a desire to return to the controlling person: the desire to prevent further trauma may be one of them.

10.31 Court proceedings are unlikely to address the client's therapeutic needs. Lawyers can take further practical restorative steps, including:

(a) inviting the court to instruct an independent expert to provide an opinion on the client's presentation, suitable therapy modalities, prognosis, and whether treatment is available in the NHS or only in the private sector;

(b) advocating for and ensuring appropriate support is put in place, whether from a psychologist, specialist domestic abuse organisation, or another support service;

(c) retrieving any possessions of the victim/survivor that the controlling person may still have;

(d) ensuring that social workers or others help the victim/survivor re-establish relationships with people the controlling person cut out of their life;

(e) helping the victim/survivor report incidents to the police if criminal offences may have been committed; and

(f) advising on a civil claim against the controlling person, including consideration of the Protection from Harassment Act 1997, s 3.

10.32 The victim/survivor is entitled to a nuanced understanding of their difficulties, suitable assessments, diagnostic formulation, and care and treatment plans. Without therapy, the victim/survivor of trauma may be at risk of relational trauma on repeat. Psychologist Peter Levine explains why accessing appropriate therapy is so important:

> We may erase a memory of abuse, but without full integration and restored agency, we will continue to have diminished capacity to respond effectively to similar situations in the future. Without this ability we may be strangely drawn to endangering situations and repetitive relationship failures that could have been addressed with interpersonal awareness and then integrated with new skills, reflection, and empowerment.[15]

10.33 While neither the Court of Protection nor the Family Division of the High Court can direct a public body to provide services that are not on offer, the court can direct the public body to file evidence setting out consideration of interventions and decision-making as to the sorts of services they (or the appropriate health body) will provide or commission, including from the independent or charity sector.

10.34 The court can make holistic best interests decisions which explore interventions that help the victim/survivor accept what has happened (and accept what is), even if they do not (yet) approve of it. An example is the case of *Re*

15 Levine (n 9).

BU, discussed in Chapter 5, where even after a year without contact with the abuser, he still occupied a place in Ms BU's mind because the trauma bond bound them together 'even in absentia'.[16] The psychologist explained that Mr NC was 'a dominating part of BU's psychological identity',[17] and his influence was likely to endure for a considerable period. Helping Ms BU gain insight would be a 'Herculean task',[18] but with intensive counselling and psycho-education, she could benefit. The initial stages of therapy could take up to six months, and would focus on helping Ms BU understand why she found herself in this situation and Mr NC's role in it. The court decided it was in Ms BU's best interests to offer her therapy to help her make informed decisions about any future contact with Mr NC.

10.35 Trauma requires targeted therapy rather than general counselling. The main treatment offered by the NHS for complex trauma is psychotherapy, often cognitive behavioural therapy that is trauma-informed. Therapy may help the victim/survivor overcome autonomic trauma responses that cause avoidance of situations associated with the trauma. If trauma occurred later in life (such as through coercive control as an adult, rather than, for example, as a result of adverse childhood experiences), therapy is likely to address 'how the trauma *conflicted with and changed* initial belief structures, and focusing on reformation of a healthy and realistic set of post traumatic beliefs'.[19]

10.36 Coercive control specialists Jeanette Roddy and Rod Dubrow-Marshall endorse the 'Power, Threat, Meaning' framework developed by the British Psychological Society.[20] This helps victims/survivors understand what has happened to them, rather than the suggestion that something is wrong with them. The model enables insight into 'threat responses'. For example, anxiety is seen as a natural response to threats, and depression as a response to being in a trauma bond. The therapeutic approach includes psychoeducation which can help victims/survivors understand the dynamics of their coercive and controlling relationship, increasing their agency in recovery.

10.37 Other treatment approaches for trauma include the following:

(a) Cognitive processing therapy (CPT). This is a structured psychotherapy usually over 12 weeks. It is a cognitive-behavioural treatment that targets the negative beliefs and feelings associated with traumatic events and helps process and reduce the impact of traumatic memories. It seeks to identify and change stuck points that are irrational, or distorted beliefs related to the trauma such as excessive guilt, shame, or self-blame. It encourages reflection on the trauma's meaning and its effects in the context of the person's life.

16 *Re BU* [2021] EWCOP 54, at para 89.
17 Ibid, para 63.
18 Ibid, para 67.
19 Guha (n 5), 59.
20 Jeanette Roddy and Rod Dubrow-Marshall, 'Understanding domestic abuse', in Jeannette Roddy (ed), *Working with Client Experiences of Domestic Abuse: A Handbook for Counsellors, Psychotherapists, and other Mental Health Professionals*, (Routledge, 2023).

(b) Eye movement desensitisation and reprocessing (EMDR) therapy. Here, the victim/survivor is asked to focus on a traumatic memory while simultaneously engaging in bilateral movements such as eye movements in a process which stimulates neural pathways and leads to healing. EMDR is informed by the Adaptive Information Processing model, in which symptoms such as flashbacks are considered to be caused by trauma memories remaining unprocessed. By processing these memories, the symptoms aim to be alleviated.[21]

(c) Imagery rescripting and reprocessing therapy (IRRT). This is 'an imagery focused cognitive behavioural treatment originally developed for treating adult survivors of childhood trauma suffering from post-traumatic stress disorder'.[22] It has also been reported to reduce intrusive symptoms of C-PTSD including nightmares and flashbacks and likewise cognitive distortions about the self, such as maladaptive schemas, and is similarly helpful in increasing emotional regulation.

(d) Dialectical behaviour therapy (DBT). While not a trauma-specific therapy, DBT may be offered to a trauma victim/survivor where trauma has contributed to emotional instability or interpersonal problems. Its focus is not on processing traumatic events, but rather on balancing acceptance and change. It includes mindfulness, distress tolerance (developing strategies to cope with pain or crisis without engaging in harmful behaviours), emotion regulation (to identify, understand, and manage intense emotions effectively), and interpersonal effectiveness (communication, setting boundaries, and maintaining relationships).

Adjunctive to the above are sensorimotor therapies that focus on the body and its movements to heal, such as yoga.[23] In addition, there are a range of other approaches including music therapy, art therapy and gardening therapy. Equine therapy is also used in trauma healing as horses are highly sensitive to human emotions and movement.

10.38 The National Institute for Health and Care Excellence (NICE) takes the view that PTSD is a serious condition but can respond well to treatment, even years after the trauma. For individuals with additional needs, including C-PTSD, NICE recommends increasing the number of therapy sessions based on the person's needs. It also advises helping individuals manage barriers to engaging with trauma-focused therapies, such as substance misuse, dissociation, emotional dysregulation, interpersonal difficulties, or negative self-perception.[24] A victim/

21 F Shapiro, *Eye Movement Desensitisation and Reprocessing: Basic Principles, Protocols and Procedures* (Guildford Press, 3rd edn, 2018).

22 M Smucker and A Boos, 'Imagery rescripting and reprocessing therapy', in A Freeman, M Stone and D Martin (eds), *Comparative Treatments for Borderline Personality Disorder* (Springer, 2nd edn, 2007), pp 215–237.

23 See van der Kolk (n 10) for body-based therapies in trauma recovery.

24 National Institute for Health and Care Excellence, 'Post-traumatic stress disorder: NICE guidance', NG116, 5 December 2018.

survivor of coercive control may therefore require more sustained support than the standard 12-week programme of CBT.

10.39 Many of the trauma therapies described above are available on the NHS, although accessing specialist therapy may involve long waiting times. Domestic abuse organisations have pointed out the difficulties survivors face, especially Black and minoritised women, when trying to access mainstream services, and how mental health services can create further trauma for survivors.[25]

10.40 Should therapy commence during proceedings? It might be said that therapy could impact on the victim'/survivor's account of their experiences, and may therefore undermine the court process. A response to that argument is that significant damage can be caused by leaving a survivor without access to therapy, and it cannot be in a person's best interests to be denied access to treatment if it is available. Decisions about treatment modality and timings need to be clinically informed and offered to the survivor in a therapeutic manner. If there is a risk of therapy impacting legal proceedings, the risk should be brought to the attention of the victim/survivor's litigation friend for consideration of next steps.

PHYSICAL HEALTH

10.41 The effects of traumatic stress are far reaching and do not impact the victim/survivor's mental health only. Lawyers should also be aware of the traumatic impact on the victim's physical health needs.

10.42 We all have experienced how our mind and body are connected when other people have caused our body to react in a way over which we have no control: a churning in our stomach before a meeting with a horrible person, or an increased heartrate when we think about a lover. Gabor Maté has written powerfully of the need for *doctors* to have a holistic approach to victims of trauma, citing research that analysed 148 published studies which showed that deficient interpersonal relationships are a risk factor as deadly as tobacco and alcohol.[26]

10.43 This book suggests that *lawyers* should also be attuned to the trauma victim's needs in a holistic manner. We know that traumatic stress – including that caused by experiencing coercive and controlling behaviour – can have a profound impact on a person's mental health, but also on their physical health too.[27] Stress causes profound changes to the body:

25 Jenny Birchall and Lizzie McCarthy, *Reframing the Links: Black and Minoritised Women, Domestic Violence and Abuse, and Mental Health – A Review of the Literature* (Women's Aid, 2021).

26 J Holt-Lunstad, TB Smith and JB Layton, 'Social relationships and mortality risk: a meta-analytic review' (2010) Jul 27; 7(7) *PLoS Med*, https://doi.org/10.17615/jccz-7473.

27 AC McFarlane, 'The long-term costs of traumatic stress: intertwined physical and psychological consequences' (2010) Feb; 9(1) *World Psychiatry* 3–10.

> ... the brain is a biological organ that changes in its architecture and its molecular profile and its neurochemistry under acute and chronic stress and directs many systems of the body—metabolic, cardiovascular and immune—that are involved in the short- and long-term consequences of being "stressed out" and the consequent health-damaging behaviors.[28]

10.44 Poor interpersonal relationships are as deadly a risk factor as tobacco and alcohol.[29] Persons with traumatic stress are at increased risk of cardiovascular diseases, including coronary heart disease and possibly stroke.[30] Persistent stress can cause chronic, low-grade inflammation, leading to various health conditions such as atherosclerosis, which increases the risk of heart attacks. Metabolic disorders, like type 2 diabetes, are also linked to stress-induced inflammation. This persistent inflammation can impair insulin signalling, leading to insulin resistance and difficulty regulating blood sugar. Chronic inflammation can trigger or worsen these conditions, resulting in increased pain and tissue damage.

10.45 Traumatic stress also raises the risk of autoimmune disorders, including rheumatoid arthritis and lupus, where the immune system mistakenly attacks the body's own tissues. Autoimmune symptoms can be difficult to identify and may not be immediately apparent in someone who has experienced trauma and is showing other trauma-induced symptoms. Additionally, there is a connection between chronic inflammation and mental health conditions, particularly depression, where neuroinflammation in the brain is a contributing factor.[31]

10.46 Further, a perpetrator may have denied the victim/survivor of coercive control access to health services, potentially for a long time. This includes dental health, and optometry. As a result, their health may have been long neglected. Pre-existing health problems may have worsened, they may have missed regular dental check-ups, screening programmes (mammograms, cervical smears, faecal immunochemical tests for bowel cancer etc). They may also have abuse-related injuries.

10.47 Although this may seem outside the ordinary ambit of lawyers, it is suggested that lawyers representing victim/survivor of coercive control should ensure that the full array of physical health needs of their client is being met, if the social workers have not already arranged these. This begins with a physical examination by the GP, who should be informed that the client has endured significant trauma, has been denied access to healthcare, and may have developed physical health conditions as a result.

28 BS McEwen, 'Neurobiological and systemic effects of chronic stress' (2017) 1 *Chronic Stress*, https://doi.org/10.1177/2470547017692.

29 L Rebecca, Jayesh Kamath Acabchuk, John D. Salamone and Blair T. Johnson, 'Stress and chronic illness: The inflammatory pathway' (2017) 185 *Social Science & Medicine* 166–170.

30 SS Coughlin, 'Post-traumatic stress disorder and cardiovascular disease' (2011) 5 *Open Cardiovasc Med J* 164–170.

31 IB Kim, JH Lee and SC Park, 'The relationship between stress, inflammation, and depression' (2022) Aug 9;10(8) *Biomedicines* 1929.

10.48 Trauma, including that which is experienced by a victim/survivor of coercive control, impacts on aspects of daily life that are classified as 'social care', including sleep, diet and activity. We know the following from research:

(a) Chronic sleep deprivation can lead to elevated evening cortisol levels and increased inflammatory markers, fuelling systemic inflammation.

(b) A diet high in processed foods, refined sugars, and unhealthy fats can directly stimulate inflammatory pathways, independent of psychological stress. These foods can alter gut microbiome composition, influencing systemic inflammation.

(c) A sedentary lifestyle has been linked to higher systemic inflammation. Lack of physical activity can contribute to the accumulation of inflammatory substances, impacting the interplay between habits, stress, and the body's inflammatory response.

10.49 Sleep, diet and activity have a bidirectional impact on physical and mental health: these matters should be addressed in the local authority's needs assessment and care and support plan, documents that lawyers should ensure are filed within proceedings.

LEARNING DISABILITIES AND AUTISM

10.50 Trauma responses may be displayed by victims of coercive control who have learning disabilities, underlying mental health conditions, or are neurodiverse. Lawyers should accept their client as they are and recognise that each individual requires tailored support, and is entitled to 'reasonable adjustments' under the Equality Act 2010.

10.51 Those with severe and profound learning disabilities are at higher risk of abuse and degree of harm,[32] including by way of coercive control, yet may be the most vulnerable to being denied access to justice. Their trauma responses may be seen as behavioural, and they may attract the label 'complex', not to indicate that they may have Complex-PTSD, but that their behaviours are complex to manage, behaviours that may be better understood as indicating an unmet need.

10.52 To this end, lawyers should be aware of diagnostic overshadowing. This occurs when a professional attributes a person's symptoms or difficulties solely

32 Nigel Beail, Pat Frankish and Allan Skelly, *Trauma and Intellectual Disability: Acknowledgment, Identification and* Intervention (Pavillion, 2021), p 122.

to their disability, thereby overlooking other causes such as trauma. It stems from not listening to people.[33] A person's behaviours, sounds or overall presentation is interpreted as being part of the learning disability or neurodiversity, rather than a communication about (for example) experiencing abuse, pain or discomfort in a part of the body, fear about being in the room with a particular person, or another feeling. Disabled victims of coercive control are entitled to high-quality, trauma-informed legal representation and access to psychological and therapeutic services on an equal basis with others. Trauma therapies are increasingly available to people with learning disabilities and to autistic people, with promising outcomes. These include adjusted techniques, such as art, drama, movement, and play.[34]

10.53 Finally, lawyers can ensure that the staff providing care and support to an autistic victim/survivor of coercive control or who has learning disabilities are trauma-informed. Behavioural approaches may not be appropriate for trauma victims who do not respond to praise for doing things 'right'. Ideally, the therapist working with the victim/survivor will collaborate with the care team at a systems level, integrating a psychodynamic approach into the care provision. This involves developing the care team's understanding of the unconscious emotional meaning behind the client's behaviours and difficulties, while adapting to their communication style and cognitive profile. Erecting this psychological scaffolding ensures that trauma recovery is integrated into everyday interactions and does not take place solely in weekly psychotherapy sessions, if such sessions are available.

CONCLUSIONS

10.54 Coercive control is traumagenic. Its sustained patterns of humiliation, fear, isolation and domination frequently produce complex trauma, with consequences that reach far beyond the cessation of abuse. Trauma is distinct from ordinary stress: it diminishes and constrains a person's psychological and physical functioning over time, often undermining agency, self-worth, safety, and belonging. These effects are compounded for those with pre-existing mental health conditions, learning disabilities, cognitive impairments, or who are neurodiverse.

10.55 Lawyers should expect trauma responses (fight, flight, freeze, fawn and flop) to shape a client's presentation and engagement, including during legal meetings. Freeze and dissociative states can impair speech, memory and affect, and may be triggered in apparently safe settings. Memory of coercive control is commonly fragmentary, arising as sensations, emotions and images rather than

33 Sara Ryan, *Critical Health and Learning Disabilities: An Exploration of Erasure and Social Murder* (Routledge, 2026), p 35.

34 See Pat Frankish, *Therapeutic Care for People with Intellectual Disabilities and Emotional Needs: Exploring a Trauma-informed Approach from Professional and Personal Perspectives* (Pavilion Publishing and Media Ltd, 2025); and Angelina Veiga and Valerie Sinason (eds), *Disability Psychotherapy: What it is and Why it Matters* (Routledge, 2026).

linear chronology. The legal gold standard of a comprehensive account is rarely realistic.

10.56 Diagnostic labels can be helpful but are neither prerequisites for adjustments nor explanations of causation. Complex PTSD is often associated with relational abuse such as coercive control and captures core difficulties in affect regulation, self-concept and relationships. Access to specialist trauma-informed interventions should be prioritised and lawyers for the victim/survivor should require evidence of consideration and commissioning pathways for specialist services. Lawyers should take steps to counter the effects of the legal process which can be counter-therapeutic and reactivating for the victim/survivor.

10.57 Therapeutic support should be timely, targeted, and tailored, drawing on evidence-based modalities and psychoeducation that restore agency and meaning. Many survivors will need more sustained input than standard short programmes, and practical steps – reconnection with supportive networks, retrieval of possessions, referrals to the police and consideration of civil claims where appropriate – are part of holistic recovery.

10.58 Trauma also has health sequelae. Chronic stress and disrupted relationships are linked to inflammatory pathways, cardiovascular and metabolic risk, autoimmune vulnerability, and neuroinflammation. The abuser may have blocked the survivor from healthcare services, so a comprehensive assessment by the GP and catching-up with missed screening appointments are essential. Sleep, diet and activity can all be impacted by trauma, and can be addressed in needs assessments and care plans.

10.59 Finally, neurodiverse victims/survivors and those with learning disabilities require reasonable adjustments, vigilance against diagnostic overshadowing, and access to adapted and specialised therapies. Trauma-informed care should inform the care and support provision that is put in place to meet the person's needs and keep them safe.

10.60 The next chapter turns to practical trauma-informed approaches to legal representation, equipping legal practitioners with concrete skills to implement the insights from the trauma literature considered in this chapter.

CHAPTER 11

Representing the victim/survivor

'There is no greater agony than bearing an untold story inside you.'[1]

INTRODUCTION

11.01 Cases of coercive control in the Court of Protection or under the inherent jurisdiction usually have three core parties: a public body (typically a local authority), the abuser, and the victim/survivor. Representation of the first two parties is the subject of the next two chapters. This chapter focuses on representation of the victim/survivor ('the client').

11.02 It is sometimes suggested that representing the victim/survivor is straightforward: the lawyers can sit back and watch the local authority and the abuser fight it out in court. This mischaracterises the crucial role of the victim/survivor's lawyers and underestimates the advanced skillset required. These cases are among the most complex that lawyers representing P in the Court of Protection can be instructed in, for four main reasons.

11.03 First, victims/survivors of coercive control have often experienced significant trauma, meaning they require a level of skill beyond the usual care and sensitivity used when representing vulnerable clients. Second, these proceedings only arise because the coercive control has not been resolved.[2] During proceedings the victim/survivor may remain subject to coercive control, or – where the court has imposed interim protective measures such as prohibiting the abuser from contact or placing the client in a safe location (see Chapter 9) – there is still a real risk of the pattern recurring.

11.04 Third, cases in the Court of Protection involve clients who lack capacity to make decisions because of an impairment of, or disturbance in the functioning of, the mind or brain. This creates an additional layer of complexity, as cognitive impairments or mental health difficulties intersect with the many impacts of coercive control. And fourth, lawyers for the victim/survivor frequently face hostility and attempts at manipulation by the abuser, including vitriolic anger directed at professionals involved in the proceedings and attempts to interfere with or influence the victim's legal representation.

1 Maya Angelou, *I Know Why the Caged Bird Sings* (Random House, 1969).

2 Although it is possible for the Court of Protection to determine facts in relation to *historic* coercive control, this would be rare.

11.05 This chapter suggests trauma-informed practical approaches for lawyers to think through in preparation for and during a meeting with their client. It should be read in conjunction with the previous chapter on trauma and coercive control.

PREPARING FOR THE MEETING WITH THE CLIENT

Reviewing records

11.06 Accounts of trauma may be recorded in local authority records (including safeguarding documents), hospital records, GP notes and carers' logs. Relevant material may also be held by the police. Before visiting the client, the solicitor should read the available material, having made sure that the court has made third parties orders for disclosure, and such disclosure has been speedily obtained. Rolling disclosure is likely to be required until the conclusion of the case.

Obtaining mental health and other advice

11.07 The client may be in a poor psychological state, with low self-confidence, reduced self-esteem, impaired decision-making, and feelings of exhaustion. All these factors can affect how they communicate with their lawyer. In Court of Protection cases, it is also likely that the client has a mental health condition, learning disability, cognitive impairment, or form of neurodiversity that may affect communication. For this reason, the lawyer should gather as much relevant information as possible before meeting the client (see para 11.06).[3]

11.08 Before visiting the client, the lawyer could contact a mental health professional or speech and language professional who knows the client. That person may be able to advise on communication approaches, the subjects the client may and may not be able to talk about, and how to support the client when discussing distressing topics.

Determining methods of communication

11.09 Lawyers should also be flexible in offering different methods of communication. Face-to-face meetings are likely to be appropriate in most cases to ensure safety and promote relationships of trust, but there will be cases where a client prefers alternatives. For example, a client may choose asynchronous text-based communication, where they are given time to respond to questions

3 Helpful resources include The Advocate's Gateway, 'Toolkit 2: General principles from research, policy and guidance: planning to question a vulnerable person or someone with communication needs' (2015), 'Toolkit 3: Planning to question someone with an autism spectrum disorder including Asperger syndrome' (2016) and 'Toolkit 4: Planning to question someone with a learning disability' (2015).

later and at their own pace: working on a shared online document can allow the lawyer to post prompt questions that the client can answer when they are able. Neurodiverse clients may prefer text-based communication over speech. Other clients may prefer to express themselves through photographs or sketches, especially as much trauma memory is non-verbal. Online meetings are dealt with below (at para 11.23).

Avoiding a power dynamic

11.10 Depending on the client's circumstances, they may have recently met (and been assessed by) several people who are new to them. The lawyer will be another stranger who wants information from them. Often the lawyer will not have been chosen by the client, but imposed upon them: this dynamic may invoke a memory of how coercive control felt to the client. The client therefore may be sceptical of revealing anything to the lawyer, or reluctant to speak to the lawyer at all.

11.11 For many people (including those who have not experienced domestic abuse), speaking to a lawyer about legal matters is likely to provoke anxiety and perhaps fear that the client has done something wrong, or that they will have to face the abuser, or that they will be judged or punished. The emergence of traumatic memories may be distressing for the client, and the lawyer should be prepared to react in a supportive and non-judgmental manner.

Arranging the appointment

11.12 Gabor Maté has observed that, 'Because our nature is so influenceable, different conditions evoke different versions of us, from benign to disastrous'.[4] With this in mind, the lawyer should work with the client – and, where appropriate, others – to identify the most suitable time and place for meetings, and to establish whether the client would feel more comfortable with a trusted person present. Trauma-attuned lawyering requires careful planning and consideration of practical steps to create conditions where the client can speak as safely, comfortably and openly as possible.

4 Gabor Maté, *The Myth of Normal* (Penguin, 2022), p 117.

11.13 A client who has experienced trauma will not disclose their wounds or tell their story until they are ready – and readiness depends on many factors outside the lawyer's control. The day, time, location, the client's sense of current safety, their assessment of the risk of further abuse, and the presence of others can all influence how much they share and in what way. For this reason, the lawyer should remain flexible, willing to adapt their approach in the moment or return another day if needed.

Preparing questions

11.14 While a trauma therapist aims to 'negotiate a safe passage between the twin dangers of constriction and intrusion',[5] a victim/survivor's lawyer should try to avoid asking too many questions, or asking questions in an inappropriate way, that risks re-traumatisation.

11.15 It is important that the lawyer elicits – insofar as it is possible – an accurate account from the client. This will form part of the evidential canvas from which the court will determine capacity (see Chapters 3 and 4), determine facts if it needs to (see Chapter 8), and make best interests decisions (see Chapter 9). The court will be assisted in these tasks if the lawyer approaches their work in trauma-conscious ways. The lawyer should be aware of the problems with the way the victim/survivor's wishes and feelings are captured, and these are discussed below (under 'attendance notes, at para 11.107).

Ensuring consistency

11.16 It is important that the lawyer engages with the client in a consistent way from the start of proceedings and commits to seeing the client through. It is poor practice for a lawyer to meet the client once, then send other colleagues to the next meeting, and someone different to attend the hearing. Building safety and trust takes time; it cannot be achieved in a single meeting or by ever-changing people.

11.17 Trust is relational, develops gradually, and must be maintained through ongoing, proactive effort. For this reason, consistency of solicitor and counsel should be prioritised, because a change of legal representatives might trigger or reinforce feelings of abandonment, and broken promises. While the court may

5 Judith L Herman, *Trauma and Recovery* (Basic Books, 2022).

be reluctant to schedule hearings around lawyers' availability, it is counsel's responsibility to explain to the court why continuity of representation is so important, drawing out the key reasons in each case.

Being prepared to meet the client

11.18 In summary, all the above preparatory work is important, as it will enable the lawyer to:

(a) avoid systems abuse where the client is asked to repeat histories to different persons;

(b) become aware of potential traumatic incidents in the history and prepare for them;

(c) more readily situate the client's account and identify areas of difference;

(d) understand the client's potential communication needs and prepare adaptations in advance; and

(e) gain an insight into the client's welfare needs.

AT THE MEETING

Small choices increase agency

11.19 The lawyer should consult with others in advance about the precise location of the meeting. When the lawyer arrives at that location, they should review the layout, temperature, brightness of the room, and ensure that others will not be able to overhear the conversation. Furniture arrangements suggestive of power (such as the lawyer sitting behind a desk, or on a taller chair) should be avoided.

11.20 When meeting the client, the lawyer should check-in and monitor the client's comfort and welfare. The client may not be used to be speaking up about their physical comfort, especially if their abuser controlled the home environment. Where is the toilet and can the client use it any time? Would they like a drink? Would they like to sit in the sun? Is the temperature okay? Should the door be left open so the client doesn't feel confined, or closed for privacy? Would the client like breaks?

11.21 It is the lawyer's duty to make an accurate note of the meeting: often turns of phrase will become crucial evidence, and the lawyer can build the client's case around the client's own words. The lawyer may want to take notes, or record the meeting. They will need to explain this to the client and gain their consent.

11.22 The lawyer should be aware of the surroundings and attuned to the client's needs. A client may ask the lawyer to meet a need that is unrelated to legal proceedings, such as reducing the noise during the night, or asking for Earl Grey tea. With the client's consent, the lawyer could mention these requests to those able to make the changes. Demonstrating a proactive interest in meeting immediate practical needs may not be important for the lawyer, but may well be for the client.[6] Supporting the client to make choices and assert their needs even about these small things can empower the client to rebuild agency.

Online meetings

11.23 If the client would like to have an online meeting, the lawyer should carry out the same level of planning as for a face-to-face meeting, but with adjustments.[7]

11.24 The lawyer should not speak to a client if the abuser is anywhere near them, because not only is the risk of listening in too great, the client will not be psychologically free to talk. If the abuser insists on being in the house when the client is having a meeting with the lawyer, the lawyer can return the matter to court and seek the court's assistance in creating a safe environment in which the client can speak to their lawyer.

11.25 It is helpful if the client is by themselves in a room (eg, in a care home) but with support nearby to deal with the technological blips or other needs. The lawyer can check in about the client's comfort, and make sure they have a drink available.

11.26 The lawyer should be in a quiet environment with a calm background, with good lighting so that the client can see the lawyer's face clearly. The lawyer should plan each sentence in advance and enunciate words slowly and clearly, particularly if the client is not used to online meetings. Silence is much more difficult to cope with online, but the lawyer should resist talking into natural gaps. The lawyer should ask a question and then stop talking to let the client think: there is no need to repeat or rephrase the question, unless the client asks or it is clear that they have not understood.

6 Rachel Witkin and Katy Robjant, *The Trauma-Informed Code of Conduct – For all Professionals Working with Survivors of Human Trafficking and Slavery* (Helen Bamber Foundation, 2018).
7 Ibid, pp 48–53.

11.27 The lawyer should try to focus on the screen, as looking away regularly can come across as if the lawyer is disinterested. The lawyer should allow sufficient time for the meeting. Ending abruptly because the lawyer has to join another meeting sould be avoided.

Grounding

11.28 At the beginning of an interview, the lawyer might be tempted to stick to the safe territory of the present, asking questions such as, 'Are the staff nice?' or 'Is the food tasty?' However, this approach has limitations. Psychologist Peter Levine has explained that trauma creates a 'tyranny of the past', where shocking events – or patterns of events – can disrupt a person's biological, psychological, and social equilibrium so profoundly that memories of those events overshadow and distort all other experiences, making it difficult to engage with the present.[8]

11.29 Similarly, Gabor Maté has observed, 'Trauma, until we work it through, keeps us stuck in the past, robbing us of the present moment's riches, limiting who we can be'.[9] Thus, while lawyers may encounter a range of trauma responses in how clients talk about abuse, it is also important to recognise that the client's mind may be caught in a 'physio-emotional time warp',[10] preventing full engagement with the present, including engagement with the lawyer's questions, including initial 'chit chat'.

11.30 At the start of a meeting therefore, the lawyer could do some grounding with the client, enabling the client to feel the chair they're sitting in, feel their feet touching the floor, and that here and now they are not in danger. The lawyer could provide clarity by explaining their role (using non-technical language), the purpose and intended duration of the meeting briefly and then stop to see if the client has understood and appreciated the parameters of the meeting, and whether they have any initial questions.

8 Maté (n 4), 16.
9 Ibid, 21.
10 Ibid, p 16.

Introductions and explaining the process

11.31 At the first meeting it may not be clear to the lawyer that the client has experienced any coercive control, as the papers may contain incomplete information. There is no disadvantage in the lawyer proceeding slowly. If the client does not want to talk about what has happened to them, the lawyer could make useful inroads by simply seeing the client (being totally present and grounded with the client) and getting to know the client, which should be more than a superficial 'how are you?'.

11.32 The lawyer should be clear about what topics the meeting might cover. If the lawyer meets with a client to talk through the court process and the client thinks at some point they are going to be asked about a terrifying abuse situation, they may not take in the information as they may be worrying throughout the meeting about when the frightening part is coming.

11.33 During the first meeting therefore, the lawyer could say that they are not going to ask about any of the abuse today. The first meeting can be usefully limited to introductions, getting to know each other, perhaps explaining the basics of court proceedings, what they are for and who is involved, and then arranging a follow-up meeting. This approach may run counter to the lawyer's desire to 'obtain' wishes and feelings there and then, but the client's needs are the priority, and a smooth and slow start may enable the lawyer to obtain much fuller wishes and feelings in due course.

11.34 Depending on the client, the lawyer could go into further detail about the nature of the case, the parties involved (carefully explaining how the abuser might participate in proceedings), the role of the judge, possible outcomes, and how the information that the client tells the lawyer will be used. Follow-up meetings can be arranged to speak about specific incidents, patterns of abuse and so on, giving the client advance notice that the lawyer would like to ask questions about those difficult subjects.

Explaining the litigation friend role

11.35 A difficult concept to explain is that of the litigation friend (see below at para 11.99). Usually, by the time the lawyer meets their client, the court will have made an order joining the client as a party to the proceedings and appointing a litigation friend to act on their behalf. In coercive control cases, the litigation friend is typically the Official Solicitor (or in some areas including Wales, a local lay advocate). The lawyer has a duty to explain who this person is, what they know about the client, if they are not present why not, and what their role entails.

11.36 It may be disempowering for the client to hear they are not in control of their own legal representation. It may mirror the feeling of being subject to coercive control, robbing the client of their autonomy and wounding their sense of self, triggering negative emotions. Even more difficult is explaining that, if the court deems the client to lack capacity, the litigation friend may disagree with the client about what is in their best interests. To minimise distress, the lawyer should convey information sensitively, clearly and without jargon.

Starting before the abuse

11.37 Due to the fragmentary nature of trauma recall, some therapists approach traumatic events incrementally from the vantage of the present state, working with the more recent events first.[11] This is one approach for a lawyer to consider. However, it may be simpler, and less confusing for the client, to orient the client at a time before the abuse (or the relationship with the abuser) started, and work forwards from there. That may help ground the client in that earlier reality. Many people like to talk about their childhood and growing up: depending on the individual client, that may be a place to start.

11.38 Whether to use open questions or gently put findings to the client will depend on the stage of the case, how well the lawyer knows the client, and the client's ability and willingness to discuss their trauma, taking into account the fragmented nature of traumatic memories mentioned in the previous paragraph and discussed in Chapter 10.

Active listening

11.39 The lawyer should listen actively and non-judgmentally. This requires refraining from speaking or commenting unnecessarily – skills that do not come naturally to some lawyers. Active listening involves observing the client's facial expressions and body language during moments of silence and being comfortable with pauses rather than feeling the need to fill them with speech.

11.40 The lawyer should act with compassion and empathy but must not presume the client's emotions. The lawyer should tune into the client's emotional

11 Peter A Levine, *Trauma and Memory: Brain and Body in a Search for the Living Past* (North Atlantic Books, 2015), p 63.

needs, distinct from their own. Lawyers may naturally feel sympathy or relief that the client is now safe, but the client may instead feel shame, grief, rage, panic, sadness, or other emotions. The solicitor should make no assumptions about the client's feelings and should focus on creating a space where the client feels safe to express themselves in their own way, including through non-verbal communication.

11.41 It may be tempting for a lawyer to respond to a disclosure of abuse with a comment such as: 'That must have been terrible for you!' Such phrases should be avoided, as they are speculative, prescriptive, suggestive and patronising. An alternative might be, 'What happened was not your fault. I am interested in hearing more about what you've experienced.'

Suggestibility

11.42 The lawyer should avoid leading questions that may prompt the client to provide the answer they think the lawyer wants to hear. This mirrors patterns in coercive control, where one person dominates the other. And if the client has a learning disability or other vulnerability, they may be particularly suggestible to authority figures such as lawyers. Chapter 10 deals with how an abuser may weaponise the client's disability, a tactic of coercive control that lawyers should be aware of.

11.43 Lawyers may have to seek alternative ways for the client to communicate information. The client may struggle to identify their own thoughts separate from the abuser's influence, and the lawyer may have to ask clarificatory questions sensitively.

Discussing abuse

11.44 It can be intensely distressing for a victim/survivor of abuse to discuss harm with a person they barely know. That is why the lawyer should proactively build trust, at a pace chosen by the client. It is important that the client feels no pressure to disclose details, and that the meeting has purposes other than discussing the traumatic events or abusive relationship.

11.45 The lawyer might start by explaining the topic and seeking the client's consent to proceed. For example: 'I have some questions about John's behaviour: is that okay?', or 'I'd now like to ask about the lasting power of attorney.' As noted above, trauma can fragment memory, making it difficult for a client to provide a clear or chronological account of events. The lawyer may have to check whether the client can recall dates or approximations of when things happened, and use gentle prompts to explore topics and themes, for example: 'Could you tell me a little about how he controlled your money?'

11.46 When discussing traumatic events, an approach to consider is 'radical acceptance', wherein the lawyer adopts a mindset that acknowledges what happened and the reality of the situation, without approving or endorsing it.[12] A brief acknowledgment of the harm might be sufficient for the conversation to move on. Rather than responding in a way that risks the client internalising the response, the lawyer could say something like, 'Thank you for trusting me with something this difficult' or I'm sorry this has happened to you'. In this way, rather than leaving the client thinking: 'This terrible thing happened to me and I hate it', radical acceptance enables the client to reframe their thought to: 'I had no control over this, but it happened. I can decide what to do next.'[13]

11.47 The client may struggle to articulate their wishes fully, including because the abuser may have limited their autonomy to express their wishes or make choices for a long time. Certain expressions of feelings may require psychological expertise to interpret. The danger of the lawyer reconstructing the narrative themselves, is that they unintentionally impose their own (different) perspective. Hence it is probably wise for the lawyer to avoid conveying a judgment wrapped in a question such as 'Why didn't you leave?' or 'Was that domestic abuse?'.

11.48 Where the client does not have access to psychological support, the lawyer may be the only person with whom they can speak about their experiences. The client may disclose information that was previously unknown to the lawyer or to the local authority. Lawyers should avoid forcing memory retrieval or applying pressure. Instead they may (with the client's permission or after discussing the matter carefully with the litigation friend) triangulate information through friends, neighbours, or other third-party accounts, as well as reviewing documents such as medical records received through third-party disclosure orders.

Physical contact

11.49 Trauma-informed practice prioritises creating a safe space where the client feels in control of interactions. Except in very limited circumstances where the client initiates and consents to non-intrusive contact (such as a handshake), a lawyer should never physically touch a client. This maintains a professional boundary to avoid actual or perceived exploitation, misunderstanding, or allegations of misconduct.

12 The term *radical acceptance* was originally developed as a mindfulness-based distress tolerance skill in dialectical behaviour therapy by Marsha Linehan, *Cognitive-behavioral Treatment of Borderline Personality Disorder.* (Guilford Press, 1993).

13 Ahona Guha, *Reclaim: Understanding Complex Trauma and Those Who Abuse* (Scribe, 2023), p 99.

11.50 Touch can be a sign of warmth and affection, but it can also be a sign of hostility and threat.[14] The lawyer holds the power in the dynamic, and a client who has experienced trauma may perceive touch as coercive or controlling, which could be retraumatising and trigger flashbacks or intense emotional reactions. Inappropriate physical contact, especially if unwanted, could amount to professional misconduct, depending on the circumstances. However, some clients may request physical contact, like a firm hug, for sensory reasons. The lawyer must decide what seems appropriate in the circumstances and record it in an attendance note.

THE EFFECTS OF TRAUMA DURING THE MEETING

11.51 The client's mood and behaviours may cycle through different phases, which may be brought about by being removed from coercive control and placed in a safe environment. Behaviours may also be affected by other mental health or neurological conditions, including neurodiversity, dissociation, anxiety, depression, dementia, or psychosis. Behaviours may include reduced food intake, hypersexualised behaviour, verbal or physical aggression or withdrawal from social activities.

11.52 In some cases, trauma responses (see Chapter 10) may cause the client to spend long periods in bed, sleeping for many hours. Legal appointments may have to be rescheduled as a result. A client may recognise that the trauma has happened, but is unable to acknowledge that it has ended, and that life continues. This prevents full processing of the experience and can make it difficult for the client to provide an account.

11.53 Concentration can also be impacted by mental health presentations, but trauma can affect concentration too. During the meeting, the lawyer could check-in with the client and ask whether a change of subject or a break would help. The lawyer may need to help orient the client to the 'here and now'. To aid in this process, the lawyer could identify objects in the room to, or take objects to the meeting such as photographs, a bracelet, beads etc.: these provide a focal point for distraction and discussion.[15]

14 Andrew McDonnell, *The Reflective Journey: A Practitioner's Guide to the Low Arousal Approach* (Studio3, 2019), p 225.
15 Witkin and Robjant (n 6), 21.

11.54 The following commentary provides examples of how trauma responses might appear, together with suggested trauma-informed approaches a lawyer might consider using. These are suggestions only and are not intended to be prescriptive stock phrases to be parroted verbatim. They are illustrations as to how a lawyer might go about meeting their client's trauma-related needs.

Emotional shut down

11.55 The client may be reluctant to engage with the questions being asked, or unable to recall events. This may be because the client is experiencing emotional shut-down as a protective response to trauma, where the mind and body switch off feelings to avoid the unbearable stress or fear associated with the trauma. This is an autonomic response that helps the person survive in the moment, but can leave them appearing detached, numb, or unresponsive even in the safe environment of speaking with a lawyer.

11.56 The client may say:

- What do you mean how do I feel? I don't feel anything.
- It's easier if I don't speak about that.
- Yes/no/I don't know (one-word answers).

11.57 The lawyer could respond: It's okay if emotions aren't coming up right now: that's a normal response to trauma. You don't have to feel or show anything; your experience still matters. We can pause, or I can ask about something different – whatever feels easier for you. If it helps, take a moment to feel your feet on the floor before we continue.

Dissociation

11.58 Trauma causes dissociation, which accounts for many of the emotions discussed in this section. Dissociation is a natural autonomic response to trauma that an individual has no control of or is necessarily aware of. It can cause a person to feel unsafe in the present. It is a 'temporary detachment of a person's mind from their emotional state and body which can manifest in various ways'.[16] It renders a person 'unable to put the actual event, the source of those memories, behind them',[17] and integrate the traumatic event into their life story.

11.59 The lawyer may notice the client

- zoning out, becoming detached from their thoughts, emotions, or environment;
- giving vague, repetitive or contradictory answers; and
- losing the thread of the discussion

11.60 The lawyer could respond: Why don't we take a small break right now? Shall we make a cup of tea: how do you take yours? Would it help if we talked about something else for a moment? You're in control here – we can stop or go at your own pace.

Flashbacks

11.61 Post-traumatic stress may give rise to flashbacks, which are intense, intrusive recollections that make the client feel as if they are reliving the event currently occurring in the present. Flashbacks often lack context, reflecting the fragmented nature of traumatic memory. They can be intensely disabling: 'The more we try to rid ourselves of these flashbacks, the more they haunt, torment, and strangle our life force, seriously restricting our capacity to live in the here and now'.[18]

11.62 The lawyer could prepare for the possibility of flashbacks by asking the client if they experience feeling 'lost' in a memory and asking them what works for them in bringing them back to the present.

11.63 Traumatic memories can resurface unexpectedly and may be triggered by questions, actions or sensory stimuli that remind the client of their trauma. If a client experiences a flashback, the lawyer's role is not to take a note of the content of the flashback as if it is an accurate account of the abuse, but to maintain safety and support the client's grounding in coming back into the room and into the present.

11.64 The client may say:

16 Witkin and Robjant (n 6), 7.
17 Bessel van der Kolk, *The Body Keeps the Score* (Penguin, 2014), p 217.
18 Levine (n 11).

- I can feel his breath against my neck.
- I'm back in the room with him.
- I can hear him shouting and the door slamming.

11.65 The lawyer could respond: You're safe here. It's just you and me in this room. That's your memory, but you are not in danger now. It makes sense that your memory feels so real: many people experience flashbacks this way. You don't have to say anything until you feel ready.

11.66 The lawyer could try to bring the client away from the flashback and into the room: Let's focus on your feet on the floor or your hands in your lap. The plant in the corner of the room has lovely leaves: do you like plants? I've brought this object (bracelet, pebble, beads, photograph etc) with me, shall we have a look?

Shame

11.67 Feelings of shame are common among trauma victims/survivors and can profoundly affect how a person perceives themself. A trauma survivor may feel responsible for getting into a coercive situation, for not escaping, for their post-trauma psychological or practical needs, or for being involved in court proceedings. Shame reflects a sense of unworthiness and can be intensified by disability; for example, the client may believe that being different would have prevented the abuse, or its traumatic effects.

11.68 Despite its painful nature, shame can serve a protective function. First, it can shield the client from confronting the full impact of traumatic experiences. If they believe they, rather than the abuser, are at fault, shame can become a focal emotion, protecting against feelings of helplessness and powerlessness. Second, although deeply painful, shame may be easier to manage than other overwhelming emotions, such as grief or rage. Third, the client may feel that carrying shame is the only way to avoid becoming like the abuser, fearing that without it they might become harmful themselves.[19]

11.69 The client may say:

- I'm a terrible person, weak and useless.

19 See the podcast series 'Complex trauma recovery' by Kina Penelope.

- I don't deserve help.
- I cannot be fixed.

11.70 The lawyer could respond: Your experience doesn't define your worth. You deserve to be heard, and it's my job to make sure this happens in the court proceedings. Shall I see how to make a referral for you to get professional psychology support for how you are feeling?

Guilt

11.71 Self-blame is not a sign of truth or responsibility; it is a symptom of trauma. The internalised sense of personal responsibility for abuse or its consequences often arises from the abuser's manipulations: the abuser will blame the victim/survivor until they absorb the narrative as truth. It may also arise from social expectations, or the client's own adaptive responses (where the abuser is also a carer, the victim/survivor may feel guilty for holding negative feelings toward them), even though the abuse is not their fault.

11.72 The client may say:

- It's my fault.
- Why didn't I escape?
- I made this happen.

11.73 The lawyer could respond: What happened was not your fault. I understand you feel responsible but only the abuser was responsible for what they did to you.

Intrusive thoughts

11.74 Trauma can lead to persistent, distressing thoughts which may 'come from nowhere'. Individuals may also unconsciously avoid or suppress painful emotions, which can result in withdrawal from social interactions and intimate relationships. Trauma survivors may remain hyper-aroused – constantly on guard and jumpy – even in safe environments. This hyper-arousal can cause sleep problems, which in turn affect cognition, mood, and physical health.

11.75 The client may say:

- I can't stop thinking about what happened. I can't focus on anything else.
- I'm useless for not being able to move on.

- Everyone will think I'm overreacting … they'll think it's all my fault.

11.76 The lawyer could respond: It's understandable that your mind keeps returning to these thoughts. Intrusive thoughts are a common response to trauma. They don't mean you're responsible or weak. We can pause if these thoughts feel overwhelming. We can focus on what feels safe to discuss.

Grief

11.77 Trauma can also manifest as intense feelings of loss, including loss of significant periods of life, the relationship with the abuser (whom they may still love), certainty, autonomy or aspects of self. The client may experience grief if assessed as lacking capacity to make decisions, including decisions regarding legal proceedings.

11.78 The client may say:

- I don't have any friends left … I pushed everyone away because of [the abuser].
- I've missed so much of my life: birthdays, holidays, my son's graduation.
- I feel like I've lost myself. I don't know who I am anymore.

11.79 The lawyer could respond: It makes sense that you feel that way. What you've been through is a huge loss, and it's normal to grieve. You don't need to talk about everything at once. We can focus on what feels most important to you today.

Rage

11.80 The client may experience intense anger. This can feel frightening and endless. Rage may be in relation, for example, to the abuse, the abuser, being removed from the controlling environment, or the legal process. It can sometimes result in challenging behaviour or disengagement from professionals, including legal representatives.

11.81 The client may say:

- Why didn't anyone help me?
- I hate it how [the abuser] controlled my life.
- I can't get over how furious I am.

11.82 The lawyer could respond: It makes sense that you're feeling angry about what happened. You can share what happened with me when you're ready.[20]

11.83 If the client displays intense emotion such as rage, the lawyer should remind themselves that it is not directed against them (see 'Lawyer self-care', at para 11.126 below). The lawyer should recognise their own limits and find a way to take a moment if they need to.

Confusion

11.84 The client may display confusion when speaking about their experiences of abuse, because trauma can disrupt memory, attention, and cognitive processing.

11.85 The client may say:

- I can't think straight.
- I don't know what to think or how I'm feeling.
- Sometimes I think I imagined it.

11.86 The lawyer could respond: Let's start with something you can remember: could you tell me where you were, was anyone else there? You can share memories with me as they emerge, when you are ready. Perhaps you could sketch a picture.

Minimising

11.87 A client may downplay or understate the severity, significance, or impact of the trauma or otherwise rationalise it, as a way of making it more manageable. Minimising is not a denial of reality; rather, it is a protective strategy that enables the individual to cope with overwhelming emotions, preserve a sense of safety, and navigate the ongoing effects of abuse.

11.88 The client may say:

- It wasn't really that bad: it could have been worse.
- [The abuser] didn't mean it. Everyone gets angry sometimes.

20 If the client displays intense emotion such as rage, the lawyer should remind themselves that it is not directed against them. The lawyer should recognise their own limits and find a way to take a moment if they need to.

- I don't want to make a fuss.

11.89 The lawyer could respond: What you experienced matters, and no one deserves to be treated that way. Being controlled was not your fault. It's understandable to feel that way – many people who have been controlled downplay what happened to cope with it.

Other presentations

11.90 While not necessarily related to trauma specifically, when speaking to the lawyer, the client may use words or phrases they have recruited from the abuser, such as: 'I know I'm "a useless sod".' The client may even emphasise the abuser's positive traits, for example, 'Derek can make a tasty casserole!'

11.91 The lawyer should take a note, if possible, of the precise words that the client uses. The lawyer will need to take care when acknowledging the abuser's positive attributes and the client recalling happy memories with the abuser that they do not affirm perspectives held by the client that this may 'make up for' the abuse or make it any more acceptable.

ENDING THE MEETING

Summing up with positivity

11.92 The lawyer should avoid leaving a client in the middle of a difficult trauma narrative or with heightened emotions, and should endeavour to bring the client back into the present. This can be done by wrapping up the discussion of past trauma, and spending a few minutes discussing the here and now: for example, by talking about food, activities, friends, the weather and plans for tomorrow.

11.93 The lawyer could summarise what has been achieved in the meeting, ending on positive topics of safety, agency and aspirations. The lawyer could emphasise that it has been a difficult meeting, and with the client reflect on the work they have done to get here, and think through with them what they will do to take care of themselves. These can be small items such as listening to their favourite music, going for a walk in the sun, drinking an exotic herbal tea, or enjoying some pampering.

11.94 The lawyer should remind the client how to contact the lawyer before the next planned meeting, if needed. The lawyer could summarise the support that is available to the client and consider any additional needs that the client has identified during the meeting that should be put in place for subsequent meetings.

Forthcoming court hearings

11.95 If there is a hearing coming up, the lawyer should ask the client if they would like to attend and, if yes, the lawyer could discuss special measures (see at para 11.120 below). The client may not need disability-related adjustments in the ordinary course of their life, but courtrooms are stressful places and depending on contact arrangements, the court hearing may be the first time since the separation that the client might have seen or been in the same room as the abuser.

Story stewardship

11.96 A lawyer might leave an initial meeting feeling empty-handed, having been unable to gather the client's wishes and feelings about the past abuse, or about their future aspirations. This is not a failure on the part of the lawyer or, of course, the client.

11.97 No meeting with the client is purposeless: by spending time with them and by asking even a small number of relevant questions in a sensitive way, the lawyer is likely to be able to provide a trauma-informed judge with an account of the client's current presentation, their perspective on what has happened, and their sense of where they are now. This forms part of the lawyer's role in 'story stewardship': honouring and sharing the victim/survivor's narrative.[21] The story can be built up during each meeting.

What happens next

11.98 Two important principles of trauma-informed approaches to legal practice are clear communication and keeping promises. Therefore, when leaving the client, the lawyer should tell the client what will happen next, and when the lawyer will next be in touch. A related consideration is consistency of legal representation (and avoiding delegating the next visit to a different lawyer), as highlighted earlier in the chapter. The client has been let down by other people, so it is important that the lawyer keeps to their word.

21 See Brené Brown, *Atlas of the Heart: Mapping Meaningful Connection and the Language of Human Experience* (Random House, 2022).

THE LITIGATION FRIEND

11.99 If an application has been made to the Court of Protection, there will be some evidence that the victim/survivor lacks subject matter capacity, and the court will routinely read across from that evidence and note in the first court order that there is reason to believe that the victim/survivor lacks capacity to conduct proceedings. In such situation, the court will invite the Official Solicitor to be the litigation friend if there is no other suitable person to act in this role.[22] The Official Solicitor is likely to accept the invitation if funding is in place (see below at para 11.103) and then then allocate the case to a solicitor. Given the nature and complexity of coercive control cases, the Court of Protection is unlikely to appoint an Accredited Legal Representative.[23]

11.100 As noted in Chapter 6, inherent jurisdiction cases are governed by the Civil Procedure Rules (CPR). Part 21 CPR provides that the court can appoint a litigation friend to a party only if that party lacks capacity to conduct proceedings pursuant to the Mental Capacity Act 2005 (MCA 2005). If the party is disabled from making capacitous decisions because of constraint, coercion or undue influence but retains capacity pursuant to the MCA 2005, it appears that the court has no power to appoint a litigation friend.

11.101 It is not uncommon in coercive control cases for the abuser to try to be appointed as the litigation friend, claiming that they know the victim/survivor the best. The abuser may produce a certificate saying that the victim/survivor has capacity to conduct proceedings, the certificate having been signed by a professional (such as a GP or solicitor) arranged by the abuser, who may not have seen all the relevant materials.[24] Lawyers representing the victim/survivor should be aware of the potential for these coercive tactics to be deployed, call them out, and resist them as appropriate.

11.102 It is a core duty of the litigation friend to facilitate the victim/survivor's access to justice and ensure that their voice is heard in the proceedings. A litigation friend may advance arguments in the Court of Protection in relation to capacity and/or best interests that do not align with P's wishes and feelings. Explaining the position at which the litigation friend has arrived on P's behalf will need to be explained in a trauma-informed manner.

22 Pursuant to the Court of Protections Rules (COPR 2017), r 17.4. See also Official Solicitor, 'Practice Note: Appointment as litigation friend in personal welfare proceedings in the Court of Protection', 3 February 2021.

23 See Practice Direction (PD) 1A, paras 9 to 11.

24 See, for example, 'When two legal teams turn up in court to represent P: Disputed capacity to conduct proceedings', 18 March 2024, openjusticecourtofprotection.org.

FUNDING

11.103 In Court of Protection proceedings, the Official Solicitor will agree to act as the victim/survivor's litigation friend only if the acceptance criteria are met, including security for the cost of the solicitor that the Official Solicitor will retain on P's behalf. Where P is subject to an urgent or standard authorisation under the Deprivation of Liberty Safeguards (DoLS) and an application has been made under MCA 2005, s 21A, P will qualify for non-means-tested legal aid. Legal aid is otherwise subject to a means test in all other welfare applications in the Court of Protection where the client is over 18.

11.104 The merits test of legal aid funding applies in all circumstances. Legal aid is generally granted if the case has at least a 'moderate' prospect of success (ie, 50% or greater chance). However, for certain categories of cases including those involving breaches of rights under the European Convention on Human Rights (ECHR), legal aid may also be available for cases assessed as borderline, marginal or even unclear.[25]

11.105 One of the first challenges for a solicitor representing a victim/survivor of coercive control is obtaining evidence of their financial means, in order to make an application for legal aid. This can be difficult if the abuser has taken charge of the victim/survivor's money and refuses to share information. The abuser may find it excruciating to be directed to do something as this is a loss of their control. Their reluctance may also be because sharing financial information would reveal that they have committed criminal offences.

11.106 In the Court of Protection, P's lawyer may apply for a financial investigation order, requiring the person with access to P's funds to provide detailed accounts and supporting documents relating to P's financial affairs. If necessary, the court can also grant an injunction directing that person to disclose the information and attach a penal notice so that failure to comply is likely to be contempt of court. The court may, on its own motion, order any person holding information on P's finances to provide to P's solicitor with copies of bank or building society account statements. This allows P's solicitor to obtain statements from financial institutions, but only if the account is in P's name. A difficulty arises if the account is in the name of the abuser only, even if P's welfare benefits are paid into that account.

25 Civil Legal Aid (Merits Criteria) Regulations 2013 (SI 2013/104), reg 69.

ATTENDANCE NOTES OF THE CLIENT'S WISHES AND FEELINGS

11.107 In the inherent jurisdiction of the High Court, the victim of coercive control will be joined as a party to the proceedings. They can instruct a lawyer or act as a litigant in person. They can take steps such as drafting witness statements themselves or with legal assistance.

11.108 In the Court of Protection, where a litigation friend has been appointed, the court will direct P's solicitor to file and serve a witness statement exhibiting an attendance note of a meeting with P during which the solicitor is expected to have obtained P's wishes and feelings on relevant matters. This assists the judge in considering P's wishes and feelings when making best interests decisions, which is required by MCA 2005, s 4(6).

11.109 As this chapter has explained, gathering the client's wishes and feelings can be a complex and lengthy process, due to the impact of trauma and its interaction with mental disability. An unusual aspect of Court of Protection proceedings is that a conversation between P and their lawyer is not protected by legal privilege, because technically the lawyer's client is not P, but the litigation friend. Attendance notes are filed with the court and served on all parties, including – if they have been joined as a party – the abuser. The abuser will therefore be able to read P's views about the abuser's behaviours, the relationship, P's current views and their healing process.

11.110 P's lawyer may feel that disclosing this information to the abuser is a betrayal of the trust they are delicately building with their client. When filing an attendance note, it is therefore incumbent on the lawyer to ensure they are not placing P at risk of further harm if the abuser still has contact, or future harm after proceedings end. Although due to the fragmentary nature of traumatic memory recall the note may not contain P's full views about the allegations against the abuser, it may contain information that is likely to be met with the abuser's disapproval. When reading an attendance note, the abuser may:

- feel betrayed: 'How dare you tell them that without my permission!';
- chastise or punish the client;
- coach the client about what to say next time: 'Just say you want to return to me!';
- claim that *they* are the victim of gaslighting;
- accuse the author of the attendance note (P's lawyer) of lying;
- say that the lawyer (or social worker etc) has coerced the client into making false accusations; or
- question the client's credibility by citing, for example, their mental illness or worsening dementia.

11.111 Lawyers for the victim/survivor should be mindful that the abuser may behave in the above (and other) ways. Therefore, the attendance note should be a carefully curated summary of wishes and feelings prepared in accordance with the legal representative's duties to the court. It need not be a transcript of the whole conversation. Lawyers can take inspiration from other areas of law where, arguably, the victim is better protected. For instance, in criminal proceedings, a victim impact statement is a brief document outlining how the offence has affected the victim: it does not disclose all the victim's thoughts, wishes, feelings, own account of their healing journey, current vulnerabilities or future aspirations.

11.112 Judges in the Court of Protection are likely to be sympathetic to an application to make sensible case management directions that minimise the risk of harm to the victim/survivor. While solicitors commonly file wishes and feelings evidence before each case management hearing, the content of the attendance note is decided by the litigation friend. Court proceedings often span several months or years, and if there are multiple case management hearings before a fact-finding hearing (see Chapter 8), the litigation friend could seek the court's permission to file one extended attendance note before the fact-finding hearing outlining the client's responses to each item on a schedule of allegations gathered over several meetings. This approach exemplifies trauma-informed practice, as it adapts court procedures to account for the time and care needed to build trust with a trauma victim and the fragmentary effect of trauma on memory recall that require several meetings to piece together the victim's account of the pattern of coercive and controlling behaviour.

PARTICIPATION IN PROCEEDINGS

11.113 Court of Protection judges have a duty to ensure the participation of P by joining them as a party and appointing a litigation friend.[26] The court must, as far as reasonably practicable, permit and encourage P to participate, or improve their ability to participate, as fully as possible in any act done for them and any decision affecting them.[27] Judges are generally flexible in accommodating P and will be guided by P's lawyers as to how their client remains central to the proceedings. Options include:

26 COPR 2017, r 1.2 and Part 17.
27 MCA 2005, s 4(4).

(a) **Attendance note**: As noted above, the court usually directs P's lawyer to file a witness statement exhibiting an attendance note of a meeting (or meetings) with P. This is a vehicle for P's wishes and feelings to be communicated to the judge without P needing to attend court.

(b) **Judicial visit**: The judge may visit P at their home (or online), typically before a hearing where best interests decisions will be made. P's lawyer attends the meeting and prepares a note of the visit, and after the judge approves the note, the lawyer circulates it to the other parties. The visit is not for gathering formal evidence but it may highlight aspects of the evidence already heard, reinforcing oral evidence from experts or family members.

(c) **Meeting the judge at court**: P may attend court and have a brief conversation with the judge before proceedings, accompanied by their lawyer, in the otherwise empty courtroom. Again, a note is circulated. P may then leave or stay for the hearing, as they wish.

(d) **Participation in the hearing in-person**: P may attend the hearing. They may sit next to their solicitor, who should remain responsive to P's needs, such as arranging breaks to explain proceedings.

(e) **Participating in the hearing remotely**: P could join the hearing remotely, from their home or other setting, and participate as they wish, with their camera turned on or off. This can be more comfortable for P, but may present challenges for legal representatives in communicating with P during the hearing. If this is P's wish, their lawyers will have to make arrangements in advance with the court.

(a) **Non-participation**: P may choose not to meet the judge, attend court, or participate at all. Their choice should be respected.

SUPPORTING THE CLIENT AT COURT

11.114 Lawyers should make logistical arrangements with their client in advance, and, where relevant, the people who will bring the client to court and support them.

11.115 Before a hearing there are usually 'pre-hearing discussions', involving lawyers only. Lawyers representing P should make sure that P knows about these discussions so that they do not think discussions are happening behind their back. Lawyers should report back to P after these discussions have taken place.

11.116 Lawyers should avoid the traumatised client meeting their barrister for the first time on the day of the hearing itself. It is good practice for the barrister to meet their client with their instructing solicitor well before the hearing. Time will need to be set aside for the client to meet with the barrister and ask any questions.

11.117 The client may appreciate being invited into the courtroom to see how it is laid out, before everyone else goes in. This is an opportunity for the lawyer to explain where the client will sit, where the abuser will sit, where others will be, who the judge will be, and how the hearing will work.

11.118 If the client and their abuser are still in contact, there are risks that the abuser will try to control the client at court. The abuser may try to sit close to the client, hold their hand, wave at them or make other performative actions to showcase to the judge how much the abuser loves and cares for the client. The abuser may seek to limit the client's participation or tell them what to say and how to act. It is important that the lawyers anticipate and prevent these controlling behaviours, especially in the court building, which is supposed to be a safe space. Lawyers should alert the judge to any efforts the abuser makes to control the victim in the courtroom or the court process more generally. The court has the power to eject the abuser from the building if they cause disruption or distress.

11.119 By the time of the court hearing, the client may have had no contact with the abuser for some time, and may not want to see them. If the abuser is also due to attend court, it is the responsibility of lawyers to carefully stage-manage the entries, exits and waiting areas so that the client does not see the abuser. Lawyers can communicate with the judge's clerk or other court staff before the hearing and request 'special measures directions'. This is available to any party or witness who is, or is at risk of, being a victim of domestic abuse.[28]

11.120 Special measures are tailored to the circumstances of the case, and might include:

(a) the client using a different entrance to access the courtroom than the abuser;

(b) if there is only one entrance, the client entering or exiting the court before or after the abuser;

(c) the court designating a conference room near the courtroom for the client and their team to minimise contact with the abuser;

(d) having a security guard present in the courtroom; and

(e) using a screen in the courtroom to prevent the client and the abuser from seeing each other.[29]

28 Domestic Abuse Act 2021, s 64.
29 See the Judicial College, *Equal Treatment Bench Book*, Chapter 4 on mental disability.

11.121 The court should send written confirmation from court staff that the requested measures will be in place. Lawyers can then inform the client that the court has directed the measures to be in place, which may help reduce feelings of anxiety.

11.122 If the abuser is giving evidence during the hearing, the client may choose not to be present. They may want their lawyer to relay what was said. Or they may want a summary only, or not to be told or informed about the content at all. Similarly, at the end of the case, the judge may hand down a 'ex tempore' judgement which the client may wish to hear. Alternatively, the client may prefer to go home and receive the outcome via a call, text, email or visit from their lawyer. Legal representatives should offer options.

11.123 It is natural for parties to have emotional reactions when the judge delivers a decision. The client may feel relief, numbness, or find the end of a hearing anticlimactic. If the court finds coercive control proved, the client may might feel anything from shock, grief, loss or disbelief to relief, gratitude and joy.

11.124 When leaving court, lawyers should again ensure that the client is protected: if the client does not want to see the abuser, the lawyers should ensure this. The abuser may be hanging around the corner from the courtroom, so the lawyers should ensure that the client's journey is planned in advance. If the abuser does not know where the client is currently living (having been temporarily removed to a place of safety), then security measures have to be put in place to ensure that the abuser is unable to follow the client.

11.125 Finally, the lawyer should provide clear information to the client about the next steps in the case, and when their next meeting will be, and follow up in writing.

LAWYER SELF-CARE

11.126 A fundamental part of responsible legal practice with traumatised clients is self-care. Any lawyer dealing with trauma should be aware of vicarious trauma, which may arise from the cumulative negative effects of being immersed in their client's (or clients') trauma. Lawyers may experience being irritable for no reason, waking up in the middle of the night, feeling unable to cope at work or at home, memory loss, dreading working on certain cases or meeting certain clients, intrusive thoughts and other symptoms. Lawyers may say they are professionals who can 'compartmentalise' their work so it doesn't affect them. Such assertions are doubtful. Indeed, failure to acknowledge and recognise the potential impacts of work with traumatised clients may lead to the effects being expressed unconsciously, for example, through detachment or case-hardening.

11.127 Supporting a traumatised client can take an emotional toll, as can the responsibility of advising on life changing decisions such as whether it is in the client's best interests to continue (or resume) contact with the abuser. Advocating for a best interests outcome that goes against the client's wishes and feelings is particularly difficult. It is also not uncommon for the lawyer representing the victim/survivor to be on the receiving end of harassment and complaints by the abuser, including threats to the lawyer's employer/Chambers or regulator, and abusive emails.

11.128 It is important to adopt a proactive approach to promoting self-care and wellbeing when working with traumatised clients as well as to use support services when needed. Lawyers are advised to seek the many resources available, in particular those from LawCare, the mental health charity for everyone in the legal sector.

CONCLUSIONS

11.129 This chapter has explained the myriad impacts of trauma on a person who has experienced coercive control, including how a victim/survivor sees themselves in the world, and their sense of trust, safety and autonomy. It has suggested that because of the fragmentary nature of traumatic memory recall, a lawyer should expect their client to explain their trauma by way of a collage rather than a neat chronology. The client's account may appear inconsistent, disjointed, or incomplete, and may be compounded by cognitive impairment or a mental health condition. The lawyer is required to tolerate a degree of uncertainty and to work within the inherent messiness of trauma narratives.

11.130 By adopting thoughtful trauma-informed approaches, a lawyer representing a victim/survivor of coercive control can be a therapeutic agent in the justice system. They can encourage the law and the legal process to be applied in a more healing way, while respecting the principles of justice and fairness.[30] The use of trauma-informed approaches enables a lawyer to hold their client's anguish tenderly and respond in a psychologically-informed manner. Engagement with a client's experience of trauma is a dynamic process, through which a lawyer might expand the possibility of healing.

30 Originating in the United States in the late 1980s, the field of *therapeutic jurisprudence* has been developed by jurists. See David Wexler, 'Therapeutic jurisprudence: An overview' (2000) 17 *Thomas M. Cooley Law Review* 125.

CHAPTER 12

Representing the local authority

> 'If only there were evil people somewhere insidiously committing evil deeds, and it were necessary only to separate them from the rest of us and destroy them. But the line dividing good and evil cuts through the heart of every human being. And who is willing to destroy a piece of his own heart?'[1]

INTRODUCTION

12.01 The last chapter offered suggestions for lawyers representing victims/survivors in cases in the Court of Protection and under the inherent jurisdiction. This chapter considers social work practice and legal representation of the local authority. In coercive control cases, social workers are often in the driving seat because the local authority will make the court application. When facts are required to be found (see Chapter 8), the local authority's role is quasi-prosecutorial, and those representing the local authority must act with speed, precision and fairness when putting their case. The chapter starts by considering legal strategy (at para 12.02), then addresses problems with accessing the victim/survivor (at para 12.15), the need to act with speed and creativity (at para 12.20), gathering evidence (at para 12.29), the role of healthcare professionals (at para 12.33), and issues that arise during proceedings (at para 12.34).

LEGAL STRATEGY

12.02 It is incumbent on the local authority, and those who represent it, to set the tone. Although social workers are likely to be heavily invested in the case, lawyers should act in a manner that reduces the temperature of the 'high octane lawfare'[2] that often characterises coercive control litigation. This can increase the psychological safety of the victim/survivor, and make the proceedings less stressful for everyone involved. A polite and respectful manner should not, of course, be at the expense of failing to tackle, head-on, the abuse.

1 Aleksandr Solzhenitsyn, *The Gulag Archipelago* (Penguin, 2024).
2 *An ICB v G & Ors* [2024] EWCOP 13, para 195.

12.03 Social workers and their in-house solicitors face ethical and legal challenges litigating coercive control cases. An in-depth meeting between P's social worker, the team manager, the in-house solicitor and external counsel can provide different perspectives that may enable a legal strategy and next steps to be agreed.

12.04 Social care professionals and the lawyers who represent them should be aware that victims/survivors of coercive control may be a 'muted group' whose voice, experiences and harms are undervalued or risk not being sufficiently important to be acted upon, especially so when intersectional considerations of gender, disability and social status are considered.[3]

12.05 While those who commit 'evil deeds', to use Solzhenitsyn's words, should be treated with fairness, it is also the case that the deeds are sometimes so peculiar and egregious, that professionals fail to hear victims/survivors, or act promptly as a result. Within the system of adult social care, practitioners may become desensitised by seeing cases with a slow trickle of controlling behaviours that such abuse becomes normalised. Further, the tactics of control may be so far outside the everyday experience of the social workers that they find it difficult to comprehend that what is reported to have taken place might actually be true, that the victim may be at imminent risk of serious harm, and that an application to the Court of Protection or under the inherent jurisdiction should be made without delay.

12.06 Social workers risk being drawn in by the explanation offered by the controlling person. Social workers may have thoughts about the alleged abuser, as follows. They seem loving and decent person. They are assertive, antagonistic and like to make complaints which take a lot of social work time to resolve, but aren't we demonising them by accusing them of coercive control? The disabled person loves them!

12.07 In relation to coercive control, the judiciary has recognised that, 'it is often difficult for professionals to identify this type of abuse and to be most effective in their investigations', especially where the perpetrator casts themselves as a victim.[4]

12.08 Social workers' disbelief may hold them back from taking prompt action,[5] as may a belief that the evidence is insufficient to make an application to the Court of Protection. This is especially so when police have refused to be involved (see para 12.09). Research has found that a person exhibiting coercive and controlling behaviour can be 'highly manipulative in presenting

3 See Martina Caterini, 'Moving towards more inclusive definitions of femicide: Intersectionality and marginalised identities' (2023) 4 *Contemporary Challenges: The Global Crime, Justice and Security Journal*.

4 *F v M* [2021] EWFC 4, para 110.

5 Jane Monckton Smith, *Control: Dangerous Relationships and How they End in Murder* (Bloomsbury Publishing, 2022), p 177.

the circumstances of what has happened', and the police has observed that 'this has been found to lead to dual arrests, the denial of victim status for women and the misidentification of the primary perpetrator.'[6] An application to the Court of Protection or under the inherent jurisdiction may involve information-sharing with the police, or run alongside a police investigation.

12.09 Although since 2015 when some forms of coercive and controlling behaviour were criminalised (see Chapter 2), it is unfortunately the case that social workers may face some reluctance persuading the police to investigate coercive control against disabled persons. In the author's experience, this is especially so where the victim has a cognitive impairment, where there is a caring relationship between alleged abuser and victim, where another organisation (eg. the Public Guardian) is undertaking an investigation, or the crime is classed as low-level (eg. a person acting as appointee is not giving the disabled person the welfare benefits to which they are entitled).

12.10 Where a victim/survivor of coercive control has learning disabilities or another cognitive impairment, they may be viewed as lacking credibility. This may be due to societal stigma in general, or more specially because the abuser has exploited the victim/survivor's communication support needs or manipulated their understanding of available support.[7]

12.11 Given that abusers are often master manipulators, local authorities are advised to focus on the person who is understood to be the *victim* by using the statutory guidance (discussed in Chapter 2), highlighting the impact of any coercive or controlling behaviours, and document these from the victim's perspective.

12.12 If possible, the social worker should complete a capacity assessment about the relevant domains (commonly these are capacity to decide on care, and to decide on contact with others). If the social worker is unable to meet the victim because of gatekeeping by the controlling person (see under heading 'Access to the victim/survivor' at para 12.15 below), a desk-top capacity assessment can be completed, and shared in draft with colleagues so that gaps can be identified and dealt with.

12.13 During safeguarding enquiries, the social worker should seek information, as relevant, from the victim's GP, hospital staff community health providers (eg, district nurses, community mental health), domiciliary care providers, and the police. It may also be appropriate to gather information from other data points such as neighbours, family and friends. These people may be able to give information about the sorts of coercive control the adult is experiencing.

6 Charlotte Barlow, Sandra Walklate and Emma Finnegan, *Who is the Victim? Identifying Victims and Perpetrators in Cases of Coercive Control* (University of Liverpool and N8 Policing Research Partnership, 2023).

7 Home Office, *Statutory guidance: Controlling or coercive behaviour: statutory guidance framework*, para 84.

12.14 Crises can unexpectedly reveal abuse. For instance, a disabled person might suffer an injury for which they are admitted to hospital where they may disclose their experiences. Alternatively, a life-changing injury might lead to assessments and interventions by mental health and social care professionals who were otherwise absent from the person's life, prompting disclosures of abuse. As part of their adult safeguarding enquiry, social workers should gather information from a variety of sources and see if there is a pattern of behaviour. This should be done rapidly: if the victim/survivor will be discharged from hospital to an abusive home environment, an application can be made inviting the court to prevent the person from being returned while investigations continue.

ACCESS TO THE VICTIM/SURVIVOR

12.15 Chapter 9 noted that without access to the adult, it is difficult for a social worker to:

(a) accurately assess the situation generally;

(b) assess the adult's social care needs;

(c) assess their capacity to make relevant decisions;

(d) assess material relevant to a safeguarding enquiry, or assess the ways in which the person is under undue influence or control of another person; or

(e) obtain their wishes and feelings about these matters.

12.16 If the controlling person is blocking a social worker's access to an adult who may be a victim of coercive control (or any other type of abuse), the local authority could send a letter by registered mail to the controlling person. The letter would invite the controlling person to a meeting at a set time and date, or to otherwise respond in writing, and set out that if no response is received by a certain date, the local authority will make a court application without further notice. A parallel letter can be sent to the person considered to be the victim explaining that the social worker's concerns, giving the social worker's details, and the steps they are taking. Social workers should assess the risk of further harm to the victim if such letters are sent, and put in place measures that mitigate identified risks.

12.17 If no response is received, the local authority should consider making an application under the inherent jurisdiction without delay if there is insufficient evidence to displace the presumption of capacity to decide on care or contact with others, at least on an interim basis. If there is sufficient capacity evidence, the application can be made to the Court of Protection noting that if the court determines P *has* capacity to make the relevant decisions, the local authority is likely to make a parallel application under the inherent jurisdiction.

12.18 Working as part of a multi-agency approach to safeguarding, the local authority could ask the GP to make an appointment with the person who is thought to be a victim of coercive control at the GP's surgery. The social worker can wait in the consulting room so that they can have direct access with the victim without the controlling person (see also 'Role of healthcare professionals' at para 12.33).

12.19 Chapter 9 explained the range of legal remedies available. In its application, the local authority should be clear as to the terms of the order being sought, and the evidential basis upon which that request rests.

SPEED AND CREATIVITY

12.20 Chapter 2 explained that the nature of coercive and controlling behaviour is a *pattern* of behaviour. This poses a challenge to a local authority to determine when to make an application. How bad does the situation need to become for an application to be made? Financial pressures under which adult social care departments operate and the cost of legal proceedings may impede prompt action.

12.21 Sometimes there is a stand-out incident over and above the invidious, slow-burn control that the social worker may have been keeping under review. An example is the case of *Re CA*,[8] considered in Chapter 7, where after many low-level incidents within a pattern of controlling behaviour, the daughter tipped a bowl of lasagne over her mother's head. This incident constituted an assault with the useful outcome of police bail prohibiting contact between them. This enabled social workers to meet with Mrs CA without the presence of the daughter and then make an application to the Court of Protection.

12.22 A local authority may be wary of making an application to the Court of Protection or under the inherent jurisdiction 'too soon', without sufficient evidence, and without giving the controlling person one more chance to engage: these are all judgment calls that have to be made in each case. Social workers will want to avoid acting prematurely and over-protectively which may make the victim/survivor's situation worse, and may damage relationships with professionals. Acting in the least restrictive way is both an operating principle of the Mental Capacity Act 2005 (MCA 2005),[9] and a fundamental approach in social care. It might be said that adherence to this principle means that all possible steps should be exhausted before legal action is taken, but this is a misnomer. A court application should be made as soon as there is sufficient evidence, because a legal remedy can prevent further harm to the victim/survivor.

12.23 Social workers and their in-house legal team should be mindful of their response in the worst-case scenario, where no steps are taken and as a result, the victim dies through homicide or by suicide (these risks are considered in

8 *In the Matter of CA (Fact Finding – Capacity – Inherent Jurisdiction – Injunctive Relief)* [2024] EWCOP 64 (T3).

9 MCA 2005, s 1(6).

Chapter 2). How would the social workers explain the local authority's decision-making at the inquest?

12.24 By the time social workers have sought legal advice on the merits of making an application, it is likely that an application should be made swiftly. There are no reported coercive and controlling cases either in the Court of Protection or under the inherent jurisdiction where the court has criticised a local authority for making an application 'too soon'. If the application is supported by cogent evidence (see 'Gathering evidence' at para 12.29), criticism is unlikely.

12.25 Conversely, judges have castigated local authorities for delays in making an application. It has been held that although the avoidance of delay is not prescribed by the MCA 2005, 'the precept should be read in to the proceedings as a facet of Art 6 ECHR' which is the right to a fair trial, and that, '[a]ny avoidable delay is likely to be inimical to P's best interests'.[10]

12.26 An example of judicial criticism of delay in a coercive control case is *Re LW*, considered in Chapter 5. There, Ms LW was detained in a mental health unit. Her partner visited regularly where he made her recite prayers making her agitated and anxious. With typical focus on the impact on P, Hayden J criticised the local authority for not making an application sooner, expressing his 'concern that this contact has been permitted to continue for as long as it has'.[11]

12.27 A local authority is permitted to take steps to resolve the dilemma before issuing an application. An example is *Re TP*,[12] where the Official Solicitor raised a concern about delay. The judge noted nuanced dilemmas faced by the local authority: 'It is always very easy with hindsight. The local authority was trying to manage the case without coming to court'. The judge noted the incremental nature of a pattern of coercive and controlling behaviour causes problems for a local authority to decide when enough is enough and an application should be made: 'The extent of FW's dominance over TP only became apparent by degrees' and that it took an expert to fully understand the extent of the interference.

12.28 A Family Division judge (and therefore a tier 3 judge of the Court of Protection) is available 24 hours a day, 365 days a year.[13] Where an application cannot reasonably be made during court hours, and is of such urgency that it requires determination before a court sitting on the next working day, an out-of-hours telephone hearing can be arranged. An example is *Re FH* (considered in Chapter 7), where Cobb J (as he then was) annexed to his judgment a previous *ex*

10 *A local authority v NP (by her litigation friend* the Official Solicitor) and others [2019] EWCOP 48, para 31.
11 *A County Council v LW & Anor* [2020] EWCOP 50, para 11, considered in Chapter 5.
12 *Newcastle-Upon-Tyne City Council v TP (Capacity of TP No. 2)* [2016] EWCOP B4, para 40.
13 Practice Guidance: Urgent applications, out of hours applications and bundles in the Family Division of the High Court, 10 May 2024.

tempore judgment in the same case that he had handed down during an evening telephone hearing some three years previously.[14]

GATHERING EVIDENCE

12.29 While a local authority should make an application without delay, it must do so with grounds that are well-drafted, with draft orders that are comprehensive, and with evidence in support that is cogent and compelling and presented in an accessible way in a paginated and bookmarked electronic bundle. Preparation of a chronology can make the case easier to understand. A chronology can be exhibited to a statement by the social worker. Those representing the local authority will want to be sure that the relevant steps have been taken, especially if the application is to be issued without notice.[15]

12.30 Judges have criticised local authorities for making applications without sufficient scrutiny of the evidence in support of an application, or finding practical alternative solutions to litigation. Three examples:

(a) In *Re G*, the family wanted to send Ms AG to Pakistan to get married. The judge was highly critical of the applicant local authority, noting its 'failure [...] to properly investigate and analyse the evidence, or keep it under review'.[16]

(b) In *Re Mazhar*, the Court of Appeal chastised those representing the local authority for making a rushed and ill-considered out-of-hours application: 'the information given to the judge was woefully inadequate. As a result, he was placed in an invidious position'.[17]

(c) In *Re KR*, the judge criticised the local authority for not providing the adult with a cheap mobile phone to solve the problem of him being alone without means to contact anyone. The local authority was worried about setting a 'precedent' and incurring cost. The judge found it, 'difficult to overstate how misjudged this approach was, given the colossal interference that the [local authority] then saw fit to pursue through this litigation, not to mention the cost of that litigation.'[18]

12.31 The case of *Hillingdon v Neary* is an example of a local authority taking invasive action without making an application. In his eviscerating judgment, Peter Jackson J encouraged local authorities to make applications:

14 *Wakefield Metropolitan District Council v FH and others* [2024] EWHC 830 (Fam).

15 Without notice applications are covered in Chapter 6 at para 6.67.

16 *Luton Borough Council v G and others* [2024] EWCOP 18, [2024] All ER (D) 07 (May), para. 134 (see Chapter 5).

17 *Mazhar v Birmingham Community Healthcare Foundation NHS Trust and others* [2020] EWCA Civ 1377, para 55 (see Chapter 6)

18 *Croydon LBC v KR* [2019] EWHC 2498 (Fam), para 67 (see Chapter 6).

> Where a dilemma exists, the court provides an accessible forum. Often, parties will have a clear view of what they are proposing, but if a party needs more evidence or is uncertain about the best outcome in a difficult case, it is no shame to say so. Proceedings in the Court of Protection need not be adversarial. The fact that these have been is no more than the consequence of Hillingdon's stance. It is a great pity that it did not issue proceedings at least six months earlier, and regrettable that when it finally did so it did not share its internal doubts with others, instead pitching its case as high as it did.[19]

12.32 The key takeaway is to gather evidence quickly and logically, instruct counsel to provide advice and draft the grounds, and file the application promptly. While the local authority should have a plan, it need not have *all* the answers. A benefit of making an application is that it brings more minds to focus on solving the problem. Additionally, the case is passed from the hands of the social worker to the judge. Lady Hale has said in the context of child abuse, that 'it is for the social workers to bring the cases before the courts and it is for the judges to decide what the risks are and whether they should be taken. We are there to protect the child but we are also there to protect the family from the well-meaning but overmighty state'.[20] Those sentiments apply equally to safeguarding the rights and interests of vulnerable adults.

THE ROLE OF HEALTHCARE PROFESSIONALS

12.33 Chapter 1 described Mary's case. There, hospital clinicians and social workers played a crucial role in listening to Mary and acting on her disclosures, thereby ensuring her safety, so too with Mrs CA described in Chapter 7.[21] The Domestic Abuse Commissioner has found that not only are health settings primary places for disclosure of domestic abuse; they are also crucial services for victims/survivors.[22] The National Police Chiefs' Council endorses a cross-agency approach, so that perpetrators are intercepted not only by police, but by healthcare, substance misuse and mental health services.[23] It is incumbent on social workers to work with health colleagues. Similarly, social workers should ensure that the victim/survivor has access to appropriate health assessments and treatment: see Chapter 10.

19 *Hillingdon London Borough Council v Neary* [2011] EWHC 1377 (COP), para 142.
20 Brenda Hale, *Spider Woman* (Penguin Random House, 2021), p 141.
21 *Re CA* (n 8).
22 Domestic Abuse Commissioner, *A Patchwork of Provision*, 2022.
23 National Police Chiefs' Council, *Multi-agency approach crucial to prevent domestic abuse deaths*, 25 March 2025.

ISSUES THAT ARISE DURING PROCEEDINGS

12.34 If the local authority is unsure whether the adult has or lacks capacity to conduct proceedings, it can invite the court to make a *Harbin v Masterman* order: see Chapter 6.

12.35 The local authority should know how P's legal representation will be funded. In applications under MCA 2005, s 16, the Legal Aid Agency requires means testing before providing funding. This may pose challenges where there are allegations of financial abuse, where P's finances are controlled by the abuser, or where P's finances are unknown. The court may grant the Official Solicitor (or the Accredited Legal Representative) an order to investigate P's finances. This may not be possible – especially in cases that require the court's urgent attention – in which case the local authority may be invited to fund P's legal representation. If P is in a hospital or care home and an application is made as a challenge under MCA 2005, s 21A to deprivation of liberty, P's means are not tested, so P will automatically be eligible for legal aid.

12.36 Those representing local authorities have responsibilities to litigate the case in an even-handed and calm way, always placing the victim/survivor in focus. Judges and lawyers should be aware of the 'slow violence' of coercive control and the incremental erosion of the victim/survivor's autonomy. Court timetables can unintentionally mirror and reinforce abusers' control through procedural delay. Those representing a local authority should be aware of the myriad delaying tactics that the controlling person may deploy during proceedings and make appropriate submissions in response.

12.37 Lastly, social workers and those representing the local authority should be aware of the traumatic effect of coercive control on the victim, dealt with in Chapter 10, and ensure access to specialist trauma support where appropriate. Given that psychological trauma is often accompanied by illness, social workers should take a biopsychosocial approach to the adult's welfare and ensure that any physical health needs are investigated. This will entail working in a multi-disciplinary team with the GP, mental health professionals and other agencies. These professionals may not have had contact with the victim if the controlling person has denied them access.

CONCLUSIONS

12.38 This chapter has suggested pragmatic ways in which social workers and legal representatives of a local authority can address coercive and controlling behaviour. The key messages are to act swiftly but with cogent, well marshalled evidence; to maintain focus on the victim's lived experience; and to use the full range of safeguarding enquiries and legal remedies to secure access and protection. The chapter has also highlighted common professional pitfalls – disbelief, deference to an abuser's narrative, and delay – and the need for early, multidisciplinary coordination, capacity assessments, and careful case presentation.

12.39 The case law underscores that timely applications grounded in proper evidence are unlikely to attract criticism, whereas avoidable delay, ill-considered without-notice approaches, and applications with insufficient evidence will. Procedurally, vigilance against the controlling person's litigation tactics is essential to prevent the court process from becoming derailed and replicating control that compounds the victim's trauma. Above all, adherence to the principle of least restrictive measures does not mean inertia: once there is sufficient evidence to support an application, decisive action is required to prevent further harm, preserve autonomy, and promote the proper administration of justice.

CHAPTER 13

Representing the controlling person

'He spoke as though the world were his to name, and she, merely, to listen.'[1]

INTRODUCTION

13.01 A controlling person is entitled to representation, regardless of the allegations against them, without discrimination and without fear or favour. However, providing legal advice and representation to a controlling person can be extremely difficult. The challenges facing a lawyer instructed by a controlling client are quite different from the challenges addressed in the preceding two chapters which discussed representation of the victim/survivor in Chapter 11, and of the local authority in Chapter 12.

13.02 A lawyer representing a controlling person should become familiar with the nature of coercive control (see Chapter 2) and of common perpetrator tactics,[2] as these may continue throughout court proceedings. There are several excellent sources of information written for frontline staff engaging with (usually male) perpetrators of domestic abuse,[3] and this chapter does not seek to repeat or summarise the useful advice in those documents. Instead, it offers reflections specifically in the context of representation in coercive control cases in the Court of Protection and under the inherent jurisdiction. In this chapter, 'client' refers to the controlling person.

THE CONTROLLING CLIENT

Typologies of those who harm

13.03 Categorising and seeking to understand the controlling person risks both over-pathologising or humanising the perpetrator without accountability, and missing the insight that coercive control is not just an interpersonal dynamic or a loss of temper: it is a 'liberty crime',[4] a structural pattern of domination rooted in gender and entitlement.

1 Arundhati Roy, *The God of Small Things* (Harper Perennial, 1997).
2 Home Office, *Controlling or coercive behaviour: statutory guidance framework*, paras 83–84.
3 European Commission, *ENGAGE Roadmap for frontline professionals interacting with male perpetrators of domestic violence and abuse to ensure a coordinated multi-agency response to perpetrators* (Brussels, 2019). See also the engaging with perpetrators resources on the website of the charity respect.org.uk.
4 Evan Stark, *Coercive Control: How Men Entrap Women in Personal Life* (2nd edn, OUP, 2023).

13.04 Having acknowledged those risks, why do people perpetrate domestic abuse? The forensic psychologist Ahona Guha suggests three domestic abuser typologies. A person may harm for *predatory* reasons, deliberately overriding the victim's rights, to achieve gratification; a person may harm in an *uncontrolled* way, for example, someone who becomes triggered and dysregulated and lashes out; and a person may harm *unconsciously*: they are likely to have little ability to understand the objectively foreseeable negative consequences on other people, and 'may be driven by a sense of deep moral righteousness ("I'm doing this for a valid and virtuous reason") or fragile narcissism ("How dare you call me selfish, I will destroy you")'.[5] Guha notes that these categories are porous and allow for some interplay.

13.05 A lawyer representing a controlling client should understand that the effect of coercive control on the victim/survivor can be severe, regardless of the controlling person's presentation in conference, likeability or stated motivation. People of any age, race or ethnicity, religion, socioeconomic background, disability status, education level or relationship status (spouse of the victim/survivor, or their parent, sibling or child) can be perpetrators of domestic abuse.

13.06 Lawyers should remain alert to the possibility that *their* client has experienced trauma, which may help explain – but does not excuse – coercive or controlling behaviour. The client may have mental health problems or alcohol or substance use issues. Although recognising these features can foster empathy, trauma-informed practice should prioritise harm reduction and victim/survivor safety over rehabilitative empathy of the abuser. Seeking to understand the perpetrator is not a substitute for holding them accountable.[6] The lawyer may signpost the client to appropriate services, including domestic abuse perpetrator programmes.

Controlling the proceedings

13.07 The 2023 statutory guidance on coercive control notes that '[p]erpetrators may also be particularly adept at manipulating professionals, agencies and systems'.[7] This includes their own lawyers as well as lawyers representing other parties. It is particularly important therefore that the lawyer representing the controlling client acts with integrity and communicates with the client clearly, always following up any verbal communication in writing. Ground rules should be established in each conference with the client, such as no one is allowed to raise their voice, or talk over another person, and that the purpose of the meeting is for the lawyers to provide advice and obtain instructions.

5 Ahona Guha, *Reclaim: Understanding Complex Trauma and Those who Abuse* (Scribe, 2023), p 160.
6 Fiona Vera-Gray, *The Right Amount of Panic: How Women Trade Freedom for Safety* (Policy Press, 2018).
7 Home Office (n 2), para 84.

13.08 The client may seek to control other aspects of the proceedings as demonstrated in the following examples, all taken from cases in the Court of Protection or under the inherent jurisdiction:

- Swearing, shouting, and being verbally aggressive with lawyers.
- Interrupting others, including their own lawyers, during conferences, round table meetings and hearings.
- Giving inconsistent instructions or those which are not supported by the evidence.
- Drafting lengthy witness statements with unfounded allegations in a hyperbolic or accusatory tone.
- Attempting to expose others as liars through the proceedings.
- Editing a barrister's draft position statement, adding unarguable points thereby preventing its submission bearing the barrister's name as doing so would constitute a regulatory breach.
- Filing their own position statement without consulting their lawyers.
- Using artificial intelligence to alter legal documents or 'correct' drafts.[8]
- Demanding to join advocates' meetings' which are meant only for lawyers.
- Labelling other people's views of best interests as dishonest or malicious.
- Altering post-hearing draft orders to reflect what the client wanted to happen during a hearing rather than judicial decisions made.
- Insistently trying to use the proceedings to litigate irrelevant issues, for example, complaints about care providers several years ago.
- Rejecting legal advice on applications that have low prospects of success, such as disclosure of care records going back many years, or reliance on covert recordings.
- Criticising their own lawyers for not presenting the case strongly enough.
- Becoming angry at their lawyers for not achieving what the client wanted, including when previously advised that there were low prospects of success.
- Denying facts despite overwhelming evidence.
- Claiming they did not behave in a coercive or controlling way because they have not been prosecuted.
- Objecting to expert opinions as to whether the victim has been subject to undue influence or coercive control.
- Wanting to appeal minor case management decisions.

8 Using some AI models to analyse case papers involves uploading information about P to a large language database, likely in breach of the transparency order.

- Claiming to be a victim of injustice and demanding investigations.[9]
- Filing court applications without consulting lawyers.
- Contacting the judge directly.
- Sharing case details on social media (including uploading videos of contact with P), thereby breaching orders.
- Rejecting the court's legitimacy and saying that orders (including injunctions) do not apply to them.
- Becoming indignant when committal proceedings are initiated because they have knowingly breached an injunction.
- Lodging complaints about, or firing, their solicitor or barrister.
- Accusing the judge of bias and seeking recusal.

Perpetrator views of the victim/survivor

13.09 According to the statutory guidance, the client may try to minimise allegations, normalise their behaviour, and discredit or undermine the victim/survivor's account or credibility. In Court of Protection cases where there is a caring relationship between the client and victim/survivor, the client may claim they are the only person who truly understands the victim/survivor's wishes, feelings and needs, or that the victim/survivor does not know what they need or what is best for them.

13.10 If the victim/survivor has made disclosures of abuse, the client may dismiss these as manipulations by biased individuals. The client might believe that their familiarity with the victim/survivor and their desire to protect them (in their own way) makes them the only person truly acting in the victim/survivor's best interests, negating the need for external scrutiny. They may therefore be resentful of court proceedings unless the proceedings serve one of the client's own aims (eg, to ventilate criticisms of someone else) and may make vexatious allegations against the victim/survivor or others such as social workers or care staff.

13.11 Clients with a high sense of self-regard and entitlement may believe their needs and views should take precedence over the victim/survivor's. Admitting any sort of wrongdoing or fault threatens the client's self-image, so they may blame others (eg. 'I had to shower her because the carers were useless'). Or the client may resort to victim-blaming, invoking the victim/survivor's perceived incapability or uselessness to explain their dependence on the client.

9 An example is the family law case of *F v M* [2021] EWFC 4, where at para 110 Hayden J found that the controlling father 'repeatedly cast himself as a victim'.

13.12 It is common for a controlling client to test whether they can successfully control the lawyer. They may ask the lawyer: 'You believe me, don't you?' The lawyer should not get drawn in or otherwise collude with, or risk being perceived as condoning, their client's discourse of denial, minimisation, excuses or victim-blaming. Instead, the lawyer could explain that their role is to provide legal advice on the basis of evidence, and provide representation in court.

Conspiracies

13.13 Delays or poor communication from local authorities, unclear care provisions, or uncertainty about the victim/survivor's decision-making capacity can lead to misunderstandings. These may escalate, causing the controlling person to resort to conspiracy as the only logical explanation. Social media can fuel these theories, and the client may also seize upon other material that purports supports them, to bolster their conspiratorial worldview.

13.14 These perceptions can spiral, and it is not uncommon for the client to allege a conspiracy in which public bodies, carers, doctors, and sometimes lawyers and judges have conspired with each other to misreport and misconstrue events to further their own agenda and to persecute the controlling client.[10]

13.15 Sometimes, there is a grain of truth in the client's account: a delay might have occurred, the social worker might have misheard what the controlling person said, the needs assessment may contain errors or other mistakes may inadvertently have been made. The controlling person's lawyer could make a list of the complaints and ask the local authority to address them in evidence. That is a way to tie up the 'loose-ends' in the client's mind, which may help them focus on the needs of the victim/survivor, rather than returning to the issues that fuel the client's feelings of unfairness and injustice.

Fighting all the way

13.16 A client might argue that the local authority lacks *concrete evidence*, such as video recordings of violent behaviour, and may dismiss other evidence, including witness statements, as *hearsay* – while insisting their own statements are truthful. If the client believes the evidence against them is fabricated, it becomes challenging for a lawyer to discuss the merits of the case with the client and develop a coherent case theory.

13.17 The client may hold onto their beliefs despite the sacrifices involved, driven by 'a deep fear of rejection and loss and will cling desperately to avoid

10 An example is *Re CA* [2024] EWCOP 64 (T3) where the judge noted at para 24 that the controlling person 'made general allegations that there was a conspiracy between the local authority and others which led to complaints being made […]. I cannot see how it can be said that these reports by the hospital staff are untrue. It would involve too many staff who had no motive to lie.'

this loss, abusing [P]'s rights and free will in the process'.[11] Controlling clients commonly see court hearings as a forum to prove that they are right. As a result, they commonly instruct their lawyers to fight *all* points, including inconsequential factual disputes, and in this way it may be challenging to discuss the many types of behaviour that make up a pattern of behaviour that will be central in each case of coercive control. Similarly, the client may be opposed to all suggestions by other parties as they consider agreement as weakness. As such, they may instruct their lawyers to oppose sensible case management steps suggested by other parties.

13.18 Lawyers have to act on instructions, but only after providing advice, including on the merits of successfully arguing a point, the costs of doing so, the risk of adverse costs, the reputational damage to the client by their inappropriate conduct which can be observed by the judge and potentially by any journalists or bloggers who attend public hearings. When taking instructions therefore, lawyers should be alive to which points they can credibly put and which are unarguable. It is worth sending the client written advice on the evidence, so that if the client submits a complaint, the lawyer has a written account of the advice provided and instructions received.

Complaints and being dismissed

13.19 A controlling client may never be satisfied with their legal representation: their lawyers can rarely achieve outcomes that the client wants. The client may be displeased that their lawyers have declined to put the client's case in the manner and tone that the client considers appropriate. Complaints from controlling clients are therefore common, and law firms should consider the risks involved before accepting a new client.

13.20 Being fired is also an occupational hazard for lawyers who take on controlling clients. It is not uncommon for lawyers representing a local authority or the victim in coercive control cases to see an ever-changing parade of lawyers representing the controlling person at hearings, especially if the controlling person is funding their own representation.

COMPLIANCE WITH ORDERS

13.21 If the client has been granted *supervised* contact with P, they should view it as an opportunity rather than a burden. It is their chance to demonstrate that they are neither controlling nor abusive in other ways. Lawyers can advise the client to be mindful of any behaviour that might be misinterpreted as inappropriate. If the court has directed the client to avoid certain topics of conversation, they must comply. As someone who cares for P, it should be straightforward for the client

11 Guha (n 5), 149–151.

to refrain from discussing certain subjects or behaving inappropriately, and the client should be advised to put to one side their irritation or rage about being told how to behave by a judge. Positive contact reports will reflect well on the client and support their case. Conversely, negative reports could lead the local authority to argue that even supervised contact is detrimental to P's well-being, potentially resulting in no contact at all.

13.22 The Court of Protection will have issued a transparency order that prohibits publishing any material that could identify P. Similarly, a reporting restrictions order will be issued by the Family Division in inherent jurisdiction cases. Given the allegations of coercive control, it is crucial for the lawyer to review the terms of the order with the client thoroughly. The judge should ask the client directly whether they understand the order and consequences of breaching it. These include a finding of contempt of court which is punishable by imprisonment, a fine, and/or seizure of assets.

13.23 It is sometimes unbearable for a controlling person to be told what to do by a judge. The client may feel utterly aggrieved, believing that *they* have been the victim of an egregious injustice, that their behaviours are reasonable in the circumstances of such injustice, and that the law is an ass and does not apply to them. Some clients wilfully breach court orders and believe that they are immune from punishment.

13.24 If the client indicates that they will ignore prohibitions directed by the court, the lawyer should tell them in clear and unequivocal terms that the client *must* comply with all directions of the court,[12] even if they disagree with them. The lawyer should remind the client of the consequences, and that breaching the rules or a court order without reasonable excuse can lead the court to depart from the general rules about costs.[13]

13.25 Controlling persons can act in unpredictable ways. Their lawyers should anticipate the unexpected. This could include returning to court for urgent directions, being notified that their client has breached orders, or being fired.

ACTIONS THE LAWYER CAN TAKE

Risk assessments

13.26 The lawyer should carefully analyse any risk to themselves before meeting with a potentially abusive client, in accordance with their regulator and their employer or Chambers. Risks include physical harm to the lawyer, which can be mitigated by having a conference with the client with a colleague, sitting closest to the door, and recording the conference. There may be a financial risk

12 Court of Protection Rules 2017 (SI 2017/1035) (COPR 2017), r 1.4(2)(e).
13 COPR 2017, r 1.4(3).

to the firm if the lawyer is on a fixed fee, but has to spend many hours handling an abusive client and fixing problems the client has created. Other risks include the client's instructions turning into a direction to their lawyer to control the proceedings or make unarguable submissions: there are considered above.

Funding

13.27 The client may approach a solicitor on a privately-funded basis. They may be eligible for legal aid if they satisfy a means test and a merits test, especially if proceedings relate to their right to family life.[14] In assessing the merits of a legal aid application on behalf of the person considered to be the abuser, the Legal Aid Agency will consider the specific allegations made against the client and whether legal representation is justified for the client to respond. The Agency will also review the potential consequences of litigation for the client, including, for example, the risk of losing the home that they share with the person considered to be the victim.

13.28 It is not uncommon for a controlling client to reject the advice of their legal representatives. If the client's case has low prospects of success, it is generally understood that counsel should draft a written advice on merits which should be sent to the client: this may help bring home the reality to the client, even if it has been discussed beforehand in conference. The solicitor should send counsel's advice to the Legal Aid Agency, which may review and withdraw funding.

13.29 The Legal Aid Agency may cease funding if the client changes their solicitor without good reason. This prevents public money from being wasted on a new solicitor and counsel team who would have to spend time reviewing potentially thousands of pages of documents which previous lawyers have already done.

Evidence

13.30 When representing a person accused of coercive control, proceedings are likely already in progress, either in the Court of Protection or in the Family Division. The client may have the application papers and initial orders, including a directions order (or 'case management order') listing the first hearing, and a transparency order. To minimise the risk of acting on cherry-picked papers, the lawyer should take steps to formally go on record and then seek the papers from the applicant local authority.

13.31 The lawyer should explain to the client how the court will make decisions, namely by evaluating the evidence and applying the law. The lawyer

14 The Civil Legal Aid (Merits Criteria) Regulations 2013 (SI 2013/104), reg 52.

may have to repeat several times that the parties may have different opinions of the evidence, and that it does not matter how strongly those opinions are held, or how loudly they are expressed: the judge will determine the matter on the basis of the evidence, and their focus will be P (in the Court of Protection) or the vulnerable adult (under the inherent jurisdiction).

Signposting to services

13.32 Lawyers can encourage the client to seek professional, specialised help from perpetrator programmes and to stop their abusive behaviours. It may be difficult to get past the client's denials that they have acted in a coercive or controlling manner or have abused the victim. The lawyer should advise the client that coercive and controlling behaviour – like other abusive behaviour – is a *choice*, so the client can choose to behave in differently.

Capacity concerns

13.33 It requires skill to advise a client that has rigid views or obsessive traits and refuses to engage with the evidence, and it is difficult for a lawyer (who is not a mental health professional) to discern when fixed beliefs become delusional beliefs that may impact on the client's capacity to conduct proceedings (considered in Chapter 4). If a lawyer considers their client may lack capacity to conduct proceedings, then the lawyer should take steps in line with their regulatory obligations, which may include raising the matter with the court at an early stage and arranging for a capacity assessment.[15] Further, the client may require an intermediary.[16]

Fact-finding

13.34 During a fact-finding hearing (see Chapter 8), the client may want to 'have their day in court' and tell the judge their side of the story. However, lawyers must carefully consider whether their client should give oral evidence. In some cases, it may not be beneficial for the client to do so, while in others, there may be little to lose if the written evidence is already unfavourable. Each situation depends on the facts and how the client is likely to come across. While lawyers cannot coach their clients, they can advise on maintaining calmness and how different behaviours and speech may be perceived. This guidance can help the client present themselves effectively if they decide to go into the witness box.

15 See capacity to conduct proceedings discussed in Chapter 4 at para 4.26, and the process to appoint a litigation friend covered in Chapter 11 at para 11.99. The procedure to be followed is set out in the Bar Council's document 'Client Incapacity', February 2014. See also *MacPherson v Sunderland City Council (Rev1)* [2024] EWCA Civ 1579.

16 See *Re N (A Child)* [2019] EWCA Civ 1997.

CONCLUSIONS

13.35 To effectively represent a controlling client, lawyers could consider the following approaches:

(1) **Explain how the lawyer works.** The lawyer should establish communication methods, response times, and the frequency and length of conferences. The lawyer should remind the client that they do not become the client and will not use the client's words or tone; that their job is to advance the client's case by maintaining a respectful and professional demeanour, to provide legal advice to the client, and conduct advocacy in a manner that the lawyer (not the client) chooses. The lawyer should refuse to a client's request to bully, intimidate, or harass a witness, or be rude to an opponent.

(2) **Avoid traps.** The lawyer should look out for the client's attempts to manipulate them, for example, by asking the lawyer to agree with the client's negative views about the social worker, or the judge.

(3) **Advise on court perception.** The lawyer should explain that coercive and controlling behaviour will harm the client's case, and that professional and courteous behaviour is to be expected.

(4) **Establish ground rules in conferences and meetings.** The lawyer should set behavioural expectations for conferences round table meetings where the client can participate. These could include muting or removing any person who shouts or interrupts another speaker.

(5) **Focus on P's best interests**. The lawyer can explain how the Court of Protection is independent from all the parties. It is an inquisitorial forum[17] which takes a holistic view of best interests, and must consider 'all the relevant circumstances'.[18] The court is focused on the victim/survivor's welfare, not the client's.

(6) **Emphasise evidence over opinion.** The lawyer can remind the client that the court makes decisions based on evidence, not opinions. It is entitled to reach a conclusion that is different from the client's preferred outcome. Parties' views, however firmly held, do not dictate the outcome.

(7) **Communicate red lines.** The lawyer should state their boundaries in first-person terms: 'I will not act for any client who shouts at or is rude to me' or 'I will retain editorial control of the position statement', rather than seeking to change behaviour by making requests such as: 'Please stop shouting!' or 'Don't edit the position statement five times!'[19]

(8) **Take action if the client crosses the red line.** The lawyer may wish to discuss the matter with a senior colleague before making this decision; however, if the client is repeatedly aggressive, verbally abusive or threatening towards

17 In *Local Authority v B* [2024] EWCA Civ 572, the Court of Appeal held, 'while the Court of Protection's role is not supervisory, it is inquisitorial.'
18 Mental Capacity Act 2005, s 4(2).
19 For more on boundary formation, see Guha (n 5), Ch 8.

the lawyer (or anyone else) causing a serious breakdown of trust, the lawyer can stop acting for the client. There is no shame in having reached this point: it is important that the lawyer protects their own mental health and wellbeing (see 'Lawyer self-care' in Chapter 11 and para 11.126).

13.36 These strategies can help maintain a professional relationship while ensuring effective representation. When representing a controlling client, a lawyer must navigate complex challenges while maintaining professional integrity. It is crucial for lawyers instructed by a person who is accused of behaving in a coercive or controlling manner to understand the dynamics of coercive control and the potential for manipulation within legal proceedings. Lawyers should establish clear communication, set firm boundaries, and focus on evidence over opinion. By prioritising the best interests of the victim/survivor, legal representatives can effectively advocate for their controlling client while ensuring justice and accountability are upheld.

CHAPTER 14

Conclusions

'… the importance of the modern judiciary having a proper understanding of the nature of domestic abuse and in particular of controlling and coercive behaviour and of its impact on both the victims and the children caught up in the atmosphere engendered in such a household.'[1]

14.01 The family courts are increasingly having to deal with coercive control, especially when the abuse affects children. In the family law case of *F v M*, Hayden J highlighted the insidious nature of this type of domestic abuse, the lack of reported case law, and called for greater awareness and training for professionals.[2] Two months later, three judges of the Court of Appeal, including the author of the foreword to this book, Lady Justice King, were in no doubt that 'central to the modern definitions of domestic abuse is the concept of coercive and/or controlling behaviour'.[3] The court endorsed 'the plea contained within [*F v M*] urging greater prominence to be given to coercive and controlling behaviour in Family Court proceedings'.[4]

14.02 There has not (yet) been an express judicial request for such prominence with respect to the Court of Protection and the inherent jurisdiction of the High Court, but I hope that this book contributes to raising awareness of these accessible legal fora that can bring about safety, healing and justice for victims/survivors of coercive control.

14.03 This conclusions chapter aims to bring together some of the strands of the book. My starting point is the victim/survivor of coercive control. Chapter 2 highlighted how a victim/survivor is subject to a pattern of intimidation tactics designed to create fear and humiliation which impacts the person's security, dignity, liberty, and autonomy. It is autonomy to which the courts frequently return when considering cases of coercive control.

14.04 Mainstream liberal philosophy posits a subject as autonomous if they make a decision by themselves, uninfluenced by others, putting out of their mind prejudices and biases. Justitia – known as 'Lady Justice' – is traditionally depicted wearing a blindfold to symbolise impartiality. She, and the legal system she represents, is immune to influence and she makes decisions based solely on

1 The President of the Family Division, Lady Justice King and Lord Justice Holroyde in the Court of Appeal case of *Re H-N and others (Children) (Domestic Abuse: Finding of Fact Hearings)* [2021] EWCA Civ 448, para 224.

2 *F v M* [2021] EWFC 4 (Fam), para 4.

3 *Re H-N* (n 1), para 29.

4 Ibid.

the facts.[5] Feminist approaches challenge the liberal notion that humans make decisions in such a machine-like fashion, blindfolded from external influence or distraction. To do so would be to lead our lives behind an artificial veil of ignorance where we ignore vital aspects of our personhood: our social influences, histories, culture, values, beliefs and interests.

14.05 From the time we are born, we are wired to attach, and to connect and interact with others. We learn to communicate by looking at and interpreting facial and bodily movements, listening to sounds that people, animals and objects such as computers make, touching people and things around us, and using our senses of smell and taste. We grow and learn with, and in relation to, others. As such, our autonomy is 'relationally constituted'.[6] We live in co-dependence with others who influence us, and who we seek to influence. We navigate the give and take of relationships with others – the exchange of perspectives and insights – while remaining attentive to the risk that influence may cross the threshold into control.

14.06 The global disability rights movement places human interdependence and relational autonomy at the heart of their call for action. The first principle of the UN Convention on the Rights of Persons with Disabilities 2006[7] (CRPD) is, 'Respect for inherent dignity, individual autonomy including the freedom to make one's own choices, and independence of persons.'[8] The two key advocacy goals achieved in the CRPD are the right to live independently and be included in the community in Article 19,[9] and the right to legal capacity in Article 12.

14.07 Recognising legal capacity entails including moving away from substituted decision-making (the model adopted in the Mental Capacity Act (MCA 2005)) and towards supported decision-making whereby it is recognised that some people may require support when exercising their legal capacity. To protect against abuse, measures in support of decision-making are to have built-in safeguards so that such measures are, among other things, 'free [...] of undue influence'.[10] The international disability rights framework requires supports to be offered but not imposed.

14.08 In contrast, courts in England and Wales can authorise state intervention against a person's wishes and in their best interests. While the MCA 2005 does not contain the word 'autonomy', the courts use it to mean two different things. First,

5 The version atop the Old Bailey does not wear a blindfold.

6 Jennifer Nedelsky, 'Reconceiving autonomy: Sources, thoughts, and possibilities' (1989) 1(1) *Yale Journal of Law and Feminism* 7–36.

7 Convention on the Rights of Persons with Disabilities (CRPD), adopted by UN General Assembly Resolution 61/106 on 12 December 2006. The UK ratified the CRPD in 2009.

8 CRPD, Article 3(a).

9 Oliver Lewis and Genevra Richardson, 'The right to live independently and be included in the community' (2020) 69 *International Journal of Law and Psychiatry* 101499.

10 Anna Arstein-Kerslake and Elionor Flynn, 'The right to legal agency: Domination, disability and the protections of Article 12 of the Convention on the Rights of Persons with Disabilities' (2016) 25(3) *Social & Legal Studies* 397–418.

it is used as a synonym for capacitous decision-making, or for the presumption of capacity (see Chapter 3, at para 3.08). The Supreme Court has said that when a person makes a capacious unwise decision, they 'suffer the consequences if and when things go wrong', and that a person 'can learn from mistakes and thus attain a greater degree of independence'.[11]

14.09 Described as 'capturing and distilling the true essence' of the principle of the presumption of capacity,[12] the President of the Family Division, McFarlane LJ has held that:

> there is a space between an unwise decision and one which an individual does not have the mental capacity to take and … it is important to respect that space, and to ensure that it is preserved, for it is within that space that an individual's autonomy operates.'[13]

14.10 Similarly, during his tenure as Vice-President of the Court of Protection from 2018 to 2023, Hayden J championed capacitous decision-making. He held that, 'paternalism has no place; protection of individual autonomy is the magnetic north of this court'.[14] The Court of Protection acts as guardian against the 'ever-present danger' of the protective instinct which 'corrupts the integrity of an objective assessment of capacity'.[15] Further, Hayden J has held that the preservation of capacity is itself a form of protection:

> The omnipresent danger in the Court of Protection is that of emphasising the obligation to protect the incapacitous, whilst losing sight of the fundamental principle that the promotion of autonomous decision making is itself a facet of protection.[16]

14.11 The second way that the courts use the concept of autonomy is as a shorthand for P's incapacitous wishes and feelings.[17] This arises at the best interests stage. Having declared that a person lacks capacity to make the relevant decision, the court must take that person's wishes and feelings into consideration.[18] The Supreme Court has endorsed this version of autonomy when it said that a function of the Court of Protection is to 'balance the promotion of the autonomy

11 *A Local Authority v JB* [2021] UKSC 52, para 51.
12 *London Borough of Tower Hamlets v PB* [2019] EWCOP 27, para 7.
13 *PC v City of York* [2013] EWCA Civ 478, para 54.
14 *Warrington Borough Council v Y & Ors* [2023] EWCOP 27, para 29.
15 Ibid.
16 *London Borough of Tower Hamlets v PB* (n 12), para 27, cited by the Supreme Court in *A Local Authority v JB* [2021] UKSC 52, para 71.
17 An example is the eating disorders case *Z NHS Foundation Trust & Anor v Patricia & Ors* [2023] EWCOP 41 where Moor J found that Patricia (the pseudonym for P, a young woman with anorexia) lacked capacity to make the material decisions but 'it was important to give Patricia her autonomy' (para 8). Giving judgment in a renewed application two years later, Arbuthnot J held that 'respecting Patricia's autonomy had not worked' (para 155), finding that by 'respecting [Patricia's] autonomy, the court [in 2023] had permitted her anorexia to call the shots' (para 167).
18 MCA 2005, s 4(6).

of vulnerable persons with their protection from harm'.[19] Best interests may align with wishes and feelings, but this is not always so. Chapter 5 summarised several cases where the Court of Protection made a decision that the person did not want.

14.12 Autonomy is at the core of both civil law jurisdictions in England and Wales considered in this book. The first is the 'uniquely fact sensitive jurisdiction' of the Court of Protection,[20] which applies the MCA 2005, an empowering piece of legislation whose aim is: 'ultimately, to promote equality for the incapacitous to the same degree as their capacitous coevals'.[21] Chapter 3 explained how the Court of Protection can make a declaration that a person lacks capacity to make a decision only if P's inability to make that decision is 'because of an impairment of, or a disturbance in the functioning of, the mind or brain'.[22] Coercive control may be relevant in the assessment of capacity if, for example, a person's impairment means they are unable to use and weigh the fact that they are subject to coercive and controlling behaviour.

14.13 However, if a person is unable to make a decision not because of an impairment of, or a disturbance in the functioning of, the mind or brain, but because they are a victim of coercive and controlling behaviour of another, they have capacity in MCA 2005 terms. It is in these cases where a High Court judge exercising the inherent jurisdiction in relation to vulnerable adults can step in.

14.14 Critics of the inherent jurisdiction include prominent jurists, and their analysis was outlined in Chapter 6. That critique notwithstanding, the Court of Appeal has long ago noted the 'sound and strong public policy justification' for the inherent jurisdiction,[23] and there is no sign either of the judiciary narrowing its availability, or of the UK Government placing the inherent jurisdiction on a statutory footing or abolishing it. This judge-made area of the law therefore remains available for the protection of victims/survivors of coercive and controlling behaviour and the restoration of their authentic and autonomous decision-making.

14.15 Munby J decided the seminal case of *Re SA* in 2005 (see Chapter 6 at para 6.16),[24] A year later, he held in another inherent jurisdiction case that, 'the law must always be astute to protect the weak and helpless, not least in circumstances where, as often happens in such cases, the very people they need to be protected from are their own relatives',[25] adding 'partners or friends' to relatives in a case the following year.[26] As the selected cases in Chapter 7 sought to illustrate, the judiciary will intervene, including in intimate relationships, if it

19 *Re JB* (n 16), para 107.
20 *Re PB* (n 12), para 51(iii).
21 *Cumbria County Council v A* [2020] EWCOP 38, para 33.
22 MCA 2005, s 2(1).
23 *A Local Authority v DL* [2012] EWCA Civ 253, para 63.
24 *Re SA (Vulnerable Adult with Capacity: Marriage)* [2005] EWHC 2942 (Fam).
25 *NS v MI* [2006] EWHC 1646 (Fam), para 8.
26 *Re MM (An Adult)* [2007] EWHC 2003 (Fam), paras 118–119.

is necessary to protect a 'vulnerable' adult from the risk of harm. This requires a real possibility – rather than a merely fanciful risk – of future harm.

14.16 Orders under the inherent jurisdiction are made *for* (rather than *on behalf of*) a person whose 'will to decide has been sapped and overborne by the improper influence of another'.[27] The courts have held that voluntariness is an essential element of decision-making: 'choice where rational, informed and un-coerced is the essence of autonomy'.[28] *Re SA* cited the 1992 Court of Appeal judgment of *Re T*, where it was held that consent must be voluntarily given and free from undue influence, because 'for an apparent consent … to be less than a true consent … there must be such a degree of external influence as to persuade the patient to depart from her own wishes, to an extent that the law regards it as undue'.[29] Whether influence is ordinary or undue will turn on the facts of each case.

14.17 Vulnerability is a core precept in the inherent jurisdiction, yet the meaning of the concept remains unclear. In the case of *Re DL* in 2012, the Court of Appeal observed that, 'it is not easy to define and delineate this group of vulnerable adults'.[30] The judiciary has subsequently been reluctant to specify how it measures a person's vulnerability, or indeed explain the purpose of categorising people as 'vulnerable' in the first place.

14.18 There is an extensive academic literature on the ethics of vulnerability from which I wish to draw out one insight. Martha Fineman has posited the notion of 'universal vulnerability' wherein each person experiences illness, dependence, ageing and change. Vulnerability is part of what it means to be human. The 'vulnerable subject' is properly understood as 'unavoidably and inherently dependent throughout life on social institutions and relationships, which are the mechanisms for gaining essential resources and capacities (or resilience) that allow us to survive and even thrive given our vulnerability'.[31] In this framework, a person is not vulnerable because they have an illness or a disability or because they are being coerced into making a particular decision, as Munby J suggested in *Re SA*.

14.19 An application of universal vulnerability to coercive control would require consideration of barriers inherent in social structures including gender, ethnicity, disability and mental health and how those factors contribute to a person's experience of coercive control (see Chapter 2 in the context of women's experience of domestic violence). Rather than a focus on the victim/survivor's inherent vulnerability (or weaknesses or failings), it is the abuse in

27 *Re SA* (n 24), para 78.
28 *Re N* [2015] EWCOP 76, para 72.
29 *Re T (Adult: Refusal of Treatment)* [1992] EWCA Civ 18 at para 57. The Court of Appeal judgment records that James Munby QC represented Ms T who successfully resisted the appeal brought by Ms T's controlling mother.
30 *A Local Authority v DL* (n 23), para 68.
31 Martha Fineman, *Vulnerability Theory and the Trinity Lectures* (Bristol University Press, 2025), p 92.

combination with structural factors that are exposed through interpersonal or social relationships.[32]

14.20 Assessing a person's 'vulnerability' in the context of the inherent jurisdiction may therefore become otiose. Moving away from the language of individual vulnerability would also help prevent a victim/survivor of coercive control from bearing the additional burden of shame and stigma associated with the pejorative label of 'vulnerable', on top of the already significant challenges of coping with the effects of abuse and navigating the court process.

14.21 Coercive control may 'corrode'[33] a person's ability to act autonomously and may vitiate their decision-making because such abuse compromises trust, mutual respect and recognition of personhood. Judges have emphasised that protective orders under the inherent jurisdiction are made in the service of autonomy as they are 'in part aimed at enhancing or liberating the autonomy of a vulnerable adult whose autonomy has been compromised by a reason other than mental incapacity'.[34] In this way, the inherent jurisdiction mounts a mission to rescue the adult from their abuser and offers them sanctuary.

14.22 An order under the inherent jurisdiction overrides a capacitous person's decisions. In this way, the court can 'protect a person from themselves' where necessary in a particular case because 'the state's duty to protect an individual will override that individual's stated wishes and feelings'.[35] Such orders aim to create an environment in which the victim/survivor can regain their autonomy and make uncoerced decisions, for example, about whether to end the relationship with the abuser, whether to apply for a non-molestation order, and/or whether to seek trauma therapy.

14.23 Legal scholar Lucy Series has described the inherent jurisdiction as using 'coercion and control [...] to foster and enhance autonomy'.[36] She has noted that while an order under the inherent jurisdiction 'rests on the plausible intuition that sometimes we experience temporary disturbances in authentic and autonomous agency', it does not follow that a judge knows an adult better than they know themselves, and that this approach is 'prone to subjective and arbitrary interpretation'.[37] A partial response to this valid critique is in Chapter 11 where it was suggested that representation of a traumatised client who has been the victim of abuse is challenging and requires trauma-aware adjustments in legal representation which can bolster the voice of the victim/survivor and may in turn

32 C Mackenzie, 'The importance of relational autonomy and capabilities for an ethics of vulnerability', in C Mackenzie, W Rogers and S Dodds (eds), *Vulnerability: New Essays in Ethics and Feminist Philosophy* (Oxford University Press, 2014).

33 *F v M* (n 2), para 4.

34 *A Local Authority v DL* (n 23), para 53.

35 *Re K (Forced Marriage: Passport Order)* [2020] EWCA Civ 190, para 36.

36 Lucy Series, 'Relationships, autonomy and legal capacity: Mental capacity and support paradigms' (2015) 40 *International Journal of Law and Psychiatry* 80–91.

37 Ibid, p 87.

may reduce judicial subjectivity, an element of which is inevitable in this most human area of the law.

14.24 Philosopher Camillia Kong has cautioned against focusing solely on whether a person's choices are 'autonomous'. Instead, she has suggested that decisions should help an individual exercise their own agency free from harmful or coercive influences. This involves being careful not to make assumptions about their inner life, respecting their uncertainties, and understanding their unique perspectives, even if it means intervening in situations that the person consents to, but are fundamentally harmful or neglectful to them.[38] Kong places an emphasis on the vital task of listening to and centring the person's subjective experience – their feelings, relationships, and perceptions – as the moral foundation of any protective intervention.

14.25 If the state is to justify removing a vulnerable adult from their loved ones, Munby J noted, it must provide a better quality of care than they previously received.[39] He warned that in making protective orders, the court must ensure that rescuing a vulnerable adult from a one type of abuse does not expose them to treatment that, despite good intentions, could undermine their dignity, happiness, and human rights.[40] After all, state-sanctioned abuse is no better than private abuse. In a section of his judgment in *Re MM* that has achieved totemic status in the Court of Protection, Munby J suggested *sensible* risk appraisal. This entails:

> being willing to tolerate manageable or acceptable risks as the price appropriately to be paid in order to achieve some other good — in particular to achieve the vital good of the elderly or vulnerable person's *happiness*. What good is it making someone safer if it merely makes them miserable?[41]

14.26 I have suggested that lawyers representing the public body, and those representing the victim/survivor take a biopsychosocial approach, ensuring that the victim/survivor has access to social support, to healthcare services and, crucially, to trauma therapy. Healing may seem impossible, but therapy can make it tangible. For many, therapy is key to restoration of autonomous (uncoerced) decision-making, the very aim of protective orders in the inherent jurisdiction. A victim/survivor of coercive control who will not regain capacity to make relevant decisions (because of, for example, a cognitive impairment) is also entitled to therapy to address their trauma. Therapy may achieve the vital good of happiness even in cases where it cannot restore capacity.

14.27 Chapter 10 on trauma drew from the work of clinicians including psychiatrist Gabor Maté. He has described trauma therapy as 'a direction not

38 Camillia Kong, 'The phenomenology and ethics of P-centricity in mental capacity law' (2023) 42 *Law and Philosophy* 145–175, at 173.
39 *Re MM (An Adult)* [2007] EWHC 2003 (Fam), para 117.
40 Ibid, para 118.
41 Ibid, para 120.

a destination; a line on a map, not a dot'.[42] Judges and lawyers tend to view the conclusion of legal proceedings as a destination dot, after which they turn to the next case. While the end of a court case may be a significant milestone for the victim/survivor because it created the environment for safety and autonomous decision-making, a final court order will, at best, be part way along a line on the map towards healing.

14.28 As with other areas of law, it is rare for a judge in the Court of Protection or a High Court judge exercising the inherent jurisdiction to provide a follow-up judgment explaining what happened next. Was the abuser referred to a perpetrator programme? Did the statutory bodies arrange therapy for the victim/survivor?[43] Was 'happiness' achieved? Listing a review hearing some months after authorising an intervention is a practical way for the parties and the court to assess the wellbeing of the victim/survivor and the ongoing need for protective orders, including injunctions. If the case is in the inherent jurisdiction, evidence provided at a review hearing can address whether the victim/survivor's autonomous decision-making has been restored, and if not, what else can be done to assist.

14.29 I was motivated to write this book because of the extreme nature of harm experienced by victims of coercive control such as Mary and Jessica, whose cases I described in Chapter 1, because of the human rights turnaround that can be achieved in court proceedings, and because of the dearth of guidance available for lawyers instructed in these challenging cases.

14.30 Chapter 1 also set out the three objectives of the book. The first was to improve awareness of coercive and controlling behaviour and how people with mental disabilities can become victims. Chapter 2 on coercive control and Chapter 10 on trauma sought to explain the behaviour of abusers and the impact on victims/survivors. The second objective was to make accessible the law in relation to coercive control in the Court of Protection and under the inherent jurisdiction of the High Court. In this regard, Chapters 3 to 9 have explained the relevant legal principles and procedures: how capacity is assessed and determined, the legal tests which courts use in making decisions on behalf of or for the victim/survivor, how the courts establish facts, and the available legal remedies.

14.31 The third and most important objective of this book was to strengthen the skillset of legal practitioners representing the three main parties in coercive control cases: the victim/survivor, the local authority, and the perpetrator. Chapters 11 to 13 suggested that by adopting trauma-aware approaches, lawyers can shine a light on this devastating form of domestic abuse that unfolds behind closed doors and casts hidden shadows.

42 Gabor Maté, *The Myth of Normal* (Penguin, 2022), p 361.
43 A notable exception is *WU v BU* [2021] EWCOP 54, considered in Chapter 5.

14.32 Legal representatives of the local authority can draft applications in a timely manner on the basis of clear and cogent evidence. Those representing the perpetrator can ensure fair and safe proceedings. Lawyers for the victim/survivor can facilitate access to justice by restoring the voice of their client who has been silenced, entrapped, dominated, manipulated, humiliated and denied their rights. And they can advocate for the victim/survivor of coercive control to be afforded the space, safety, and therapeutic support to heal.

Index

[all references are to paragraph number]

Ability of P to make the decision
communication of decision, 3.38—3.39
introduction, 3.25—3.27
overview, 3.40
retain information, 3.32—3.33
understand information relevant to decision, 3.28—3.31
use of information, 3.35—3.38
use or weigh information, 3.37—3.37
Abuser
terminology, 1.07
Adult
terminology, 1.06
Agreements
legal remedies, 9.36
'All practicable steps'
capacity, 3.13—3.16
Attendance notes
of wishes and feelings, 11.107—11.112
Autism
trauma, 10.50—10.53
Behaviours
elements of coercive control, 2.03—2.06
Best interests decisions
care, 9.13
conduct of proceedings, 9.10
contact with other persons, 9.14—9.17
generally, 9.05—9.09
information sharing, 9.18
internet use, 9.20—9.21
lasting powers of attorney, 9.22—9.24
property and financial affairs, 9.19
residence, 9.11—9.12
sexual relations, 9.25
social media use, 9.20—9.21
Brain function
trauma, 10.13—10.14
Capacity
See **Ability of P to make the decision**
'all practicable steps', 3.13—3.16
coercive control, and, 3.04—3.07
Court of Protection Visitor, 3.69—3.71
declarations of
final, 3.51
generally, 3.50
interim, 3.52

Capacity – *contd*
determining lack
ability of P to make decision, 3.25—3.40
because of an impairment or disturbance, 3.41—3.49
generally, 3.21—3.24
evidence
Court of Protection Visitor, from, 3.69—3.71
generally, 3.53—3.55
independent expert, from, 3.72—3.76
local authority, from, 3.59—3.68
NHS body, from, 3.59—3.68
party, from, 3.56—3.58
s 49 orders, 3.59—3.68
social workers, from, 3.56—3.58
final declarations, 3.51
inability of P to make decision because of an impairment or disturbance, 3.41—3.49
independent expert, 3.72—3.76
inherent jurisdiction, and, 6.64—6.65
interim declarations, 3.52
introduction, 3.01—3.03
presumption, 3.08—3.12
relevant information
care, 4.35—4.43
conduct of proceedings, 4.23—4.32
contact with others, 4.44—4.49
disclosure of information to others, 4.50—4.51
execution of LPA, 4.61—4.65
internet use, 4.57—4.60
introduction, 4.22
marriage, 4.68—4.71
property and financial affairs, 4.52—4.56
residence, 4.33—4.34
revocation of LPA, 4.61—4.65
sexual relations, 4.66—4.67
social media use, 4.57—4.60
testamentary capacity, 4.72—4.73
s.49 orders, 3.59—3.68
social workers, 3.56—3.58
summary, 3.77—3.78
unwise decisions, 3.17—3.20

Care needs and support
assessing capacity, 4.35—4.43
best interests decisions, 9.13
Case law
bipolar affective disorder, 5.52—5.56
brain injury, 5.57—5.64
control by parent
father, 7.24—7.34
mother, 7.11—7.14
stepfather, 7.15—7.23
control of parent, 7.35—7.50
control of partner, 7.03—7.10
Court of Protection, in
brain injury, 5.57—5.64
conclusions, 5.65—5.66
elder abuse, 5.19—5.51
introduction, 5.01
learning disabilities, 5.02—5.18
mental illness, 5.52—5.56
forced relationships, 7.51—7.58
generally, 1.14—1.27
inherent jurisdiction, under
conclusions, 7.59—7.62
control by parent, 7.11—7.34
control of parent, 7.35—7.50
control of partner, 7.03—7.10
forced relationships, 7.51—7.58
introduction, 5.01
learning disabilities
introduction, 5.02
pregnancy, 5.10—5.18
sex-offender stepfather, 5.03—5.05
violent partner, 5.06—5.09
living with sex-offender stepfather, 5.03—5.05
mental illness, 5.52—5.56
overview, 1.28—1.35
pressure to become pregnant, 5.10—5.18
sex-offender stepfather, 5.03—5.05
trauma bond, 5.19—5.40
unreported cases, 1.15—1.27
wanting to see violent partner, 5.06—5.09
Chronic sleep deprivation
trauma, 10.48—10.49
Civil Procedure Rules
determination of capacity or influence, 6.64—6.65
form of application, 6.60
funding, 6.62
interim orders, 6.69
introduction, 6.58—6.59
level of judiciary, 6.61
litigation friend, 6.66
transfer of proceedings, 6.63
without notice applications, 6.67—6.68
Civil remedies
See **Legal Remedies**
Coercive control
case law
See also **Case law**
brain injury, 5.57—5.64
conclusions, 5.65—5.66
elder abuse, 5.19—5.51
introduction, 5.01
learning disabilities, 5.02—5.18
mental illness, 5.52—5.56
conclusions, 2.74—2.76
connection with trauma, and, 10.03—10.07
controlling or coercive behaviour in intimate or family relationship, 2.43—2.50
criminal law
domestic abuse, 2.41—2.42
introduction, 2.40
putting people in fear of violence, 2.51—2.55
statutory guidance, 2.56—2.58
disabled people, 2.67—2.73
domestic abuse, 2.41—2.42
elements
behaviours, 2.03—2.06
entrapment, 2.15—2.20
homicide, 2.24—2.28
post-separation abuse, 2.21—2.23
suicide, 2.24—2.28
tactics of control, 2.07—2.14
historical context, 2.56—2.66
international human rights law
Council of Europe, 2.35—2.39
introduction, 2.29
United Nations, 2.30—2.34
introduction, 2.01—2.02
putting people in fear of violence, 2.51—2.55
statutory guidance, 2.56—2.58
terminology, 1.04—1.09
trauma, and, 10.03—10.07
Conduct of proceedings
appointing litigation friend, 4.32, 6.66
capacity to conduct proceedings, 4.23—4.32
Contact with other persons
assessing capacity, 4.23—4.32
best interests decisions, 9.10
Control
parent, by
father, 7.24—7.34
mother, 7.11—7.14
stepfather, 7.15—7.24
parent, of, 7.35—7.50
partner, of, 7.03—7.10
Controlling person
terminology, 1.07

Convention on Preventing and Combating Violence against Women and Domestic Violence
international human rights law, 2.39
Convention on the Elimination of All Forms of Discrimination Against Women (CEDAW)
international human rights law, 2.30—2.34
Convention on the Rights of Persons with Disabilities (CRPD)
international human rights law, 2.66, 14.06
Council of Europe
international human rights law, 2.35—2.39
Court of Protection
case law
brain injury, 5.57—5.64
conclusions, 5.65—5.66
elder abuse, 5.19—5.51
introduction, 5.01
learning disabilities, 5.02—5.18
mental illness, 5.52—5.56
See **Fact-finding**
Court of Protection Visitor
assessing capacity, 3.69—3.71
Criminal law
controlling or coercive behaviour in intimate or family relationship, 2.43—2.50
domestic abuse, 2.41—2.42
introduction, 2.40
putting people in fear of violence, 2.51—2.55
statutory guidance, 2.56—2.58
Declarations of capacity
final, 3.51
generally, 3.50
interim, 3.52
Deny, attack, reverse victim and offender (DARVO)
perpetrator tactic, 2.22
Deprivation of liberty
Article 5 ECHR, 6.42—6.55
Court of Protection, 9.59
inherent jurisdiction, 6.42—6.57
Diet
trauma, 10.48—10.49
Disabled people
domestic abuse, 2.60
historical treatment, 2.67—2.73
international human rights law, 14.06
Disclosure of information to others
assessing capacity, 4.50—4.51
best interests decisions, 9.18
Dissociation
effect of trauma, 11.58—11.60
Domestic abuse
meaning, 2.41—2.42
Domestic Abuse Commissioner
terminology, 1.05
Domestic abuse protection notices
introduction, 1.37
legal remedies, 9.72—9.73
Domestic abuse protection orders
legal remedies, 9.69—9.71
Economic abuse
elements of coercive control, 2.03
Elder abuse
cases in Court of Protection cases, 5.19—5.51
Engaging in sexual relations
assessing capacity, 4.66—4.67
no best interests decision possible, 9.25
Entrapment
elements of coercive control, 2.15—2.20
European Convention on Human Rights (ECHR)
international human rights law, 2.35—2.38
Evidence
capacity, of
Court of Protection Visitor, from, 3.69—3.71
generally, 3.53—3.55
independent expert, from, 3.72—3.76
litigation friend, by, 3.58
local authority, from, 3.56—3.57
NHS body, from, 3.59—3.68
non-party authority, from, 3.59—3.68
P, from, 3.58
party, from, 3.56—3.58
s.49 orders, 3.59—3.68
social workers, from, 3.56—3.57
controlling person, of, 13.30—13.31
local authority, by, 12.29—12.33
Execution of LPA
Court of Protection, in, 9.22—9.24
decision-making, 4.61—4.65
inherent jurisdiction, under, 9.32
Exercise
trauma, 10.48—10.49
Fact-finding
conclusions, 8.37—8.40
Court of Protection, in
determining whether to hold hearing, 8.07—8.09
establishing facts first, 8.06
interim decisions, 8.10—8.11
purpose, 8.02—8.05
witnesses, 8.25—8.28

Fact-finding – *contd*
hearings
control by judiciary, 8.30—8.33
determining whether to hold, 8.06—8.09
introduction, 8.21
judgment, 8,34—8.36
representation of local authority, 12.37
timetabling, 8.22—8.23
witnesses, 8.25—8.29
inherent jurisdiction, under
generally, 8.12—8.14
witnesses, 8.29
introduction, 8.01
representation of controlling person, 13.34
representation of local authority, 12.37
schedules of allegations, 8.15—8.20
witnesses
Court of Protection, in, 8.25—8.28
inherent jurisdiction, under, 8.29
Final declarations
capacity, 3.51
Financial affairs
See **Property and financial affairs**
Flashbacks
effects of trauma, 11.61—11.66
Forced marriage protection orders
legal remedies, 9.65—9.66
Forced relationships
case law, 7.51—7.58
Fragmented memory recall
effects of trauma, 10.15—10.19
Freedom from torture, inhuman or degrading treatment
inherent jurisdiction, 6.32—6.34
Funding of legal representation
inherent jurisdiction, 6.62
representation of controlling person, 13.27—13.29
representation of local authority, 12.36
representation of victim/survivor, 11.103—11.106
Gender
terminology, 1.05
Grief
effects of trauma, 11.77—11.79
Guilt
effects of trauma, 11.71—11.73
Harbin v Masterman orders
considerations by local authority, 12.35
Healing
trauma, 10.30—10.40
Health services
disclosures of abuse, 12.34
Healthcare
for victim/survivor, 10.41—10.49
Homicide
following coercive control, 1.21, 2.24—2.28
Human rights
Council of Europe, 2.35—2.39
deprivation of liberty, 6.42—6.57
freedom from torture, etc, 6.32—6.34
inherent jurisdiction, 6.31—6.57
introduction, 2.29
respect for private and family life, 6.35—6.41
United Nations, 2.30—2.34
Independent expert
evidence of capacity, 3.73—3.77
Influence
inherent jurisdiction, 6.28—6.29
Information relevant for assessment capacity
across decision-making domains, 4.22—4.73
Information sharing
assessing capacity, 4.50—4.51
best interests decisions, 9.18
Inherent jurisdiction
applications
general form, 6.60
without notice, 6.67—6.68
avoiding delay, 12.25—12.27
avoiding protective imperative, 6.30
case law
See also **Case law**
conclusions, 7.59—7.62
control by parent, 7.11—7.34
control of parent, 7.35—7.50
control of partner, 7.03—7.10
forced relationships, 7.51—7.58
introduction, 7.01—7.02
See **Civil Procedure Rules**
conclusions
general, 6.70—6.73
overview, 14.13—14.30
deprivation of liberty, 6.56—6.57
determination of capacity or influence, 6.64—6.65
fact-finding
generally, 8.12—8.14
witnesses, 8.29
foundational cases, 6.09—6.15
freedom from torture, inhuman or degrading treatment, 6.32—6.34
funding, 6.62
human rights issues
deprivation of liberty, 6.56—6.57
freedom from torture, etc, 6.32—6.34
introduction, 6.31
liberty and security of person, 6.42—6.55

Inherent jurisdiction – *contd*
human rights issues – *contd*
respect for private and family life, 6.35—6.41
influence, 6.28—6.29
interim orders, 6.69
introduction, 6.01—6.08
level of judiciary, 6.61
liberty and security of person, 6.42—6.55
litigation friend, 6.66
principles
foundational cases, 6.09—6.15
influence, 6.28—6.29
protective imperative, 6.30
vulnerable adult, 6.16—6.27
private and family life, 6.35—6.41
procedure
determination of capacity or influence, 6.64—6.65
form of application, 6.60
funding, 6.62
interim orders, 6.69
level of judiciary, 6.61
litigation friend, 6.66
rules, 6.58—6.59
transfer of proceedings, 6.63
without notice applications, 6.67—6.68
right to liberty and security of person, 6.42—6.55
right to respect for private and family life, 6.35—6.41
transfer of proceedings, 6.63
undue influence, 6.28—6.29
vulnerable adult, 6.16—6.27
without notice applications, 6.67—6.68
Injunctions
controlling person, against, 9.39
generally, 9.38
just and convenient, 9.40—9.42
P, and, 9.39
wording, 9.43—9.45
Interim declarations
of capacity, 3.52, 3.55, 3.58, 4.32
Interim orders
inherent jurisdiction, under, 6.69, 7.60, 9.51—9.58
Court of Protection, in, 9.46—9.50
deprivation of liberty, 9.59
International human rights law
See **Human rights**
Internet use
assessing capacity, 4.57—4.60
best interests decisions, 9.20—9.21
Intrusive thoughts
effects of trauma, 11.74—11.76
Istanbul Convention
international human rights law, 2.39
Judicial visit
representation of victim/survivor, 11.113
Lasting power of attorney
assessing capacity, 4.61—4.65
Court of Protection, in, 9.22—9.24
inherent jurisdiction, under, 9.32
Lawyer
terminology, 1.08
Learning disability
cases in the Court of Protection, 5.02—5.18
introduction, 5.02
trauma, 10.50—10.53
Legal aid
for controlling person, 13.27—13.29
for victim/survivor, 11.103—11.106
inherent jurisdiction, 6.62
local authority considerations, 12.35
Legal remedies
agreements, 9.36
best interests decisions
care, 9.13
conduct of proceedings, 9.10
contact with other persons, 9.14—9.17
generally, 9.05—9.09
information sharing, 9.18
internet use, 9.20—9.21
lasting powers of attorney, 9.22—9.24
property and financial affairs, 9.19
residence, 9.11—9.12
sexual relations, 9.25
social media use, 9.20—9.21
care, 9.13
civil
domestic abuse protection notices, 9.72—9.73
domestic abuse protection orders, 9.69—9.71
forced marriage protection orders, 9.65—9.66
introduction, 9.60
non-molestation orders, 9.61—9.64
restraining orders, 9.67—9.68
conclusion, 9.74—9.76
conduct of proceedings, 9.10
contact with other persons, 9.14—9.17
Court of Protection, in
care needs and support, 9.13
conduct of proceedings, 9.10
contact with other persons, 9.14—9.17
generally, 9.05—9.09
information sharing, 9.18
interim, 9.46—9.50
internet use, 9.20—9.21
lasting powers of attorney, 9.22—9.24
property and financial affairs, 9.19
residence, 9.11—9.12

Legal remedies – *contd*
Court of Protection, in – *contd*
sexual relations, 9.25
social media use, 9.20—9.21
deprivation of liberty, 9.59
disclosure of information to others, 9.18
domestic abuse protection notices, 9.72—9.73
domestic abuse protection orders, 9.69—9.71
engaging in sexual relations, 9.25
execution of LPA
Court of Protection, in, 9.22—9.24
inherent jurisdiction, under, 9.32
forced marriage protection orders, 9.65—9.66
information sharing, 9.18
inherent jurisdiction, under
interim, 9.51—9.58
LPAs, 9.32
objectives, 9.26—9.31
removal from home, 9.33—9.35
injunctions
controlling person, against, 9.39
generally, 9.38
just and convenient, 9.40—9.42
P, and, 9.39
wording, 9.43—9.45
interim
Court of Protection, in, 9.46—9.50
deprivation of liberty, 9.59
inherent jurisdiction, under, 9.51—9.58
internet use, 9.20—9.21
introduction, 9.01—9.04
lasting powers of attorney
Court of Protection, in, 9.22—9.24
inherent jurisdiction, under, 9.32
non-molestation orders, 9.61—9.64
property and financial affairs, 9.19
removal from home, 9.33—9.35
residence, 9.11—9.12
restraining orders, 9.67—9.68
revocation of LPA, 9.22—9.24
sexual relations, 9.25
social media use, 9.20—9.21
undertakings, 9.37
Litigation friend
evidence of capacity, 3.59
inherent jurisdiction, 6.66
representation of victim/survivor, 11.99—11.102
Local authority
evidence of capacity, 3.57—3.58
representation of local authority
access to victim/survivor, 12.15—12.19
conclusions, 12.40—12.41
creativity of action, 12.20—12.28
Local authority – *contd*
representation of local authority – *contd*
evidence gathering, 12.29—12.33
fact-finding hearings, 12.37
funding legal representation of victim/survivor, 12.36
Harbin v Masterman order, 12.35
health services' role, 12.34
introduction, 12.01—12.02
legal strategy, 12.03—12.14
'slow violence', 12.38
speed of action, 12.20—12.28
timetabling, 12.38
trauma, and, 12.39
statutory powers, 1.36—1.47
Marriage
assessing capacity, 4.68—4.71
Memory recall
effect of trauma, 10.13—10.14
factual fragmentation, 10.15—10.19
substance abuse, 10.20
Mental health
diagnoses, 10.21—10.29
healing and therapy, 10.30—10.40
Mental illness
case law, 5.52—5.56
Micro-management of everyday life
elements of coercive control, 2.03
Non-molestation orders
generally, 9.61—9.64
introduction, 1.37
Perpetrator
terminology, 1.07
Physical health
effects of trauma, 10.41—10.49
Post-separation abuse
and coercive control, 2.21—2.23
Powers of entry
introduction, 1.36
Pressure to become pregnant
case law, 5.10—5.18
Property and financial affairs
best interests decisions, 9.19
relevant information, 4.52—4.56
Psychological manipulation
elements of coercive control, 2.03
Putting people in fear of violence
criminal offence, 2.51—2.55
Rage
effect of trauma, 11.80—11.83
Reasonably foreseeable consequences
assessing capacity, 4.14—4.17
Removal from home
legal remedies, 9.33—9.35
Representation of controlling person
best interests of P, and, 13.35
capacity concerns, 13.33

Representation of controlling person – *contd*
communication methods, 13.35
complaints against lawyers, 13.19—13.20
compliance with orders, 13.21—13.25
conclusions, 13.35—13.37
conspiracies, 13.13—13.15
control of proceedings, 13.07—13.08
controlling client, 13.03—13.25
court perception, 13.35
evidence, 13.30—13.31
fact-finding, 13.34
'fighting all the way', 13.16—13.18
funding, 13.27—13.29
ground rules, 13.35
introduction, 13.01—13.02
lawyer's actions, 13.26—13.34
legal aid, 13.27—13.29
perpetrator's view of victim/survivor, 13.09—13.12
red lines, 13.35
risk assessments, 13.26
signposting to services, 13.32
trap avoidance, 13.35
typologies of perpetrators, 13.03—13.06
Representation of local authority
access to victim/survivor, 12.15—12.19
conclusions, 12.40—12.41
creativity of action, 12.20—12.28
evidence gathering, 12.29—12.33
fact-finding hearings, 12.37
funding, 12.36
Harbin v Masterman order, 12.35
health services' role, 12.34
introduction, 12.01—12.02
legal strategy, 12.03—12.14
'slow violence', 12.38
speed of action, 12.20—12.28
timetabling, 12.38
trauma, and, 12.39
Representation of victim/survivor
active listening, 11.39—11.41
advice form mental health professional, 11.07—11.08
advocates' meeting, 11.115
appointment arrangements, 11.12—11.13
attendance notes, 11.107—11.112
borrowed words or phrases, 11.90
choices available during meeting, 11.19—11.22
communication methods, 11.09
conclusions, 11.129—11.131
conduct of meeting, 11.19—11.50
confusion, 11.84—11.86
consistency of contact, 11.16—11.17
discussion of abuse, 11.44—11.48
dissociation, 11.58—11.60
Representation of victim/survivor – *contd*
downplay of severity, significance or impact, 11.87—11.89
effects of trauma during meeting, 11.51—11.91
emotional shut down, 11.55—11.57
ending the meeting, 11.92—11.99
explanation of the litigation friend role, 11.35—11.36
explanation of the process, 11.31—11.34
flashbacks, 11.61—11.66
funding, 11.103—11.106
future court hearings, 11.95
grief, 11.77—11.79
grounding, 11.28—11.30
guilt, 11.71—11.73
introduction, 11.01—11.05
intrusive thoughts, 11.74—11.76
judicial visit, 11.113
lawyer self-care, 11.126—11.128
listening, 11.39—11.41
litigation friend, 11.99—11.102
minimising trauma, 11.87—11.89
next steps communications, 11.98
notes of meeting, 11.107—11.112
online meetings, 11.23—11.27
other presentations, 11.90—11.91
participation in proceedings, 11.113
physical contact, 11.49—11.50
positive summing up, 11.92—11.94
power dynamic, 11.10—11.11
pre-abuse recollections, 11.37—11.38
pre-hearing discussions, 11.115
preparation for meeting, 11.06—11.18
questions, 11.14—11.15
rage, 11.80—11.83
remote participation, 11.113
review of records, 11.06
shame, 11.67—11.70
story stewardship, 11.96—11.97
suggestibility, 11.42—11.43
summing up, 11.92—11.94
supporting client at court, 11.114—11.125
witness statement, 11.107—11.112
Residence
assessing capacity, 4.33—4.34
best interests decisions, 9.11—9.12
Restraining orders
legal remedies, 9.67—9.68
Revocation of LPA
assessing capacity, 4.61—4.65
best interests decisions, 9.22—9.24
Right to liberty and security of person
See **Deprivation of Liberty**
Right to respect for private and family life
inherent jurisdiction, 6.35—6.41

Schedules of allegations
fact-finding, 8.15—8.20
Section 49 orders
evidence of capacity, 3.60—3.69
Sexual relations
assessing capacity, 4.66—4.67
best interests decisions, 9.25
Sexual violence
and coercive control, 2.03
Shame
effects of trauma, 11.67—11.70
Sleep deprivation
effects of trauma, 10.48—10.49
Social media use
assessing capacity, 4.57—4.60
best interests decisions, 9.20—9.21
Special Visitor
See **Court of Protection Visitor**
Stalking
and coercive control, 2.03
Statutory guidance on coercive control
criminal law, 2.56—2.58
Structural inequality
and coercive control, 2.15—2.20
Substance abuse
trauma, 10.20
Suggestibility
effects of trauma, 11.42—11.43
Suicide
and coercive control, 2.24—2.28
Technology-facilitated control
elements of coercive control, 2.03
Testamentary capacity
assessing capacity, 4.72—4.73
Therapy
trauma, 10.30—10.40
Threats
elements of coercive control, 2.03
Transfer of proceedings
between Court of Protection and under inherent jurisdiction, 6.63
Trauma
autism, 10.50—10.53
brain function, 10.13—10.14
chronic sleep deprivation, 10.48—10.49
conclusions, 10.54—10.60
connection to coercive control, 10.03—10.07
diet high in processed foods, 10.48—10.49
elements of coercive control, and, 2.16
factual fragmentation, 10.15—10.19
generally, 10.03—10.07
Trauma – *contd*
healing, 10.30—10.40
introduction, 10.01—10.02
learning disability, 10.50—10.53
memory recall
brain function, 10.13—10.14
factual fragmentation, 10.15—10.19
substance abuse, 10.20
mental health
diagnoses, 10.21—10.29
healing and therapy, 10.30—10.40
physical health, 10.41—10.49
representation of local authority, and, 12.39
responses, 10.08—10.12
sedentary lifestyle, 10.48—10.49
sleep deprivation, 10.48—10.49
stress of everyday life, and, 10.06
substance abuse, 10.20
therapy, 10.30—10.40
Trauma bond
case law, 5.33—5.36, 9.58
psychology, 1.29, 2.17, 9.48, 10.36
Undue influence
inherent jurisdiction, 6.28—6.29
United Nations
international human rights law, 2.30—2.34
Convention on the Rights of Persons with Disabilities, 2.66, 14.06
Unwise decisions
capacity, 3.18—3.21
Victim
See also **Representation of victim/survivor**
Violence
and coercive control, 2.03
Vulnerable adult
inherent jurisdiction, 2.72, 6.16—6.27
potential for reform, 14.15—14.2
Without notice applications
inherent jurisdiction, 6.67—6.68
Witness statements
by the controlling person, 13.08
by social worker, 12.29
for the victim/survivor, 3.58, 11.107—11.112
status, 8.26—8.27
Witnesses
Court of Protection, in, 8.25—8.28
inherent jurisdiction, under, 8.29